CISSP For Dummies

Cheat Sheet

KT-223-455

Months before the test

1. **Develop your preparation strategy.** Get started by getting all your study aids lined up. *CISSP For Dummies* belongs on top of the pile.

2. **Budget your preparation time.** The breadth of the CISSP exam requires that you make time to review every aspect of the exam domains. You don't apply every aspect of the CISSP arsenal every day at work, so you can't count on it being fresh in your mind without reviewing every domain completely from the ground up. You'll be unpleasantly surprised by what you've forgotten if you don't plan to review.

3. **Schedule your exam time.** The CISSP exam is available intermittently around the world. If necessary, you need to make travel arrangements, hotel arrangements, arrange child care, and actually find an available seat in a scheduled exam. It's no more expensive to schedule the exam in advance and then reschedule than to pay the full last-minute entry fee, so don't put off signing up for the exam because your schedule is subject to last-minute work or family needs.

Weeks before the test

1. **Schedule your preparation time.** There's enough to review that you have to be completely honest with yourself about your progress. A last-moment cram will be a disaster. Book blocks of time in your schedule for review, and be honest about scheduling study.

2. **Study *CISSP For Dummies*.** This book reviews all aspects of the CISSP exam at a level that should be just right if you have any hands-on experience at all with the subject.

3. **Take practice tests and answer practice questions.** Practice questions confront you with gaps in your preparation and get you used to the brain sweat that the CISSP exam demands.

4. **Check other resources.** If there are any aspects of the CISSP exam domains that you haven't experienced up close and personal, now is the time to get that exposure.

5. **Plan your trip.** Don't count on making a long early-morning drive for an 8 A.M. exam. Make arrangements to get close to the exam site so you have a calm trip of just a few minutes to the testing room.

CISSP For Dummies®

Cheat Sheet

Night before the test

1. **Have a nutritious dinner.** Avoid spicy and rich foods. Think marathon runner for the day ahead.

2. **Double-check your admission and travel plans.** Make sure that you know exactly where you need to be, what you need for admission, when you need to be there, and how early you need to leave to arrive with time to spare.

3. **Review *CISSP For Dummies*.** Once more around the block should get your head on straight. At this point, you should know the book cold.

4. **Go to sleep.** Stretch out and get ready for an important day.

Day of the exam

1. **Double-check your exam supplies.** The CISSP exam is longer than other standard professional exams, and the testing conditions are different. You can bring snacks, beverages, tissues, and other comfort and refreshment items. In our opinion, a big bottle of water is tops on the list. Wear an analog watch; digital watches are forbidden in some testing areas.

2. **Dress in layers.** The exam room may not be the most comfortable temperature, and your needs may change during the very long exam. Give yourself some flexibility to warm up or cool down.

3. **Review *CISSP For Dummies*.** By now, you could write out this book from memory.

4. **Head to the exam room, sit down, and get the proctor's instructions.** At this point, you should be confident in your preparation, well rested, and ready to test your knowledge and skills. Good luck!

After you leave the exam room

1. **Prepare for a retest.** It's just like the Space Shuttle crew taking time to carefully shut down the bird even when they're safely on the ground. Take the time immediately to make notes about what you found most difficult about the exam. If you need to retest, those notes are your shortest, most reliable path to follow-up success.

2. **Relax and wait for your results.** At this point, there's nothing left but to enjoy the quiet after the storm. So do it. Hug your family, play with your dog, and be optimistic. You've done everything you needed to do, and now you can enjoy the quiet.

For Dummies: Bestselling Book Series for Beginners

CISSP
FOR
DUMMIES®

by Lawrence Miller and
Peter H. Gregory

Wiley Publishing, Inc.

CISSP For Dummies®

Published by
Wiley Publishing, Inc.
111 River Street
Hoboken, NJ 07030
www.wiley.com

Copyright © 2002 Wiley Publishing, Inc., Indianapolis, Indiana

Published simultaneously in Canada

No part of this publication may be reproduced, stored in a retrieval system or transmitted in any form or by any means, electronic, mechanical, photocopying, recording, scanning or otherwise, except as permitted under Sections 107 or 108 of the 1976 United States Copyright Act, without either the prior written permission of the Publisher, or authorization through payment of the appropriate per-copy fee to the Copyright Clearance Center, 222 Rosewood Drive, Danvers, MA 01923, (978) 750-8400, fax (978) 646-8700. Requests to the Publisher for permission should be addressed to the Legal Department, Wiley Publishing, Inc., 10475 Crosspoint Blvd., Indianapolis, IN 46256, (317) 572-3447, fax (317) 572-4447, e-mail: permcoordinator@ wiley.com.

Trademarks: Wiley, the Wiley Publishing logo, For Dummies, the Dummies Man logo, A Reference for the Rest of Us!, The Dummies Way, Dummies Daily, The Fun and Easy Way, Dummies.com and related trade dress are trademarks or registered trademarks of Wiley Publishing, Inc., in the United States and other countries, and may not be used without written permission. All other trademarks are the property of their respective owners. Wiley Publishing, Inc., is not associated with any product or vendor mentioned in this book.

For general information on our other products and services or to obtain technical support, please contact our Customer Care Department within the U.S. at 800-762-2974, outside the U.S. at 317-572-3993, or fax 317-572-4002.

Wiley also publishes its books in a variety of electronic formats. Some content that appears in print may not be available in electronic books.

Library of Congress Cataloging-in-Publication Data:

Library of Congress Control Number: 2002110297

ISBN: 0-7645-1670-1

Manufactured in the United States of America

10 9 8 7 6 5 4 3

1B/RV/QV/QV/IN

Wiley Publishing, Inc. is a trademark of Wiley Publishing, Inc.

About the Authors

Lawrence Miller, CISSP, MCSE+I, CCNP, and Sun Certified Systems Administrator, has worked in systems administration and information security for over nine years. His other certifications include CNA, A+, Network+, and i-Net+. He is currently working as the Information Technology Operations Manager for a major U.S. law firm. Previously he has worked as the Internetworking Security Engineer for a service provider in the U.S. retail sector and as a consultant for various multi-national clients in Tokyo, Japan. He also served as a Chief Petty Officer in the U.S. Navy in various roles including as an Information Systems Security Manager, Technical Services Department Head, and Meteorologist/Oceanographer.

Peter H. Gregory, CISSP, is the author of *Solaris Security, Sun Certified System Administrator for Solaris 8 Study Guide,* and *Enterprise Information Security.* He has been the technical reviewer/editor for over 20 business computing books over the past eight years, including *Secure Electronic Commerce, Halting the Hacker, Essential Guide to Intelligent Optical Networks,* and several of the Sun Microsystems Press system administration references and guides for Solaris. He is one of several volunteers who write some of the CISSP certification examination questions for upcoming exams.

Peter is the Logical Security Strategist at a wireless telecommunications carrier in Seattle, Washington. Prior to this, he was the Manager for Enterprise Security Architecture; and in the five years before that, he held less-glamorous IT management titles there.

In the mid-1980s he was the lead development engineer for a casino management product at Bally Systems. Then to balance his karma, he worked for almost three years at World Vision, one of the world's largest disaster relief organizations, helping to migrate its applications from mainframes to Unix.

When he pries his hands off the keyboard, Peter and his wife Corinne can be found raising their three young girls and getting dirt under their fingernails in the garden.

Peter's Web site can be found at www.hartgregorygroup.com, and he can be reached at peter.gregory@hartgregorygroup.com.

Dedication

From Lawrence Miller:
For my loving wife and children (Minda, Eric, Vick, and Ken), my parents, and my little blister (Alicia).

From Peter H. Gregory:
To those who have been heroes all along — the police, firefighters, and paramedics in New York City and everywhere.

Authors' Acknowledgments

Peter H. Gregory would like to thank Melody Layne, Acquisition Editor at Wiley, for her perseverance and patience, especially at the beginning of the project. Thank you to Pat O'Brien, Senior Project Editor at Wiley, for your help, and to Teresa Artman for copy editing. Thank you, Larry, for agreeing to coauthor a book with someone you had never even heard of.

A big thanks to my wife, Corinne, for helping me write the initial proposal, convincing me that I could write two books at once (something I'll never plan to do again), and for reading my chapters before I turned them in.

Thank you, Marsha MacInnes, for help along the way, for helping me get perspective, and for self-confidence.

And, finally, heartfelt thanks go to Liz Suto, wherever you are, for getting me into this business nine years ago when you asked me to do a tech review on your book *Informix Online Performance Tuning*.

Larry Miller would like to thank everyone at Wiley Publishing for making this a very pleasant and rewarding experience, especially Melody Layne, Pat O'Brien, and Teresa Artman. I would also like to thank Pat O'Day for your friendship and professional guidance. Finally, a very special thank you to Thad Stoner and Mica Johnson for your friendship, encouragement, and for introducing me to this wonderful opportunity!

Publisher's Acknowledgments

We're proud of this book; please send us your comments through our online registration form located at www.dummies.com/register/.

Some of the people who helped bring this book to market include the following:

Acquisitions, Editorial, and Media Development

Sr. Project Editor: Pat O'Brien

Acquisitions Editor: Melody Layne

Sr. Copy Editor: Teresa Artman

Technical Editor: Hart-Gregory Group

Editorial Director: Mary C. Corder

Permissions Editor: Laura Moss

Media Development Specialist: Angela Denny

Media Development Manager: Laura VanWinkle

Media Development Supervisor: Richard Graves

Editorial Assistant: Amanda Foxworth

Production

Project Coordinator: Dale White

Layout and Graphics: Joyce Haughey, Kristin McMullan, Jackie Nicholas, Barry Offringa, Jacque Schnieder, Erin Zeltner

Proofreaders: Laura Albert, TECHBOOKS Production Services

Indexer: TECHBOOKS Production Services

Publishing and Editorial for Technology Dummies
   Richard Swadley, Vice President and Executive Group Publisher
   Andy Cummings, Vice President and Publisher
   Mary C. Corder, Editorial Director

Publishing for Consumer Dummies
   Diane Graves Steele, Vice President and Publisher
   Joyce Pepple, Acquisitions Director

Composition Services
   Gerry Fahey, Vice President of Production Services
   Debbie Stailey, Director of Composition Services

Contents at a Glance

Cartoons at a Glance

By Rich Tennant

page 323

page 23

page 5

page 353

Cartoon Information:
Fax: 978-546-7747
E-Mail: richtennant@the5thwave.com
World Wide Web: www.the5thwave.com

Table of Contents

Introduction

●●

*W*ithin the past year, security practitioners around the world have begun pursuing a little-known but highly regarded professional title: the Certified Information Systems Security Professional (CISSP) certification.

Despite being established over 12 years ago, the CISSP certification has only recently begun to gain widespread attention. Its demand is quickly surpassing many vendor-sponsored technical certifications as the professional standard in the information security field.

About This Book

My goal in this book is simple: to help you prepare for and pass the CISSP examination. Although I've stuffed it chock-full of good information, we don't expect that this book will be a weighty desktop reference on the shelf of every security professional — although I certainly wouldn't object.

Furthermore, this isn't Wal-Mart. I don't intend for this book to be an all-purpose, be-all-to-end-all, one-stop shopping guide. I strongly believe that given the broad base of knowledge required for the CISSP examination, this goal is not achievable and to make any claim as such would be irresponsible. I liken such a huge goal to trying to put the entire Internet on a single Web site!

As a security professional, you'll find that earning the CISSP certification is only a beginning. New technology, with its associated risks and vulnerabilities, requires each of us as security professionals to constantly press forward, consuming vast volumes of knowledge and information in a constant tug-of-war against the bad guys. Thus, when preparing for your CISSP certification, you should study as much relevant information as your time and resources allow. *CISSP For Dummies* provides the blueprint for your study effort and gives you some great experience practicing for the test to boot.

How This Book Is Organized

This book is organized into four parts. I cover the Common Body of Knowledge (CBK) domains in Part II. Although this book's chapters don't necessarily have to be read in order, they're organized according to the structure of the CBK domains and follow a somewhat logical progression.

Part I: Exam Basics

In Part I, I first introduce the International Information Systems Security Certifications Consortium [(ISC)^2], the CISSP examination, and the CBK. Then we provide some helpful guidance for study.

Part II: Domains

Part II contains the domains of the CBK. A CISSP candidate will probably have had at least some practical work experience with many of the concepts and technologies that I cover in this part. Taken individually, these domains represent at least a slightly larger part of the actual CISSP exam than other domains. This is certainly true about the Telecommunications and Network Security domain and the Security Management Practices domain, which are largely introductions to basic security concepts discussed throughout the CBK.

Part III: The Part of Tens

The much loved and revered Part of Tens contains six chapters that are more than mere lists. I include information to help you prepare for the CISSP exam and to also potentially help you in your career as a security professional.

Part IV: Appendixes

Unlike reading many other books with pretty worthless appendixes — why do you think the appendectomy was invented, anyway? — you don't want to skip this part. Appendix A contains a sample test of 250 practice questions similar in format to the actual CISSP examination. Appendix B contains a glossary, but not just any ordinary glossary: The CISSP exam requires you to select the *best* answer for a given question. You definitely need to know and understand very concise terms and definitions for the exam in order to recognize any obviously wrong answers. Appendix C details all the goodies on the CD that accompanies this book; believe me, it's packed!

How the Chapters Are Organized

CISSP For Dummies is unique in the *For Dummies* series. Because the CISSP examination covers such a broad base of information, I don't recommend skipping any of the material in this book. The information presented in some of the chapters may be familiar to you or easier to understand than others, but I still recommend at least a quick, cursory read of those chapters. For this reason, I don't include a quick assessment test at the beginning of each chapter as in other *For Dummies* certification books. Instead, I chose to pack this book with as much useful information as possible to help you succeed in your quest for the CISSP certification.

Chapter introductions

The first page of each domain chapter in begins with a brief introduction to the domain covered therein. You'll also find a list of chapter objectives that closely correlates to the CISSP knowledge objectives for that domain.

Study subjects

In the heart of each CISSP domain chapter, I extensively cover the knowledge objectives listed in the CISSP CBK. These chapters provide the relevant information for the CISSP exam with enough detail to place the information into proper context. If you read a chapter and feel that you need further study to understand a topic, I list additional references at the end of each of these chapters to help guide your efforts.

Tables and illustrations

To be helpful to you in your study, I provide tables and illustrations of important information or concepts whenever I can. However, because CISSP is a vendor-neutral certification, don't expect to find screen captures or simulation-type graphics. More room for good, old-fashioned information!

Additional references

If, after reading a chapter, you feel that you need more information to fully comprehend a subject or concept, I help point you in the right direction with a list of credible references.

Prep Tests

Finally, I conclude each CISSP domain chapter with a quick, 10-question multiple-choice Prep Test. *Note:* The prep tests at the end of each of these chapters are *not* the type of questions that you find on the actual CISSP examination.

(See Appendix A and the CD-ROM for sample questions similar to those found on the CISSP exam.) Instead, the prep tests are meant to help you recall important information that I present in the chapter to help you answer questions on the actual exam.

Icons Used in This Book

Throughout this book, you'll note little icons in the left margin that act as road signs to help you quickly pull out the stuff that's most important to you. Here's what they look like and what they represent.

Instant Answer icons highlight important information to help you answer questions on the actual exam. Look for these icons to highlight critical points to succeed on the CISSP exam.

Information tagged with a Remember icon identifies general information and core concepts that you may already know but should certainly understand and review before the CISSP exam.

Tip icons include short suggestions and tidbits of useful information.

Look for Warning icons to identify potential pitfalls, including easily confused or difficult-to-understand terms and concepts.

The Cross-Reference icon points you to other areas of the book where you can find related information.

Let's Get Started!

Congratulations! You made it through the introduction to *CISSP For Dummies*. You're now in the proper mental state for mass absorption of knowledge, well on your way to becoming a Certified Information Systems Security Professional! Actually, this is only the beginning. But remember, a journey of a thousand miles begins with a heavy dose of caffeine and processed sugar, so pick your favorite and get started!

Part I
Exam Basics

The 5th Wave   By Rich Tennant

"A centralized security management system sounds fine, but then what would we do with the dogs?"

In this part . . .

1t's time to get up to speed on this whole wacky CISSP thing. One of the most unusual characteristics of the CISSP exam is that it would be really, really surprising if you have hands-on experience with every aspect of security that the exam tests. The chapters in this part describe the exam and the basic areas tested.

Chapter 1

(ISC)² and the CISSP Certification

Some say that the Certified Information Systems Security Professional (CISSP) candidate requires a breadth of knowledge 50 miles across and 2 inches deep. To embellish on this statement, the CISSP candidate is more like the Great Wall of China, with a knowledge base extending over 3,500 miles, a few holes here and there, stronger in some areas than others, and one of the Seven Wonders of the Modern World.

The problem with many currently available CISSP preparation materials is in defining how high the Great Wall actually is: Some material overwhelms and intimidates CISSP candidates, leading them to believe that the wall is as high as it is long. Other study materials are perilously brief and shallow, giving the unsuspecting candidate a false sense of confidence as he merely attempts to step over the Great Wall, careful not to stub his toe. *CISSP For Dummies* answers the question, "What level of knowledge must a CISSP candidate possess to succeed?"

About (ISC)² and the CISSP Certification

The Certified Information Systems Security Professional (CISSP) certification program was established in 1989 by the International Information Systems Security Certification Consortium [(ISC)²]. The (ISC)² is a non-profit, tax-exempt corporation chartered for the explicit purpose of developing and administering the certification and education programs associated with the CISSP (and the Systems Security Certified Practitioner, or SSCP) certification. The CISSP certification is based on a Common Body of Knowledge (CBK) identified by the (ISC)^2 and defined through ten distinct domains as follows:

- Access Control Systems and Methodology
- Telecommunications and Network Security
- Security Management Practices
- Applications and Systems Development Security
- Cryptography
- Security Architecture and Models
- Operations Security
- Business Continuity Planning (BCP) and Disaster Recovery Planning (DRP)
- Law, Investigations, and Ethics
- Physical Security

You Must Be This Tall to Ride (And Other Minimum Requirements)

The CISSP candidate must have a minimum of three years (cumulative) of professional work experience in one or more of the above domains. Beginning January 1, 2003, the minimum requirement will be four years. Also, effective June 1, 2002, (ISC)^2 has changed the CISSP examination and certification process as follows: After notified of a passing score on the CISSP examination, the candidate must submit a qualified third-party endorsement (from another CISSP; the candidate's employer; or any licensed, certified, or commissioned professional) to validate the candidate's work experience. This must be submitted within 90 days of the date of the exam results notification letter or the application and exam results are voided. A percentage of submitted applications will be randomly audited, requiring additional documentation (normally a resume) and review by (ISC)^2. Final notification of certification upon receipt of the endorsement letter will normally be sent by (ISC)^2 via e-mail within one business day (seven business days if audited).

The candidate must also subscribe to the (ISC)^2 Code of Ethics and renew certification every three years. The CISSP certification can be renewed by accumulating 120 Continuing Professional Education (CPE) credits or by re-taking the CISSP examination. You earn CPE credits for various activities, including taking educational courses or attending seminars and security conferences, membership in association chapters and meeting attendance, vendor presentations, university or college course completion, providing security training, publishing security articles or books, serving on industry boards, self-study, and volunteer work. You must submit evidence of any such activities to (ISC)^2 for determining and documenting CPE credits. In most cases, this can be done online in the secure area of the (ISC)^2 Web site. There is also an $85 US annual maintenance fee payable to (ISC)^2. Maintenance fees are billed in arrears for the preceding year and may be paid online, also in the secure area of the (ISC)^2 Web site.

Beginning January 1, 2003, the minimum requirements for CISSP certification will be four years of professional work experience. (A college degree or equivalent life experience can count as one year of experience.) This change is being implemented to maintain the integrity and value of the CISSP certification and reflects the (ISC)^2 board of directors' consensus that a broad-based education or similar life experience is necessary to excel in the information security profession.

This change won't affect CISSP candidates that certify in 2002. If you fail the exam in 2002 and don't re-take it until after January 1, 2003, you are subject to the new minimum requirements.

Registering for the Exam

You can register for the CISSP exam online, via mail, or via fax.

First, you need to find a suitable exam date and location. It's given throughout the year at various locations (typically at colleges, community centers, or convention centers) worldwide. You can find exam schedules on the (ISC)^2 Web site at www.isc2.org.

Unlike most certification exams, the CISSP examination isn't conveniently available at Prometric Testing Centers.

Some travel may be necessary, which requires advance planning for travel arrangements . . . possibly including airline, rental car, and hotel reservations. If you're traveling to another country for your CISSP examination, visa requirements may apply.

After you find a suitable exam date and location on the (ISC)^2 Web site, complete the online registration form or download a copy of the form to mail or fax. If you're registering online or via fax, you need to use a MasterCard or

Visa charge card for payment. If registering by mail, you can pay for the exam via MasterCard, Visa, personal check, or money order. The current fee to take the test is $450 if you register more than 21 days in advance. The mailing address for registrations is:

(ISC)² Services, PO Box 1117, Dunedin, FL 34697 USA

The number for fax registration is 1-727-738-8522.

When you register, you'll be required to quantify your work experience in information security. You're not required to have experience in each of the ten domains, but the cumulative total of your work experience must be at least three years (four years after January 1, 2003).

I recommend that you register early for several reasons.

- ✔ The total charge of $450 for advance registration and the $100 rescheduling fee is exactly the same as the fee for last-minute registration: $550.

- ✔ By committing to a specific testing date, you're more likely to stay focused and avoid procrastination.

- ✔ Registering early allows you to better plan your travel arrangements and possibly save some money by booking reservations well in advance.

- ✔ Space is limited at all test centers. Reservations are accepted on a first-come, first-served basis; in the case of registrations by mail, the date of the postmark is used. If the test date fills up before you register (and this is a hot certification), you may be hard-pressed to find another test date and location that suits you this year.

Great news! If you're a US military veteran and are eligible for Montgomery GI Bill benefits, the Veteran's Administration will reimburse you for the full cost of the exam, pass or fail (but not exam preparation costs).

Developing a Study Plan

Many resources are available to help the CISSP candidate prepare for the exam. Self-study will be a major part of any study plan. Work experience is also critical to success and can be incorporated into your study plan. For those who learn best in a classroom or training environment, (ISC)² offers CISSP review seminars.

I recommend that you commit to an intense 60-day study plan leading up to the CISSP exam. How intense will depend on your own personal experience and learning ability, but plan on a minimum of 2 hours a day for 60 days. If you're a slow learner or reader, or perhaps find yourself weak in many areas, plan on 4–6 hours a day and more on the weekends. But stick to the 60-day plan. If you feel you need 360 hours of study, you may be tempted to spread this out over a 6-month period for 2 hours a day. But committing to 6 months of intense study is much harder (on you, as well as your family and friends) than 2 months. In the end, you will find yourself studying only as much as you would have in a 60-day period.

Self-study

Self-study can include books and study references, a study group, and practice exams.

Begin by requesting an official *CISSP Certification CBK Study Guide* from the (ISC)² Web site (www.isc2.org). It's free and will be e-mailed to you as a password-protected Adobe Acrobat PDF document. This provides a good outline of the subjects on which you'll be tested.

Next, read this book, take the practice exam in Appendix A, and review the materials on the accompanying CD-ROM. *CISSP For Dummies* is written to provide the CISSP candidate an excellent overview of all the broad topics covered on the CISSP exam.

Next, focus on weak areas that you've identified. Read additional references; I list several great ones in Chapter 15. As a minimum, I highly recommend *The CISSP Prep Guide: Mastering the Ten Domains of Computer Security* by Ronald L. Krutz and Russell Dean Vines (John Wiley & Sons, Inc.) and the *Information Security Management Handbook,* 4th Edition by Harold F. Tipton and Micki Krause (Auerbach Publications).

You should also download and review the Tipton and Rothke presentations and the ten domain guides available at www.cccure.org/studytips.php.

You can also find several study guides at www.cissps.com, www.cccure.org, and www.cramsession.com.

Joining or creating your own study group will help you stay focused and also provide a wealth of information from the broad perspectives and experiences of other security professionals.

No practice exams exactly duplicate the CISSP exam (and forget about brain dumps). However, many resources are available for practice questions. You'll find that some practice questions are too hard, others are too easy, and some are just plain irrelevant. However, the repetition of practice questions will help reinforce important information that you need to know in order to successfully answer questions on the CISSP exam. For this reason, I recommend taking as many practice exams as possible. Use the Practice Exam in Appendix A of this book, use the Flash Cards on the CD-ROM, try the practice questions on the CISSP Open Study Guide (OSG) Web site (www.cccure.org/studytips.php), and use the Boson CISSP Exam #2 and #3 (www.boson.com).

Getting hands-on experience

Getting hands-on experience may be easier said than done, but keep your eyes and ears open for learning opportunities during your course of study for the CISSP exam.

For example, if you're weak in networking or applications development, talk to the networking group or programmers in your company. They may be able to show you a few things that will help make sense of the volumes of information that you're trying to digest.

Your company should have a security policy that should be freely available to its employees, particularly if you have a security function in the organization. Get a copy and review its contents. Are critical elements missing? Do any supporting guidelines, standards, and procedures exist? If your company doesn't have a security policy, perhaps now is a good time for you to educate management about issues of due care, due diligence, and other concepts from the Law, Investigations, and Ethics security domain.

Review your company's Business Continuity and Disaster Recovery plans. They don't exist? Perhaps this is an initiative that you can lead to help both you and your company.

Attending an (ISC)² CISSP review seminar

The (ISC)² also administers review seminars to help the CISSP candidate prepare, including a one-day "Introduction to the CISSP Exam and CBK" and a more extensive five-day "CBK Review Seminar." Schedules and registration forms for the CBK Review Seminar are available on the (ISC)² Web site at www.isc2.org.

The standard rate for the CBK Review seminar is $2,670 if you register early (16 days or more in advance). You can register for both the CBK Review Seminar and the CISSP examination for $2,995 (a $125 discount on the CISSP exam). The cost is $2,970 (or $3,195 for both the seminar and examination) if you register less than 16 days in advance. Members of the Information Systems Security Association (ISSA) also get a substantial discount. The cost for ISSA members registering 16 or more days in advance is $2,370 for the seminar and $2,695 for the seminar and examination. (All dollar amounts listed here are US currency.)

If you generally learn better in a classroom environment or find that you only have knowledge or actual experience in one or two of the domains, you might seriously consider attending a review seminar.

Are you ready for the exam?

This is a difficult question to answer and should be based on individual learning factors and study habits. I don't know of any magic formula for determining your chances of success or failure on the CISSP examination.

In general, I would recommend a minimum of two months of focused study. Read this book and continue taking the practice exam in this book and on the accompanying CD until you can consistently score 80 percent or better in all areas. *CISSP For Dummies* covers *all* of the information that you will need to pass the CISSP examination. Read this book (and re-read it) until you are comfortable with the information presented and can successfully recall and apply it in each of the ten domains.

Continue by reviewing other materials (particularly in your weak areas) and actively participating in an online or local study group. Take as many practice exams from as many different sources as possible. There are no brain dumps for the CISSP examination, and no practice test will exactly duplicate the actual exam (some are too easy, and others are too difficult), but repetition will help you retain the important knowledge required to succeed on the CISSP exam.

About the CISSP Examination

The CISSP examination itself is a grueling 6-hour 250-question marathon. To put that into perspective, in 6 hours you could walk about 25 miles, watch a Kevin Costner movie 1½ times, or sing "My Way" 54 times on a karaoke machine. Each of these feats respectively would closely approximate the physical, mental (not intellectual), and emotional toll of the CISSP examination.

As described by the (ICS)², a minimum score of "70 percent" is required to pass the examination. Not all the questions are weighted equally, so it's not possible to absolutely state the number of correct questions required for a passing score.

The examination isn't computer-based. You're given an exam booklet and an answer sheet. You can write in the exam booklet, but only answers recorded on the answer sheet are scored.

You won't find any multiple-answer, fill-in-the-blank, scenario, or simulation questions on the CISSP exam. However, all 250 multiple-choice questions require you to select the *best* answer from 4 possible choices. This means that the answer isn't always a straightforward, clear answer.

A common and effective test-taking strategy for multiple-choice questions is to carefully read each question and then eliminate any obviously wrong choices. The CISSP examination is no exception.

Wrong choices aren't so obvious on the CISSP examination. You will find a few obviously wrong choices, but they only stand out to someone who has studied thoroughly for the examination and has a good grasp of all ten of the security domains.

Only 225 questions are actually counted toward your final score. The other 25 are trial questions for future versions of the CISSP examination, but they're not identified within the exam.

The CISSP examination is currently available in English only. Foreign language dictionaries are permitted. (ISC)² also recommends that non-English speaking candidates pass the Test of English as a Foreign Language (TOEFL) exam prior to attempting the CISSP examination.

Chapter 17 covers the details of the exam environment.

Waiting for Your Results

Perhaps the most painful part of the CISSP examination is waiting for the results. You can expect to come out of the CISSP examination, at best, with no idea of whether you have passed or failed . . . or worse, with the sinking feeling that you bombed it miserably. Take heart — this is an almost universal reaction, but it's certainly not the universal result.

(ISC)² officially states that you can expect your exam results within 6 weeks of your examination date. However, (ISC)² is getting more efficient and often has results out within 1–2 weeks. Your official results are sent via regular snail mail. No results are given out via telephone or e-mail. If you don't receive your results within 6 weeks, you should contact (ISC)² to inquire about the status.

Your results will be simply *Pass* or *Fail.* No score is given, and your domain strengths/weaknesses aren't identified. You just receive an official letter informing you of your results. When you pass, you receive your CISSP certification number, CISSP certificate, wallet card, lapel pin, and username/temporary password for access to the secure (ISC)² Web site.

While waiting for your results, assume the worst and prepare for the retest. Recall specific problem areas from the examination. Write them down and study those areas again. If you fail the examination, this effort will pay huge dividends when you try again. And if you pass the examination, you'll be a better CISSP!

Chapter 2

The Common Body of Knowledge (CBK)

*T*he *Common Body of Knowledge* (CBK) defines a basic and common knowledge base for all security professionals that are commonly referred to as the *ten domains of information security*. The CBK also provides minimum knowledge requirements for the Certified Information Systems Security Professional (CISSP) exam analogous to, but distinctly different from, typical test objectives. However, rather than requiring a candidate to perform specific tasks or demonstrate skill with a specific technology, the CBK is relatively abstract and stable.

The CBK is periodically updated by the CBK Committee, which is appointed by the International Information Systems Security Certifications Consortium [(ISC)^2] Board of Directors.

The ten domains of information security, as defined in the CBK, are described below and can be found online at `www.isc2.org`.

Access Control Systems and Methodology

This domain encompasses the set of mechanisms employed to restrict or direct the behavior, use, and content of a system. It defines a user's rights on a system, including what a user can do and what resources are available to a user.

This domain is covered in Chapter 3. Major topics include

- Accountability
- Access control techniques
- Access control administration
- Access control models
- Identification and authentication techniques
- Access control methodologies and implementation
- File and data ownership
- Methods of attack
- Monitoring
- Penetration testing

Telecommunications and Network Security

This domain encompasses the structures, transmission methods, transport formats, and security measures used to provide confidentiality, integrity, availability, and authentication for transmissions over private and public networks.

This domain is covered in Chapter 4. Major topics include

- The Open Systems Interconnection (OSI) Model
- Communications and network security
- Internet/intranet/extranet
- E-mail and facsimile security
- Secure voice communications
- Network attacks and countermeasures

Security Management Practices

This domain encompasses

- **Security management:** The identification of an organization's information assets and the development, documentation, and implementation of policies, standards, procedures, and guidelines that ensure confidentiality, integrity, and availability

✔ **Risk management:** The identification, measurement, control, and minimization of loss associated with uncertain events or risks, including overall security review, risk analysis, selection and evaluation of safeguards, cost benefit analysis, management decision, safeguard implementation, and effectiveness review.

This domain is covered in Chapter 5. Major topics include

✔ Security management concepts and principles

✔ Change control and change management

✔ Information and data classification

✔ Employment policies and practices

✔ Policies, standards, guidelines, and procedures

✔ Individual roles and responsibilities

✔ Security awareness training

✔ Security management planning

Applications and Systems Development Security

This domain encompasses the controls included within systems and applications software and the steps used in their development.

This domain is covered in Chapter 6. Major topics include

✔ Application issues

✔ Databases and data warehousing

✔ Data and information storage

✔ Knowledge-based systems

✔ Systems development controls

✔ Malicious code

✔ Methods of attack

Cryptography

This domain encompasses the principles, means, and methods of disguising information to ensure its integrity, confidentiality, and authenticity.

This domain is covered in Chapter 7. Major topics include

- ✔ Use of cryptography to achieve security goals
- ✔ Cryptographic concepts, methodologies, and practices
- ✔ Private and public key algorithms
- ✔ Public Key Infrastructure (PKI)
- ✔ Cryptography in Internet and e-mail applications
- ✔ Methods of attack

Security Architecture and Models

This domain encompasses the concepts, principles, structures, and standards used to design, implement, monitor, and secure operating systems, equipment, networks, and applications.

This domain is covered in Chapter 8. Major topics include

- ✔ Common computer and network organizations, architectures, and designs
- ✔ Common security models, architectures, and evaluation criteria
- ✔ Common flaws and security issues associated with system architectures and designs

Operations Security

This domain encompasses the controls over hardware, media, and operators with access privileges to resources, including monitoring and auditing.

This domain is covered in Chapter 9. Major topics include

- ✔ Administrative management
- ✔ Security concepts

- ✔ Control types
- ✔ Operations controls
- ✔ Resource protection
- ✔ Auditing and audit trails
- ✔ Monitoring tools and techniques
- ✔ Intrusion detection
- ✔ Penetration testing
- ✔ Inappropriate activities
- ✔ Threats and countermeasures
- ✔ Violations, breaches, and reporting

Business Continuity Planning (BCP) and Disaster Recovery Planning (DRP)

This domain encompasses the preparation, testing and updating of specific actions to protect critical business processes from the effect of major system and network failures.

This domain is covered in Chapter 10. Major topics include

- ✔ Business continuity planning
- ✔ Disaster recovery planning
- ✔ BCP/DRP events

Law, Investigations, and Ethics

This domain encompasses computer crime laws and regulations, incident handling, investigative measures and techniques, evidence gathering, ethical issues and codes of conduct for security professionals.

This domain is covered in Chapter 11. Major topics include

- ✔ Major categories and types of laws
- ✔ Investigations and evidence

- ✔ Major categories of computer crime
- ✔ Incident handling
- ✔ Ethics

Physical Security

This domain encompasses the threats and countermeasures to physically protect an enterprise's resources and sensitive information including people, facilities, data, equipment, support systems, media, and supplies.

This domain is covered in Chapter 12. Major topics include

- ✔ Facility requirements
- ✔ Technical controls
- ✔ Environment and life safety
- ✔ Physical security threats
- ✔ Elements of physical security

Part II
Domains

"I can tell a lot from your resume. You're well educated, detail oriented, and own a really tiny printer."

In this part . . .

The ten chapters of this part cover all the "domains" of the CISSP exam. Buckle in. It's an exciting ride!

Chapter 3

Access Control Systems and Methodology

· ·

· ·

*A*ccess control is at the heart of information security. For that matter, access control is at the heart of *all* security.

During medieval times, castles were built to provide safety and security. The castle was normally built in a strategic location with towering walls surrounded by a moat. Battlements were positioned along the top of the wall with bastions at the corners. A heavily fortified and guarded entrance were secured by a drawbridge to control entry to (and departure from) the castle. These measures created a security perimeter, preventing hostile forces from freely roaming through the castle grounds and attacking its inhabitants. Breaching the perimeter and gaining entry to the castle was the key to victory for an attacking force. After getting inside, the castle defenses were relatively simple, and the attackers were free to burn and pillage. Hard and crunchy on the outside, chewy in the middle.

Similarly, computer security requires a strong perimeter and elaborate defenses. Unfortunately, a drawbridge doesn't suffice for access control in computer security. Threats to computer security are much more sophisticated and prevalent than marauding bandits and the occasional fire-breathing dragons. Access control is still critical to securing a perimeter, but it's not limited to a single point of entry. Instead, security professionals must protect their systems from a plethora of threats, including Internet-based attacks, viruses and Trojan horses, insider attacks, covert channels, software bugs, and honest mistakes.

Additionally, you must ensure that the drawbridge operator (the firewall administrator) is properly trained on how and when to raise or lower the drawbridge (policies and procedures), and you must be sure that he's not sleeping on the job (that is, monitor your logs). The End!

The Certified Information Systems Security Professional (CISSP) candidate must fully understand access control concepts (including control types and authentication, authorization, and accounting), system access controls (including identification and authentication techniques, methodologies and implementation, and methods of attack), and data access controls (including access control techniques and models).

Uncovering Concepts of Access Control

Access control, in the context of information security, is the ability to permit or deny the use of an object (a passive entity such as a system or file) by a subject (an active entity such as an individual or process). Such use is normally defined through a set of rules or permissions: read, write, execute, list, change, and delete.

Control types

Access control is achieved through an entire set of controls that, identified by purpose, include preventive (reduces risk) and detective (identifies violations and incidents) controls. Other types of controls include corrective (remedies violations and incidents; improves existing preventive and detective controls), deterrent (discourages violations), recovery (restores systems and information), and compensating (alternative controls).

Access controls can be administrative, technical, or physical.

Administrative controls

Administrative controls include the policies and procedures that an organization implements as part of its overall information security strategy. Administrative controls ensure that technical and physical controls are understood and properly implemented in accordance with the organization's security policy. The purpose of administrative controls is often both preventive and detective. These may include

- ✔ **Policies and procedures**
- ✔ **Security awareness training**
- ✔ **Asset classification and control**
- ✔ **Employment policies and practices** (background checks, job rotations, and separation of duties and responsibilities)
- ✔ **Account administration**
- ✔ **Account, log, and journal monitoring**
- ✔ **Review of audit trails**

I discuss administrative controls in Chapters 5 and 9.

Technical controls

Technical (or logical) *controls* use hardware and software technology to implement access control.

Preventive technical controls include

- ✔ **Encryption** (Data Encryption Standard [DES], Advanced Encryption Standard [AES], Merkle-Hellman Knapsack)
- ✔ **Access control mechanisms** (biometrics, smart cards, and tokens)
- ✔ **Access control lists**
- ✔ **Remote access authentication protocols** (Password Authentication Protocol [PAP], Challenge Handshake Authentication Protocol [CHAP], and Remote Authentication Dial-In User Service [RADIUS])

Detective technical controls include

- ✔ **Violation reports**
- ✔ **Audit trails**
- ✔ **Network monitoring and intrusion detection**

Technical controls are the focus of this chapter; I also discuss them in Chapters 4, 6, 7, and 8.

Physical controls

Physical controls ensure the safety and security of the physical environment. These can be preventative or detective in nature.

Preventive physical controls include

- ✔ **Environmental controls** (for example: Heating, Ventilation, Air Conditioning [HVAC])
- ✔ **Security perimeters** (fences, locked doors, and restricted areas)
- ✔ **Guards and dogs**

Detective physical controls include

- ✔ **Motion detectors**
- ✔ **Video cameras**
- ✔ **Environmental sensors and alarms** (to detect heat, smoke, fire, and water hazards)

I discuss physical controls in Chapter 12.

Access control services

Access control systems provide three essential services:

- ✔ **Authentication**
- ✔ **Authorization**
- ✔ **Accountability**

Authentication

Authentication (who can log in) is actually a two-step process consisting of identification and authentication (I&A). *Identification* is the means by which a user claims a specific identity to a system. *Authentication* is the process of verifying that identity. For example, a username/password combination is one common technique (albeit a weak one) that demonstrates the concepts of identification (username) and authentication (password).

Authentication determines who can log in.

Authorization

Authorization (also referred to as *establishment*) defines the rights and permissions granted to a user account or process (what you can do). After a user is authenticated, authorization determines what that user can do on a system or resource.

Authorization (or establishment) determines what a subject can do.

Accountability

Accountability is the ability to associate users and processes with their actions (what you did). Audit trails and system logs are components of accountability. An important security concept that's closely related to accountability is non-repudiation. *Non-repudiation* means that a user cannot deny an action because his identity is positively associated with his actions.

Accountability determines what a subject did.

Non-repudiation means that a user cannot deny an action.

Categories of Access Control

The two categories of access controls are

- ✔ **System access controls.** Controls in this category protect the entire system and provide a first line of defense for the data contained on the system.
- ✔ **Data access controls.** Controls in this category are specifically implemented to protect the data contained on the system.

System access controls

System access controls are the hard and crunchy outside, providing the first line of defense in information security. They protect systems and information by restricting access to the system.

Although system access controls can provide complete authentication, authorization, and accountability (AAA), it's authentication for which they are renowned.

Authentication can be based on any of three factors.

- ✔ **Something you know,** such as a password or a personal identification number (PIN): This is based on the assumption that only the owner of the account knows the secret password or PIN needed to access the account. Of course, this is not always the case because passwords are often shared, stolen, guessed, or otherwise compromised.

- ✔ **Something you have,** such as a smart card or token: This is based on the assumption that only the owner of the account has the necessary key to unlock the account. Of course, keys are often lost, stolen, borrowed, or duplicated.

- ✔ **Something you are,** such as fingerprint, voice, retina, or iris characteristics: This is based on the assumption that the finger or eyeball attached to your body is actually yours and uniquely identifies you. Of course, fingers and eyes can be lost or.... Actually, the major drawback with this authentication mechanism is acceptance — people are uneasy about using these systems.

Authentication is based on something you know, something you have, or something you are.

Two-factor authentication requires two of the three above-listed factors for authentication. *Three-factor authentication* requires all three above-listed factors for authentication.

A commonly cited example of an access control system that uses two-factor authentication is an automatic teller machine (ATM) card and a PIN. For the CISSP exam, this scenario is considered two-factor authentication. Purists might argue that the ATM card is actually a form of identification that you present to the ATM machine to establish your identity and that the PIN is the only authentication factor involved; thus, this doesn't provide two-factor authentication. Save this debate for engaging conversation at a wild party.

Identification and authentication

The various I&A techniques that I discuss in this section include passwords/ passphrases and PINs (knowledge-based), biometrics and behavior (characteristic-based), one-time passwords, tokens, and single sign-on (SSO).

The identification component is normally a relatively simple mechanism based on a username or, in the case of a system or process, based on a computer name, Media Access Control (MAC) address, Internet Protocol (IP) address, or Process ID (PID). The only requirements for identification are that it must uniquely identify the user and shouldn't identify that user's role or relative importance in the organization (such as labels like *accounting* or *ceo*). Common or shared accounts, such as *root*, *admin*, or *system*, should be avoided. Such accounts provide no accountability and are prime targets for a hacker.

"Polly wanna hacker?"

The distinction between *hackers* and *crackers* is now more commonly understood, particularly within the security community, but to ensure that there is absolutely no confusion, I shall do my civic duty here and make the distinction: Hacker=good, Cracker=bad. Hackers perform a vital role in the Internet and computing community by helping to debug source code, identify vulnerabilities, and improve software development — all of which serve the greater good. Conversely, crackers typically include script kiddies, cyberpunks, cyberterrorists, common criminals, and other vermin . . . all motivated by less noble causes.

The term *hacker* is commonly used to describe both hackers and crackers in general, much as the words *he* or *him* are used to describe people in general.

Identification is the act of claiming a specific identity. Authentication is the act of verifying that identity.

Passwords and passphrases

"A password should be like a toothbrush. Use it everyday; change it regularly; and DON'T share it with friends." –USENET

Passwords are easily the most common authentication mechanism in use today. Although more advanced and secure authentication technologies are available, including tokens and biometrics, they're typically used as supplements to or in combination with — rather than as replacements for — traditional usernames and passwords.

A *passphrase* is a variation on passwords that uses a sequence of characters or words instead of a single password. Although they're generally more difficult to break than regular passwords, they're also inconvenient to enter and share the same problems associated with passwords.

The CISSP candidate should understand the general problems associated with passwords as well as common password controls and management features.

Problems with passwords/passphrases include:

- **Insecure:** Passwords are generally insecure for several reasons, including:
  - **Human nature:** In the case of user-generated passwords, users will normally choose passwords that are easily remembered and consequently easily guessed (such as a spouse's or pet's name, birthdays and anniversaries, or hobbies). Users may also be inclined to write down (particularly system-generated passwords) or share their passwords.

- • **Transmission and storage:** Many applications and protocols (file transfer protocol [FTP] and PAP, respectively) transmit passwords in clear text. Passwords may also be stored in plaintext files or using a weak hashing algorithm.

- ✓ **Easily broken:** Passwords are susceptible to brute force and dictionary attacks (which I discuss later in this chapter in the section "Methods of attack") by readily available programs such as Crack, John the Ripper, and l0phtcrack (pronounced *loft-crack*).

- ✓ **Inconvenient:** Entering passwords can be tiresome for users who are easily agitated. In an attempt to bypass these controls, users may: select an easily typed and weak password; automate logons (or select *Remember my password* in a browser); or neglect to lock their workstations or to log out.

- ✓ **Refutable:** Transactions authenticated with only a password don't necessarily provide absolute proof of a user's identity. Authentication mechanisms must guarantee non-repudiation, which is a critical component of accountability. (For more on non-repudiation, see the earlier section "Accountability.")

Passwords have the following log-in controls and management features that should be configured in accordance with an organization's security policy and security best practices:

- ✓ **Length:** The longer the better. A password is, in effect, an encryption key. Just as larger encryption keys (such as 128-bit or 256-bit) are better, so too are longer passwords. Systems should be configured to require a minimum password length of 6–8 characters.

- ✓ **Complexity:** Strong passwords contain a mix of upper- and lowercase letters, numbers, and special characters such as # and $. Be aware that certain special characters may not be accepted by some systems or may perform special functions (that is to say, in terminal emulation software).

- ✓ **Aging:** Maximum password aging should be set to require passwords at regular intervals: 30, 60, or 90 days is usually recommended. Minimum password aging — one day is usually recommended — should also be set to prevent users from easily circumventing password history controls.

- ✓ **History:** Password history settings (five is usually recommended) allow a system to remember previously used passwords. This prevents users from circumventing maximum password aging by alternating between two or three familiar passwords when required to change their passwords.

- ✓ **Limited attempts:** This control limits the number of unsuccessful log-on attempts and consists of two components: counter threshold (3 is usually recommended) and counter reset (30 minutes is usually recommended).

✔ **Lockout duration:** When the counter threshold (that I describe in the previous bullet) has been exceeded, the account is locked out. Lockout duration is commonly set to 30 minutes or forever, which requires an administrator to unlock the account. Some systems don't notify the user when an account has been locked out but instead quietly alert the system administrator to a possible break-in attempt.

✔ **Limited time periods:** This control restricts the time of day that a user can log in. For example, limiting users to access during business hours only is very effective. However, this type of control is becoming less common in the modern age of the workaholic with erratic work hours and in the global economy.

✔ **System messages:** System messages include the following:

- **Logon banner:** Welcome messages invite criminals to access your systems. Disable any welcome message and replace it with a legal warning that requires the user to click OK to acknowledge.

- **Last username:** Many popular operating systems display the username of the last successful logon. This feature is a convenience for users (who only need to type in their password) and hackers (who only need to crack the password and not worry about matching it to a valid user account). Disable this feature.

- **Last successful logon:** After successfully logging onto the system, this message tells the user the last time that he logged on. If the system shows that the last successful logon for a user was Saturday morning at 2 a.m. and the user knows that couldn't possibly have been him because he has a life, he'll know that his account has been compromised and can report the incident accordingly.

I'm sure that you know many of the following widely available and well-known guidelines for creating more secure passwords:

✔ **Mix upper- and lowercase characters.**

✔ **Replace letters with numbers** (for example, replace *e* with *3*).

✔ **Combine two words by using a special character.**

✔ **Use the first letter from each word of a nonsense phrase from a nonsense song** (for example, "Oops! ...I Did It Again" becomes *O!Idia*).

The problem with these guidelines is that they're widely available and well known. In fact, hackers use some of these same guidelines to create their aliases or handles: *super-geek* becomes *5up3rg33k*. A password like *Qwerty12!* satisfies these guidelines, but it's not really a good password because it's a relatively simple and obvious pattern. Many dictionary attacks include not only word lists, but also patterns such as these. One solution is to employ a software tool that helps users evaluate the quality of their passwords as they create them. These tools are commonly known as *password/passphrase generators* or *password appraisers*.

Personal Identification Numbers (PINs)

A PIN in itself is a relatively weak authentication mechanism because there are only 10,000 possible combinations for a 4-digit numeric PIN. The phrase *numeric PIN* may seem redundant, but alphanumeric PINs can be used, for example, in RSA's SecurID token. Therefore, some other safeguard is normally used in combination with a PIN. For example, most ATMs confiscate your ATM card after three incorrect PIN attempts. A PIN used with a one-time token password and an account lockout policy is also very effective, allowing a user to attempt only one PIN/password combination per minute and then locking the account after three or five failed attempts as determined by the security policy.

Biometrics and behavior

The only absolute method for positively identifying an individual is to base authentication on some unique physiological or behavioral characteristic of that individual. Physiological characteristics, including fingerprints, hand geometry, and facial features such as retina and iris patterns, are used for biometric identification. Behavioral biometrics are based on measurements and data derived from an action and indirectly measure characteristics of the human body. Behavioral characteristics include voice, signature, and keystroke patterns.

Biometrics are based on the third factor of authentication — something you are. (To read about all three factors, peruse the earlier section "System access controls.") The concept of I&A is applied slightly differently in biometric access control systems depending on their use, as follows.

- ✓ **Physical access controls:** The individual presents the required biometric characteristic, and the system attempts to *identify* the individual by matching the input characteristic to its database of authorized personnel. This is also known as a *one-to-many* search.

- ✓ **Logical access controls:** The user enters a username or PIN (or inserts a smart card) and then presents the required biometric characteristic for verification. The system attempts to *authenticate* the user by matching the claimed identity and the stored biometric image file for that account. This is also known as a *one-to-one* search.

The necessary factors for an effective biometrics access control system include

✔ **Accuracy:** This is the most important characteristic of any biometric system. The *uniqueness* of the body organ or characteristic being measured to guarantee positive identification is an important element of accuracy. In common biometric systems today, the only two organs that satisfy this requirement are the fingers/hands and the eyes.

Another important element of accuracy is the system's ability to detect and reject forged or counterfeit input data. The accuracy of a biometric system is normally stated as a percentage, in the following terms.

- **False Reject Rate (FRR) or Type I error:** Authorized users who are incorrectly denied access, stated as a percentage. Reducing a system's sensitivity reduces the FRR but increases the False Accept Rate (FAR).

  The False Reject Rate (or Type I error) is the percentage of authorized users who are incorrectly denied access.

- **False Accept Rate (FAR) or Type II error:** Unauthorized users who are incorrectly granted access, stated as a percentage. Increasing a system's sensitivity reduces the FAR but increases the FRR.

  The False Accept Rate (or Type II error) is the percentage of unauthorized users who are incorrectly granted access.

- **Crossover Error Rate (CER):** The point at which the FRR equals the FAR, stated as a percentage. (See Figure 3-1.) Because FAR and FRR can be adjusted by changing a system's sensitivity, the CER is considered the most important measure of biometric system accuracy.

  The Crossover Error Rate (CER) is the point at which the FRR equals the FAR, stated as a percentage.

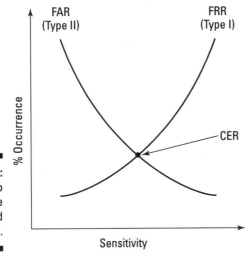

Figure 3-1:
Use CER to compare FAR and FRR.

✔ **Speed and throughput:** This describes the length of time required to complete the entire authentication procedure. This includes stepping up to the system; inputting a card or PIN (if required); entering biometric data (such as inserting a finger or hand in a reader, pressing a sensor, aligning an eye with a camera or scanner, speaking a phrase, or signing a name); processing the input data; and opening and closing an access door (in the case of a physical access control system). Another important measure is the initial enrollment time required to create a biometric file for a user account. Generally accepted standards are a speed of less than five seconds, a throughput rate of six to ten per minute, and enrollment time of less than two minutes.

✔ **Data storage requirements:** This has become a less significant but still interesting issue with the decreases in cost for data storage media. Biometric system input file sizes can be as small as 9 bytes or as large as 10,000 bytes, averaging 256–1000 bytes.

✔ **Reliability:** As with any system, reliability is an important factor. The system must operate continuously and accurately without frequent maintenance outages.

✔ **Acceptability:** Acceptance by users is the biggest hurdle to widespread implementation of biometric systems. Certain privacy and ethics issues arise with the prospect of these systems being used to collect medical or other physiological data about employees. Other factors include intrusiveness of the data collection procedure and required physical contact with common system components, such as pressing an eye against a plastic cup or placing lips close to a microphone for voice recognition.

Acceptability by users is the most common problem with biometric systems.

Table 3-1 summarizes the generally accepted standards for the above factors.

Table 3-1	Generally Accepted Standards for Biometric Systems
Characteristic	*Standard*
Accuracy	CER<10%
Speed	5 seconds
Throughput	6–10/minute
Enrollment time	<2 minutes

Common types of physiological biometric access control systems include

- ✔ **Finger scan systems:** These are the most common biometric systems in use today, accounting for approximately 78 percent of total sales in biometric technology. *Finger scan systems* analyze the ridges, whorls, and minutiae (bifurcations and ridge endings, dots, islands, ponds and lakes, spurs, bridges, and crossovers) of a fingerprint to create a digitized image that uniquely identifies the owner of the fingerprint.

  Finger scan systems, unlike fingerprint recognition systems, don't store an image of the entire fingerprint — only a digitized file describing its unique characteristics. This fact should allay the privacy concerns of most users. See Table 3-2 for general characteristics of finger scan systems.

- ✔ **Hand geometry systems:** Like finger scan systems, *hand geometry systems* are also nonintrusive and therefore generally more easily accepted than other biometric systems. These systems are also generally more accurate than finger scan systems and have some of the smallest file sizes compared with other biometric system types. Three-dimensional hand geometry data is acquired by a digital camera that simultaneously captures a vertical and a horizontal image of the subject's hand. The digitized image records the length, width, height, and other unique characteristics of the hand and fingers. See Table 3-2 for general characteristics of hand geometry systems.

Table 3-2	General Characteristics of Finger Scan and Hand Geometry Systems	
Characteristic	*Finger Scan*	*Hand Geometry*
Accuracy	<1%–5% (CER)	<1%–2% (CER)
Speed	1–7 seconds	3–5 seconds
File size	~250–1500 bytes	~10 bytes
Advantages	Nonintrusive, inexpensive	Small file size
Disadvantages	Sensor wear and tear; may be affected by swelling, injury, or wearing rings	Sensor wear and tear; may be affected by swelling, injury, or wearing rings

✔ **Retina pattern:** These systems record unique elements in the vascular pattern of the retina. Major concerns with this type of system are fears of eye damage from a laser (which is actually only a camera with a focused low-intensity light) directed at the eye and, more feasibly, privacy concerns. Certain health conditions such as diabetes and heart disease are known to cause changes in the retinal pattern, which may be detected by these types of systems. See Table 3-3 for general characteristics of retina pattern systems.

✔ **Iris pattern:** These systems are by far the most accurate on any type of biometric system. The *iris* is the colored portion of the eye surrounding the pupil. The complex patterns of the iris include unique features such as coronas, filaments, freckles, pits, radial furrows, rifts, and striations. The characteristics of the iris, formed shortly before birth, remain stable throughout life. The iris is so unique that even the two eyes of a single individual have different patterns. The iris pattern is scanned by a camera directed at an aperture mirror. The subject must glance at the mirror from a distance of approximately three to ten inches. It's technically feasible but perhaps financially infeasible to perform an iris scan from a distance of several feet. See Table 3-3 for general characteristics of iris pattern systems.

Table 3-3	General Characteristics of Retina and Iris Pattern Systems	
Characteristic	*Retina Pattern*	*Iris Pattern*
Accuracy	1.5% (CER)	< 0.5% (CER)
Speed	4–7 seconds	2.5–4 seconds
File size	~96 bytes	~256–512 bytes
Advantages	Overall accuracy	Best overall accuracy
Disadvantages	Perceived intrusiveness; sanitation and privacy concerns	Subject must remain absolutely still; colored contact lenses and glasses cannot be worn

Common types of behavioral biometric systems include

✔ **Voice recognition:** These systems capture unique characteristics of a subject's voice and may also analyze phonetic or linguistic patterns. Most voice recognition systems are text dependent, requiring the subject to repeat a specific phrase. This functional requirement of voice recognition systems also helps improve their security by providing two-factor authentication: *something you know* (phrase) and *something you are* (voice). See Table 3-4 for general characteristics of voice recognition systems.

✔ **Signature dynamics:** These systems typically require the subject to sign his name on a signature tablet. Of course, signatures commonly exhibit some slight changes because of different factors and they can be forged. See Table 3-4 for general characteristics of signature dynamic systems.

Table 3-4	General Characteristics of Voice Recognition and Signature Dynamics Systems	
Characteristic	*Voice Recognition*	*Signature Dynamics*
Accuracy	<10% (CER)	1% (CER)
Speed	10–14 seconds	5–10 seconds
File size	~1,000–10,000 bytes	~1,000–1,500 bytes
Advantages	Inexpensive; nonintrusive	Nonintrusive
Disadvantages	Accuracy, speed, file size; affected by background noise, voice changes; can be imitated	Signature tablet wear and tear; speed; can be forged

In general, the CISSP candidate doesn't need to know the specific characteristics and specifications of the different biometric systems, but you should know how they compare with other biometric system. For example, know that iris pattern systems are more accurate than retina pattern systems.

One-time passwords

A *one-time password* is a password that is valid for one log-on session only. A one-time password is considered a dynamic password; that is, it changes at some regular interval or event. Conversely, a *static password* is a password that is the same for each logon. Similar to the concept of a one-time pad in cryptography (which I discuss in Chapter 7), a one-time password provides maximum security for access control.

Two examples of one-time password implementations are tokens (which I discuss in the next section) and the S/Key protocol. The *S/Key protocol,* developed by Bellcore and defined in RFC 1760, is client/server based and uses MD4 and MD5 to generate one-time passwords (MD4 and MD5 are algorithms used to verify data integrity through the creation of a 128-bit message digest from data input. I discuss both in Chapter 7.)

Tokens

Tokens are access control devices such as key fobs, dongles, smart cards, magnetic cards, and keypad or calculator-type cards that store static passwords (or digital certificates) or generate dynamic passwords. The three general types of tokens are

✔ **Static password tokens:** Store a static password or digital certificate.

✔ **Synchronous dynamic password tokens:** Continuously generate a new password or passcode at a fixed time (for example, 60 seconds) or event (such as each time that a button is pressed) intervals. Typically, the passcode is valid only during a fixed time window (say, two minutes) and only for a single logon (that is, if logging on to more than one system, you must wait for the next passcode).

✔ **Asynchronous** (or **challenge-response**) **dynamic password tokens:** Generate a new password or passcode asynchronously by calculating the correct response to a system-generated random challenge string that's manually entered into the token by its owner.

Tokens provide two-factor authentication (*something you have* and *something you know*) by either requiring the owner to authenticate to the token first or by requiring that a secret PIN is entered along with the generated password. Both RADIUS and Terminal Access Controller Access Control System (TACACS+; which I discuss later in the upcoming section "Centralized access controls") support various token products.

Tokens can be used to generate one-time passwords and provide two-factor authentication.

Single sign-on (SSO)

The concept of single sign-on (SSO) addresses a common problem for users and security administrators alike.

Users that require access to multiple systems or applications must often maintain numerous different passwords. This inevitably leads to shortcuts in creating and recalling passwords; weak passwords with only slight variations are used and more likely to be written down. This also affects user productivity (and sanity!) by requiring multiple logons and additional support, such as resetting passwords and unlocking accounts.

See Chapter 7 for a review of the basics of cryptography.

From the security administrator's perspective, multiple accounts mean multiple vulnerabilities. Every account that exists in a system, network, or application is a potential point of unauthorized access. Multiple accounts belonging to a single user represent an even greater vulnerability, specifically for the reasons that I discuss in the preceding paragraph. And someone has to create, maintain, support, and remove (or disable) all those accounts!

Alas, SSO is that great Utopian solution that users and security administrators alike thirst for and seek. SSO allows a user to present a single set of log-on credentials, typically to an authentication server, which then transparently logs the user on to all other enterprise systems and applications for which that user is authorized. Of course, SSO is not without disadvantages, which include

✔ **Woo-hoo!:** After you're authenticated, you've got the keys to the kingdom. Read that as unrestricted access to all authorized resources!

✔ **Labor intensive:** SSO is difficult to implement. But, hey — that's why you get paid (or should get paid) the big bucks!

SSO is commonly implemented by third-party ticket-based solutions including:

✔ **Kerberos:** *Kerberos,* commonly used in the Sun Network File System (NFS) and Windows 2000, is perhaps the most popular ticket-based authentication protocol in use today. Kerberos is named for the fierce, three-headed dog that guards the gates of Hades in Greek mythology (not to be confused with Ker-beer-os, the fuzzy, six-headed dog sitting at the bar that keeps looking better and better!). This protocol is an open systems protocol that was developed at the Massachusetts Institute of Technology (MIT, also know as *Millionaires in Training*) in the mid-1980s. The CISSP exam requires a general understanding of Kerberos operation. Unfortunately, Kerberos is a complex protocol with many different implementations and no simple explanation. The following step-by-step discussion is a basic description of Kerberos operation:

1. The Kerberos client prompts the subject (such as a user) for identification and authentication (username and password). Using the authentication information (password), the client temporarily generates and stores the subject's secret key by using a one-way hash function and then sends the subject's identification (username) to the Key Distribution Center (KDC). (See Chapter 7 for a discussion of hash functions.) The password/secret key *is not* sent to the KDC. See Figure 3-2.

2. The KDC Authentication Service (AS) verifies that the subject (known as a *principal*) exists in the KDC database. The KDC Ticket Granting Service (TGS) then generates a Client/TGS Session Key encrypted with the subject's secret key, which is known only to the TGS and the client (temporarily). The TGS also generates a Ticket Granting Ticket (TGT), comprising the subject's identification, the client network address, the valid period of the ticket, and the Client/TGS Session Key. The TGT is encrypted by using the secret key of the TGS server, which is known only to the TGS server. The Client/TGS Session Key and TGT are then sent back to the client. See Figure 3-3.

3. The client decrypts the Client/TGS Session Key with the secret key that was generated using the subject's password, authenticates the subject (user), and then erases the stored secret key to avoid possible compromise. The TGT, which was encrypted with the secret key of the TGS server, cannot be decrypted by the client. See Figure 3-4.

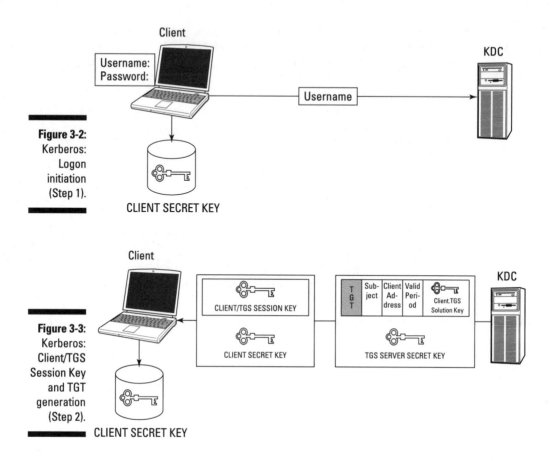

Figure 3-2:
Kerberos:
Logon
initiation
(Step 1).

Figure 3-3:
Kerberos:
Client/TGS
Session Key
and TGT
generation
(Step 2).

Figure 3-4:
Kerberos:
Logon
completion
(Step 3).

4. When the subject requests access to a specific object (such as a server, also known as a *principal*), it sends the TGT, the object identifier (such as a server name), and an authenticator to the TGS server. The authenticator is a separate message that contains the client ID and a timestamp, and it is encrypted by using the Client/TGS Session Key. See Figure 3-5.

5. The TGS server generates both a Client/Server Session Key, which is encrypted by using the Client/TGS Session Key, and a Service Ticket comprising the subject's identification, the client network address, the valid period of the ticket, and the Client/Server Session Key. The Service Ticket is encrypted using the secret key of the requested object (server), which is known only to the TGS server and the object. The Client/Server Session Key and Service Ticket are then sent back to the client. See Figure 3-6.

6. The client decrypts the Client/Server Session Key by using the Client/Server TGS Key. The Service Ticket, which was encrypted with the secret key of the requested object, cannot be decrypted by the client. See Figure 3-7.

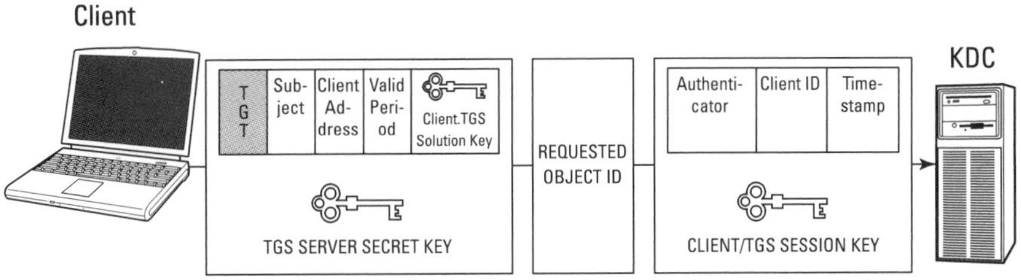

Figure 3-5: Kerberos: Requesting services (Step 4).

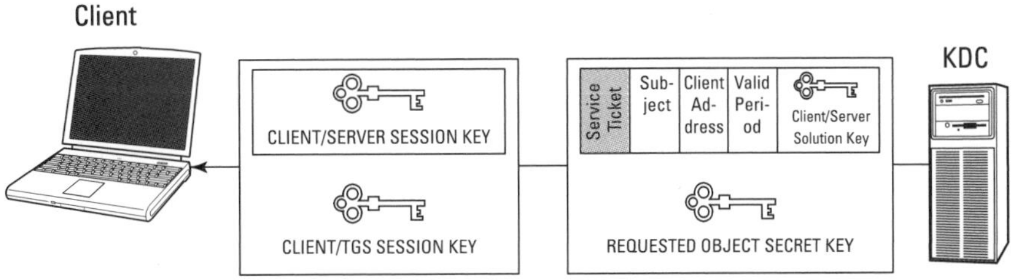

Figure 3-6: Kerberos: Client/Server Session Key and Service Ticket generation (Step 5).

Client

KDC

Figure 3-7:
Kerberos:
Decrypt
Client/Server
Session Key
(Step 6).

CLIENT/SERVER SESSION KEY

Service Ticket	Sub-ject	Client Ad-dress	Valid Peri-od	Client/Server Solution Key

REQUESTED OBJECT SECRET KEY

7. The client can then communicate directly with the requested object (server). The client sends the Service Ticket and an authenticator to the requested object (server). The authenticator, comprising the subject's identification and a timestamp, is encrypted by using the Client/Server Session Key that was generated by the TGS. The object (server) decrypts the Service Ticket by using its secret key. The Service Ticket contains the Client/Server Session Key, which allows the object (server) to then decrypt the authenticator. If the subject identification and timestamp are valid (according to the subject identification, client network address, and valid period specified in the Service Ticket), then communication between the client and server is established. The Client/Server Session Key is then used for secure communications between the subject and object. See Figure 3-8.

✔ **SESAME:** The *Secure European System and Applications in a Multi-vendor Environment* (SESAME) project, developed by the European Computer Manufacturer's Association (ECMA), is a ticket-based system, like Kerberos, with some additional security enhancements. It uses public key cryptography to distribute secret keys, incorporates a trusted authentication server at each host, employs MD5 and crc-32 one-way hash functions, and uses two separate certificates (or tickets) to provide authentication and define access privileges.

Figure 3-8:
Kerberos:
Client/Server
commu-
nications
(Step 7).

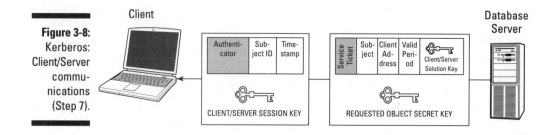

Client

Database Server

Authenti-cator	Sub-ject ID	Time-stamp

CLIENT/SERVER SESSION KEY

Service Ticket	Sub-ject	Client Ad-dress	Valid Peri-od	Client/Server Solution Key

REQUESTED OBJECT SECRET KEY

✔ **KryptoKnight:** Developed by IBM, *KryptoKnight* is another example of a ticket-based SSO authentication system that establishes peer-to-peer relationships between the KDC and its principals.

Kerberos, SESAME, and KryptoKnight are three examples of ticket-based authentication protocols that provide SSO services.

Methodologies and implementation

Access control methodologies are generally classified as either centralized or decentralized. Within each of these classifications, numerous protocols and models are available for implementation. The CISSP candidate should be able to identify the various protocols and models used in centralized and decentralized access control systems.

Centralized access controls

Centralized access control systems maintain user account information in a central location. Examples of centralized access control systems and protocols commonly used for authentication of remote users include:

✔ **RAS:** *Remote Access Service* (RAS) servers utilize the Point-to-Point Protocol (PPP) to encapsulate IP packets and establish dial-in connections over serial and ISDN links. PPP incorporates the following three authentication protocols:

  • **PAP:** The *Password Authentication Protocol* (PAP) uses a two-way handshake to authenticate a peer to a server when a link is initially established. PAP transmits passwords in clear text and provides no protection from replay or brute force attacks.

  • **CHAP:** The *Challenge Handshake Protocol* (CHAP) uses a three-way handshake to authenticate both a peer and server when a link is initially established and, optionally, at regular intervals throughout the session. CHAP requires both the peer and server to be preconfigured with a shared secret that must be stored in plain text. The peer uses the secret to calculate the response to a server challenge by using an MD5 one-way hash function. *MS-CHAP*, a Microsoft enhancement to CHAP, allows the shared secret to be stored in an encrypted form.

  • **EAP:** The *Extensible Authentication Protocol* (EAP) adds flexibility to PPP authentication by implementing various authentication mechanisms including MD5-challenge, S/Key, generic token card, digital certificates, and so forth. EAP is implemented in many wireless networks.

✔ **RADIUS:** The *Remote Authentication Dial-In User Service* (RADIUS) protocol is an open-source, User Datagram Protocol- (UDP) based client-server protocol. Defined in the RFC 2058 and 2059, RADIUS provides authentication and accountability. A user provides username/password information to a RADIUS client using PAP or CHAP. The RADIUS client encrypts the password and sends the username and encrypted password to the RADIUS server for authentication.

Note: Passwords exchanged between the RADIUS client and RADIUS server are encrypted, but passwords exchanged between the PC client and the RADIUS client are not necessarily encrypted — if using PAP authentication, for example. However, if the PC client happens to also be the RADIUS client, all password exchanges will be encrypted regardless of the authentication protocol being used.

✔ **TACACS:** The *Terminal Access Controller Access Control System* (TACACS) is a UDP-based access control protocol, originally developed for the MILNET (U.S. Military Network), which provides authentication, authorization, and accountability (AAA). The original TACACS protocol has been significantly enhanced, primarily by Cisco, as XTACACS (no longer used) and TACACS+ (which is the most common implementation of TACACS). TACACS+ is TCP-based (port 49) and supports practically any authentication mechanism (PAP, CHAP, MS-CHAP, EAP, token cards, Kerberos, and so on). The basic operation of TACACS+ is similar to RADIUS, including the caveat about encrypted passwords between client and server. The major advantages of TACACS+ are its wide support of various authentication mechanisms and granular control of authorization parameters. RADIUS and TACACS+ use dynamic passwords and TACACS uses static passwords.

RAS (PAP and CHAP), RADIUS, and TACACS are examples of centralized access control for remote access.

Decentralized access controls

Decentralized access control systems maintain user account information in separate locations by different administrators throughout an organization or enterprise. Examples of decentralized access control systems include

✔ **Multiple domains and trusts:** A *domain* is a collection of users, computers, and resources (such as a printer) with a common security policy and single administration. In smaller organizations, a single domain may be defined; this is considered a *centralized access* control. However, larger organizations or enterprises typically establish multiple domains along organizational or geographical boundaries, such as separate Marketing, Accounting, Sales, and Research domains, or separate Chicago, Seattle, Paris, and Tokyo domains. One-way *trust relationships* or *trust models* facilitate communications between multiple domains. For example, if the Marketing domain explicitly trusts the Research domain, then all users in the Research domain are permitted access to resources in the Marketing domain. Unless a trust relationship in the reverse direction is established (Research trusts Marketing), users in the Marketing domain will *not* be able to access resources in the Research domain.

✔ **Databases:** Access to databases is controlled through a *database management system* (DBMS). A DBMS restricts access by different subjects (users) to various objects (such as data and operations) in a database. A *view* is a logical operation that can be used to restrict access to specific information in a database, hide attributes, and restrict queries available to a user. Views are a type of constrained user interface that restricts access to specific functions by not allowing a user to request it. I cover additional database security methods in Chapter 6.

A database view is a type of constrained user interface.

Methods of attack

Gaining access (getting through that hard and crunchy outside) to a system or network is a hacker's first objective. Several methods of attack are commonly used against access control systems, including

✔ **Brute force or dictionary attack:** With this method, the attacker attempts every possible combination of letters, numbers, and characters to crack a password, passphrase, or PIN. A *dictionary attack* is essentially a more focused type of brute force attack in which a predefined word list is used. Such word lists or dictionaries, including foreign language and special-interest dictionaries, are widely available on the Internet for use in password-cracking utilities such as l0phtcrack and John the Ripper.

✔ **Buffer** or **stack overflow:** *Buffer overflows* constitute the most common and successful type of computer attacks today. Although often used in denial-of-service attacks, buffer overflows in certain systems or applications may enable an attacker to gain unauthorized access to a system or directory. A *teardrop attack* is a type of stack overflow attack that exploits vulnerabilities in the IP protocol.

✔ **Man-in-the-middle attacks:** This method involves an attacker intercepting messages between two parties and forwarding a modified version of the original message. For example, an attacker may substitute his own public key during a public key exchange between two parties. The two parties believe that they're still communicating with each other and unknowingly encrypt messages using the attacker's public key rather than the intended recipient's public key. The attacker can then decrypt secret messages between the two parties, modify their contents as desired, and send them on to the unwary recipient.

✔ **Packet (or password) sniffing:** In this method, an attacker uses a sniffer to capture network packets and analyze their contents, such as usernames/passwords and shared keys.

✔ **Session hijacking:** This method is similar to a man-in-the-middle attack except that the attacker impersonates the intended recipient rather than modifying messages in transit.

✔ **Social engineering:** This low-tech method is one of the most effective and easily perpetrated forms of attack. Common techniques involve dumpster diving, shoulder surfing, raiding cubicles (passwords on monitors and under mouse pads), and plain ol' asking. This latter brazen technique can simply be the attacker calling a user, pretending to be a system administrator and asking for the user's password, or calling a help desk pretending to be a user and asking to have the password changed.

Data access controls

Data access controls are, well, the hard and crunchy middle. Probably not your favorite candy, something like a freeze-dried Cadbury's Creme Egg, but effective information security requires defense in depth.

Data access controls protect systems and information by restricting access to system files and user data based on object (user) identity. Data access controls also provide authorization and accountability, relying on system access controls to provide identification and authentication.

Access control techniques

Data access control techniques are generally categorized as either discretionary or mandatory. The CISSP candidate must fully understand the concept of discretionary and mandatory access controls and be able to describe specific access control methods under each category.

Discretionary access control

A *discretionary access control* (DAC) is an access policy determined by the owner of a file (or other resource). The owner decides who is allowed access to the file and what privileges they have.

In DAC, the owner determines the access policy.

Two important concepts in DAC are

✔ **File and data ownership:** Because the access policy is determined by the owner of the resource (including files, directories, data, system resources, and devices), every object in a system must have an owner. Theoretically, an object without an owner is left unprotected. Normally, the owner of a resource is the person who created the resource (such as a file or directory), but in certain cases, the owner may need to be explicitly identified as an administrative function.

✔ **Access rights and permissions:** These are the controls that an owner can assign to individual users or groups for specific resources. Various systems (Windows-based, Unix-based, and Novell-based) define different sets of permissions that are essentially variations or extensions of three basic types of access:

- **Read (R):** The subject can read contents of a file or list contents of a directory.

- **Write (W):** The subject can change the contents of a file or directory (including add, rename, create, and delete).

- **Execute (X):** If the file is a program, the subject can run the program.

Access control lists (ACLs) provide a flexible method for applying discretionary access controls. An ACL lists the specific rights and permissions that are assigned to a subject for a given object.

ACLs are implemented differently on different operating systems. Although the CISSP exam doesn't directly test your knowledge of specific operating systems or products, you should be aware of this fact. Also, understand that ACLs in this context are different from ACLs used on routers, which have nothing to do with DAC.

Role-based access control is another method for implementing discretionary access controls. Role-based access control assigns group membership based on organizational or functional roles. Individuals may belong to one or many groups (acquiring cumulative permissions or limited to the most restrictive set of permissions for all assigned groups), and a group may contain only a single individual (corresponding to a specific organizational role assigned to one person). Access rights and permissions for objects are assigned to groups rather than (or in addition to) individuals. This strategy greatly simplifies the management of access rights and permissions.

Major disadvantages of discretionary access control techniques include

✔ Lack of centralized administration

✔ Dependence on security-conscious resource owners

✔ Many popular operating systems defaulting to full access for everyone if permissions aren't explicitly set by the owner

✔ Difficult, if not impossible, auditing

Mandatory access control

A *mandatory access control* (MAC) is an access policy determined by the system rather than the owner, in contrast to DAC. MAC is used in multilevel systems that process highly sensitive data, such as classified government and military information. A *multilevel system* is a single computer system that handles multiple classification levels between subjects and objects. Two important concepts in MAC are

✔ **Sensitivity labels:** In a MAC-based system, all subjects and objects must have labels assigned. A subject's sensitivity labe*l* specifies its level of trust. An object's sensitivity label specifies the level of trust required for access. In order to access a given object, the subject must have a sensitivity level equal to or higher than the requested object. For example, a user (subject) with a Top Secret clearance (sensitivity label) is permitted access to a file (object) with a Secret classification level (sensitivity label) because her clearance level exceeds the minimum required for access. I discuss classification systems in Chapter 5.

✔ **Data import and export:** Controlling the import of information from other systems and export to other systems (including printers) is a critical function of MAC-based systems, which must ensure that sensitivity labels are properly maintained and implemented so that sensitive information is appropriately protected at all times.

In MAC, the system determines the access policy.

Rule-based access control is one method for applying mandatory access control. Actually, all MAC-based systems implement a simple form of rule-based access control by matching an object's sensitivity label and a subject's sensitivity label to determine whether access should be granted or denied. Additional rules can be applied using rule-based access control to further define specific conditions for access to a requested object.

Lattice-based access controls are another method for implementing mandatory access controls. A *lattice model* is a mathematical structure that defines greatest lower-bound and least upper-bound values for a pair of elements, such as a subject and an object. This model can be used for complex access control decisions involving multiple objects and/or subjects: for example, given a set of files with multiple classification levels, determining what the minimum clearance level is that a user requires to access all the files.

Major disadvantage of mandatory access control techniques include

✔ Lack of flexibility

✔ Difficulty in implementing and programming for

✔ User frustration

Access control models

Models are used to express access control requirements in a theoretical or mathematical framework that precisely describes or quantifies its function. Common access control models include Bell-LaPadula, Biba, Clark-Wilson, non-interference, access matrix, and information flow. I introduce these models in the following sections and also cover them more in Chapter 8.

Bell-LaPadula (Basic security theorem)

Published in 1973, the Bell-LaPadula model was the first formal confidentiality model of a mandatory access control system. *Bell-LaPadula* is a state machine model that addresses only the confidentiality of information. A *secure state* is defined and maintained during transitions between secure states. The basic premise of Bell-LaPadula is that information cannot flow downward. Bell-LaPadula defines the following two properties:

- ✔ **simple security property (ss property):** A subject cannot read information from an object with a higher sensitivity label (*no read up*, or NRU).

- ✔ ***-property (star property):** A subject cannot write information to an object with a lower sensitivity label (*no write down*, or NWD).

Bell-LaPadula addresses confidentiality.

Biba

Published in 1977, the *Biba integrity model* (sometimes referred to as *Bell-LaPadula upside down*) was the first formal integrity model. Biba is a lattice-based model that addresses the first goal of integrity — ensuring that modifications to data are not made by unauthorized users or processes. (For more on lattice-based models, read the earlier section "Mandatory access controls." See Chapter 5 for a complete discussion of the three goals of integrity.) Biba defines the following two properties:

- ✔ **simple integrity property:** A subject cannot read information from an object with a lower integrity level (no read down).

- ✔ ***-integrity property (star integrity property):** A subject cannot write information to an object with a higher integrity level (no write up).

Clark-Wilson

Published in 1987, the *Clark-Wilson integrity model* establishes a security framework for use in commercial activities, such as the banking industry. Clark-Wilson addresses all three goals of integrity (read more about this in Chapter 5) and identifies special requirements for inputting data based on the following items and procedures:

- ✔ **Unconstrained data item (UDI):** Data outside the control area, such as input data.

- ✔ **Constrained data item (CDI):** Data inside the control area (integrity must be preserved).

- ✔ **Integrity verification procedures (IVP):** Checks validity of CDIs.

- ✔ **Transformation procedures (TP):** Maintains integrity of CDIs.

Biba and Clark-Wilson both address integrity.

Non-interference model

A *non-interference model*, in general, ensures that the actions of different objects and subjects are not seen by and don't interfere with other objects and subjects on the same system.

Access matrix model

An *access matrix model*, in general, provides object access rights (read/write/execute, or R/W/X) to subjects in a DAC system. An access matrix consists of access control lists (ACLs) and capability lists. (For more on DAC and ACLs, peruse the earlier section "Discretionary access control.")

Information flow model

An *information flow model*, in general, is a lattice-based model in which objects are assigned a security class and value and their direction of flow is controlled by a security policy.

Additional References

Krutz, Ronald L. and Vines, Russell Dean. *The CISSP Prep Guide: Mastering the Ten Domains of Computer Security,* Chapter 2. John Wiley & Sons, Inc.

Tipton, Harold F. and Krause, Micki. *Information Security Management Handbook,* 4th Edition, Chapters 1, 2, and 21. Auerbach Publications.

Pipkin, Donald L. *Information Security, Protecting the Global Enterprise,* Chapters 8–11, and 15. Prentice Hall PTR.

Kaeo, Merike. *Designing Network Security,* Chapters 1 and 2. Cisco Press.

Anderson, Ross. *Security Engineering: A Guide to Building Dependable Distributed Systems,* Chapters 2–4, 7, and 13. John Wiley & Sons, Inc.

Russell, Deborah and Gangemi Sr., G.T. *Computer Security Basics,* Chapter 3. O'Reilly and Associates.

Prep Test

1 **General purpose controls types include all the following except**

A ○ Detective

B ○ Mandatory

C ○ Preventive

D ○ Compensating

2 **Violation reports and audit trails are examples of what type of control?**

A ○ Detective technical

B ○ Preventive technical

C ○ Detective administrative

D ○ Preventive administrative

3 **"A user cannot deny an action" describes the concept of**

A ○ Authentication

B ○ Accountability

C ○ Non-repudiation

D ○ Plausible deniability

4 **Authentication can be based on any combination of the following factors except**

A ○ Something you know

B ○ Something you have

C ○ Something you need

D ○ Something you are

5 **Unauthorized users that are incorrectly granted access in biometric systems are described as the**

A ○ False Reject Rate (Type II error)

B ○ False Accept Rate (Type II error)

C ○ False Reject Rate (Type I error)

D ○ False Accept Rate (Type I error)

6 **All the following devices and protocols can be used to implement one-time passwords except**

A ○ Tokens

B ○ S/Key

C ○ RADIUS

D ○ Kerberos

7 Which of the following PPP authentication protocols transmits passwords in clear text?

A ○ PAP

B ○ CHAP

C ○ MS-CHAP

D ○ FTP

8 Which of the following is not considered a method of attack against access control systems?

A ○ Brute force

B ○ Dictionary

C ○ Denial of service

D ○ Buffer overflow

9 Sensitivity labels are a fundamental component in which type of access control systems?

A ○ Mandatory access control

B ○ Discretionary access control

C ○ Access control lists

D ○ Role-based access control

10 Which of the following access control models addresses availability issues?

A ○ Bell-LaPadula

B ○ Biba

C ○ Clark-Wilson

D ○ None of the above

Answers

1 **B.** Mandatory. Control types identified by purpose include preventive, detective, corrective, deterrent, recovery, and compensating controls. *Review "Control types."*

2 **A.** Detective technical. Preventive technical controls include access control mechanisms and protocols. Review of audit trails is a detective administrative control, but the actual generating of audit trails is a technical function (control). *Review "Technical controls."*

3 **C.** Non-repudiation. Authentication and accountability are related to but aren't the same as non-repudiation. Plausible deniability is a bogus answer. *Review "Accountability."*

4 **C.** Something you need. The three factors of authentication are *something you know*, *something you have*, and *something you are*. *Review "System access controls."*

5 **B.** False Accept Rate (Type II error). You should know the biometric error types by both descriptions. The False Reject Rate is a Type I error and describes the percentage of authorized users that are incorrectly denied access. *Review "Biometrics and behavior."*

6 **D.** Kerberos. Kerberos is a ticket-based authentication protocol. Although the tickets that are generated are unique for every logon, Kerberos relies on shared secrets that are static. Therefore, Kerberos isn't considered a one-time password protocol. *Review these three sections: "One-time passwords," "Tokens," and "Single sign-on (SSO)."*

7 **A.** PAP. The Password Authentication Protocol (PAP) transmits passwords in clear text. CHAP and MS-CHAP authenticate using challenges and responses that are calculated using a one-way hash function. FTP transmits passwords in clear text but isn't a PPP authentication protocol. *Review "Centralized access controls."*

8 **C.** Denial of service. The purpose of an attack against access controls is to gain access to a system. Brute force and dictionary attacks are both password cracking methods. Although commonly used in denial of service attacks, a buffer overflow attack can exploit vulnerabilities or flaws in certain applications and protocols that will allow unauthorized access. *Review "Methods of attack."*

9 **A.** Mandatory access control. The fundamental components in discretionary access controls are file (and data) ownership and access rights and permissions. Access control lists and role-based access control are types of discretionary access control systems. *Review "Access control techniques."*

10 **D.** None of the above. Bell-LaPadula addresses confidentiality issues. Biba and Clark-Wilson address integrity issues. *Review "Access control models."*

Chapter 4

Telecommunications and Network Security

*T*he Telecommunications and Network Security domain is easily the most extensive domain in the Common Body of Knowledge (CBK) for the Certified Information Systems Security Professional (CISSP) examination. The CISSP candidate must thoroughly understand the various networking models, protocols, standards, services, technologies, and vulnerabilities. A networking background will definitely help the CISSP candidate pass the exam and a prior networking certification such as the CompTIA Network+ or the Cisco Certified Network Associate (CCNA) is highly recommended.

Data Network Types

Data networks are generally classified as *local area* networks (LANs) and *wide area* networks (WANs). The CISSP candidate should understand the fundamental distinctions between these two types of network classifications.

Local area network (LAN)

A *local area network* (LAN) is a data network that operates across a relatively small geographic area, such as a single building or floor. A LAN connects workstations, servers, printers, and other devices so that network resources can be shared, such as files and e-mail. Two variations of basic LANs include

- ✔ **Campus area network (CAN):** Connects multiple buildings across a high-performance backbone
- ✔ **Metropolitan area network (MAN):** A LAN that extends across a large area, such as a small city

A local area network (LAN) is a data network that operates across a relatively small geographic area.

See the upcoming section "The OSI Reference Model" for a discussion of the LAN function at the Physical and Data Link layers of the OSI Reference Model.

Wide area network (WAN)

A *wide area network* (WAN) connects multiple LANs and other WANs by using telecommunications devices and facilities to form an internetwork.

A wide area network (WAN) is a data network that operates across a relatively large geographic area.

Examples of WANs include

- ✔ **Internet:** The Mother of all WANs, the *Internet* is the global network of public networks originally developed by the US Department of Defense (DoD) Advanced Research Projects Agency (ARPA). Users and systems connect to the Internet via Internet Service Providers (ISPs).
- ✔ **Intranet:** An *intranet* can be thought of as a private Internet. An intranet typically uses Web-based technologies to disseminate company information that's available only to authorized users on the company network.
- ✔ **Extranet:** An *extranet* extends the basic concept of an intranet to include partners, vendors, or other related parties. For example, an automobile manufacturer may operate an extranet that connects networks belonging to parts manufacturers, distributors, and dealerships. Extranets are commonly operated across the Internet by using a Virtual Private Network (VPN), which I discuss later in the section "Virtual private networks (VPNs)," or other secure connection.

See the next section for a discussion on the WAN function at the Physical, Data Link, and Network layers of the OSI Reference Model.

The OSI Reference Model

In 1984, the International Standards Organization (ISO) adopted the Open Systems Interconnection (OSI) reference model (or simply, the *OSI model*) to facilitate interoperability between network devices independent of the manufacturer. The OSI model defines standard protocols for communication and interoperability by using a layered approach. This approach divides complex networking issues into simpler functional components that help the understanding, design, and development of networking solutions and provides the following specific advantages:

- ✔ Clarifies the general functions of a communications process rather than focusing on specific issues

- ✔ Reduces complex networking processes into simpler sublayers and components

- ✔ Promotes interoperability by defining standard interfaces

- ✔ Aids development by allowing a vendor to change individual features at a single layer rather than rebuilding the entire protocol stack

- ✔ Facilitates easier (and more logical) troubleshooting

The OSI model consists of seven distinct layers that describe how data is communicated between systems and applications on a computer network. (See Figure 4-1.)

In the OSI model, data is passed from the highest layer (Application; Layer 7) downward through each layer to the lowest layer (Physical; Layer 1) and is then transmitted across the network medium to the destination node, where it's passed upward from the lowest layer to the highest layer. Each layer communicates only with the layer immediately above and below it (adjacent layers). This communication is achieved through a process known as *data encapsulation*. Data encapsulation wraps protocol information from the layer immediately above in the data section of the layer immediately below. Figure 4-2 illustrates this process.

Try creating a mnemonic to recall the layers of the OSI model, such as: Adult People Should Try New Dairy Products.

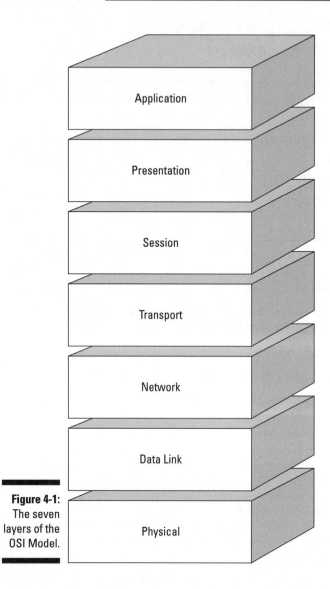

Figure 4-1:
The seven layers of the OSI Model.

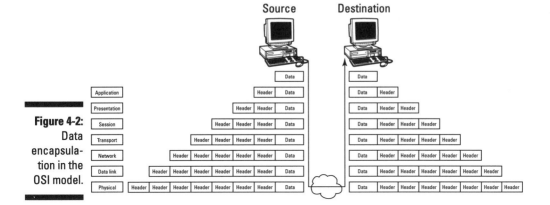

Physical Layer (Layer 1)

The Physical Layer sends and receives bits across the network.

It specifies the electrical, mechanical, and functional requirements of the network including topology, cabling and connectors, and interface types, as well
as the process for converting bits to electrical (or light) signals that can be
transmitted across the physical medium. (See Figure 4-3.)

Network topologies

The three basic network topologies in common use today are bus, star, and
ring. Although many variations of the three basic types (meshed, Fiber
Distributed Data Interface [FDDI], star-bus, star-ring) exist, I stick to the
basics here.

Bus

In a *bus* (or linear bus) topology, all devices are connected to a single cable
(the *backbone*) that's terminated on both ends, as illustrated in Figure 4-4.
Bus networks are ideal for smaller networks because they're inexpensive and
easy to install. However, in a larger environment, they're impractical because
the media have physical limitations, the backbone is a single point of failure
(a break anywhere on the network affects the entire network), and tracing a
fault in a large network can be extremely difficult.

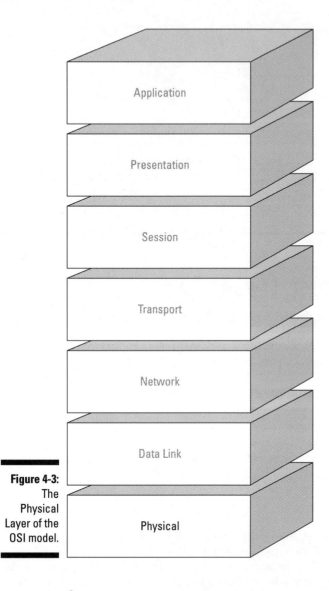

Figure 4-3:
The
Physical
Layer of the
OSI model.

Star

In a *star* topology, each individual node on the network is directly connected to a central hub or concentrator, as shown in Figure 4-5. All data communications must pass through the hub, which can become a bottleneck or single point of failure. Star topologies are more expensive than bus topologies because of the additional hardware (hubs) and cable lengths. However, a star topology is ideal for larger environments and is the most common basic topology in use today. A star topology is also easy to install and maintain, and network faults are easily isolated without affecting the rest of the network.

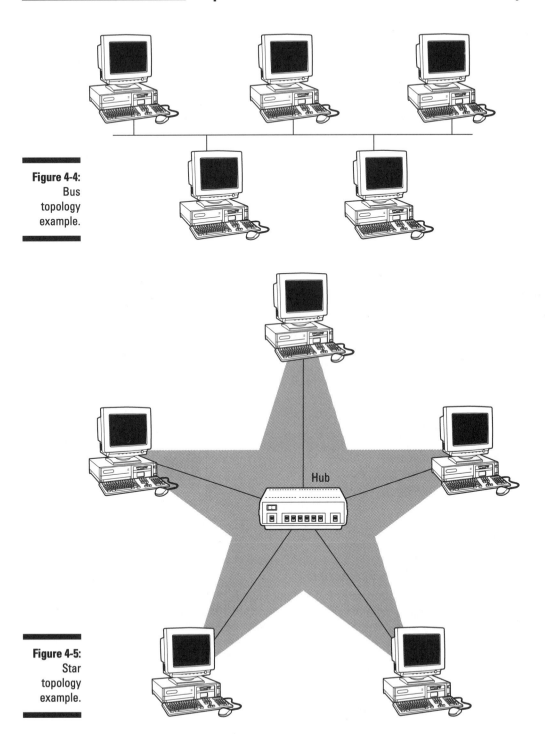

Figure 4-4:
Bus
topology
example.

Figure 4-5:
Star
topology
example.

Ring

A *ring* topology is a closed loop connecting end devices in a continuous ring, as illustrated in Figure 4-6. Functionally, this is achieved by connecting individual devices to a Multistation Access Unit (MSAU or MAU). Physically, this gives the ring topology the appearance of a star topology, as you can see in Figure 4-7. Ring topologies are common in token-ring and FDDI networks.

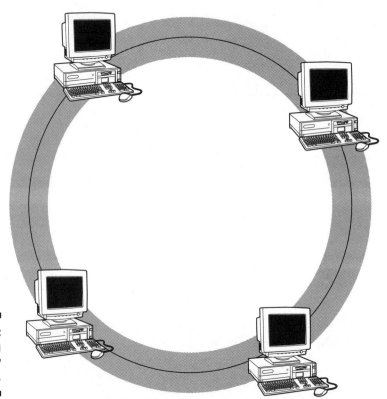

Figure 4-6:
Logical ring topology example.

Cable and connector types

Cables carry the electrical or light signals that represent data between devices on a network. Signaling over cable medium is classified as either baseband or broadband. *Baseband* signaling uses a single channel for transmission of digital signals and is common in LANs using twisted pair cabling. *Broadband* signaling uses many channels over a range of frequencies for transmission of analog signals including voice, video, and data. The three basic cable types used in networks are coaxial, twisted pair, and fiber optic.

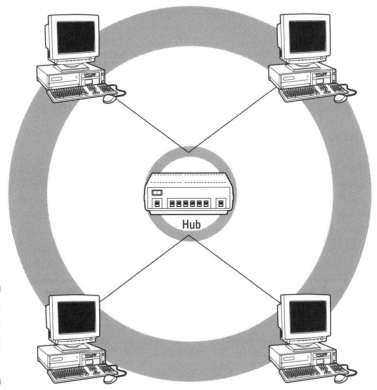

Figure 4-7:
Physical
ring
topology
example.

Coaxial cable

Using coaxial (coax) cable was very common in the early days of LANs and is rebounding (sort of) with the emergence of broadband networks. *Coax* cable consists of a single, solid copper-wire core, surrounded by a plastic or Teflon insulator, braided-metal shielding, and (sometimes) a metal foil wrap, all covered with a plastic sheath. This construction makes the cable very durable and resistant to Electromagnetic Interference (EMI) and Radio Frequency Interference (RFI) signals.

Analog and digital signaling

Analog signaling conveys information through a continuous signal using variations of wave amplitude, frequency, and phase.

Digital signaling conveys information in pulses through the presence or absence (on-off) of electrical signals.

Coax cable comes in two flavors: thick and thin.

- ✔ **Thick:** Also known as *RG8* or *RG11* or *thicknet*. Thicknet cable uses a screw-type connector, known as an *Attachment Unit Interface (AUI)*.

- ✔ **Thin:** Also known as *RG58* or *thinnet*. Thinnet cable is typically connected to network devices by using a bayonet-type connector, known as a *BNC connector*.

Twisted pair cable

Twisted pair cable is the most popular LAN cable in use today because it's lightweight, flexible, inexpensive, and easy to install. One easily recognized example of twisted pair cable is common telephone wire. Twisted pair cable consists of copper wire pairs that are twisted together to improve the transmission quality of the cable. Currently, six classes of twisted pair cable are defined. Read through Table 4-1 for the lowdown. However, only CAT-3, CAT-5, and CAT-6 cable are typically used for networking.

Table 4-1	Twisted Pair Cable Classes	
Classes	*Use*	*Example*
1	Voice only	Telephone
2	Data (up to 4 Mbps)	Token-ring at 4 Mbps
3	Data (up to 10 Mbps)	Ethernet
4	Data (up to 20 Mbps)	Token-ring at 16 Mbps
5	Data (up to 100 Mbps)	Fast Ethernet
6	Data (up to 1000 Mbps)	Gigabit Ethernet

Twisted pair cable can be either unshielded (UTP) or shielded (STP). UTP cabling is more common because it's easier to work with and less expensive than STP. STP is used when RFI or EMI is a major concern.

Twisted pair cable is terminated with an RJ-type terminator. The three common types of RJ-type connectors are RJ-11, RJ-45, and RJ-49. Although these connectors are all similar in appearance (particularly RJ-45 and RJ-49), only RJ-45 connectors are used for LANs. RJ-11 connectors are used for analog phone lines, and RJ-49 connectors are commonly used for Integrated Services Digital Network (ISDN) lines and WAN interfaces.

Fiber optic cable

Fiber optic cable, the most expensive type of network cabling but also the most reliable, is typically used in backbone networks and high-availability (FDDI) networks. Fiber optic cable carries data as light signals rather than electrical signals. Fiber optic cable consists of a glass core or bundle, a glass insulator (commonly known as *cladding*), Kevlar fiber strands (for strength) and a polyvinyl chloride (PVC) or Teflon outer sheath. Advantages of fiber optic cable include higher speeds, longer distances, and resistance to interception and interference. Fiber optic cable is terminated with an SC-type or ST-type connector.

See Table 4-2 for a comparison of the various cable types and their characteristics:

Table 4-2	Cable Types and Characteristics		
Cable Type	*Ethernet Designation*	*Maximum Length*	*EMI/RFI Resistance*
RG58 (Thinnet)	10Base2	185 meters	Good
RG8/11 (Thicknet)	10Base5	500 meters	Better
UTP	10/100/1000BaseT	100 meters	Poor
STP	10/100/1000BaseT	100 meters	Fair to good
Fiber optic	100BaseF	2,000 meters	Best (No effect)

Interface types

The interface between the Data Terminal Equipment (DTE) and Data Communications Equipment (DCE), which I discuss in the upcoming section "Networking equipment," is specified at the Physical Layer.

Network topologies, cable and connector types, and interfaces are defined at the Physical Layer of the OSI Model.

Common interface standards include

- ✔ **EIA/TIA-232:** Supports unbalanced circuits at signal speeds of up to 64 Kbps (formerly known as *RS-232).*

- ✔ **EIA/TIA-449:** Faster version of EIA/TIA-232 that supports longer cable runs and speeds of up to 2 Mbps.

- ✔ **V.24. CCITT:** (Formerly ITU-T.) A standard that's essentially the same as EIA/TIA-232 standard.

✔ **V.35. CCITT:** (Formerly ITU-T.) A standard that describes a synchronous communications protocol between network access devices and a packet network with speeds of up to 48 Kbps.

✔ **X.21bis. CCITT:** (Formerly ITU-T.) A standard that defines communications protocol between DCE and DTE in an X.25 network. It is essentially the same as the EIA/TIA-232 standard.

✔ **High-Speed Serial Interface (HSSI):** A network standard developed to address the need for high-speed (up to 52 Mbps) serial connections over WAN links.

Networking equipment

Networking devices that operate at the Physical Layer include Network Interface Cards (NICs), network media (cabling/connectors/interfaces, which I discuss in the earlier section "Cable and connector types"), repeaters, and hubs.

Network Interface Cards (NICs) are used to connect a computer to the network. NICs may be integrated on a computer motherboard or installed as an adapter card, such as an ISA, PCI, or PC card.

A *repeater* is a non-intelligent device that simply amplifies a signal to compensate for attenuation (signal loss) and extend the length of the cable segment.

A *hub* (or *concentrator*) is used to connect multiple LAN devices together, such as servers and workstations. The two basic types of hubs are

✔ **Passive:** Data enters one port and exits all other ports without any signal amplification or regeneration.

✔ **Active:** Combines the features of a passive hub and repeater. Also known as a *multi-port repeater*.

Data Link Layer (Layer 2)

The Data Link Layer ensures that messages are delivered to the proper device across a physical network link and defines the networking protocol (for example, Ethernet and token-ring) used for sending and receiving data between individual devices. It formats messages from layers above into frames for transmission, handles point-to-point synchronization and error control, and can perform link encryption.

I go into detail about this in Chapter 7.

The Data Link Layer consists of two sublayers: the Logical Link Control (LLC) and Media Access Control (MAC) sublayers, as illustrated in Figure 4-8.

The Data Link Layer is responsible for ensuring that messages are delivered to the proper device across a physical network link.

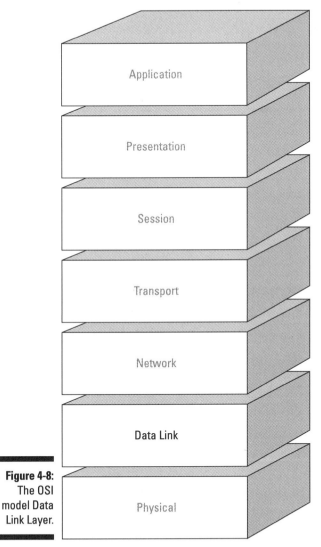

Figure 4-8:
The OSI
model Data
Link Layer.

The Logical Link Control (LLC) sublayer is defined in IEEE standards 802.1 (Internetworking) and 802.2 (Logical Link Control). See Table 4-3 for more information about the IEEE 802 standards. The LLC sublayer operates between the Network Layer above and the MAC sublayer below. The LLC sublayer performs the following three functions:

✔ Provides an interface for the MAC sublayer using Source Service Access Points (SSAPs) and Destination Service Access Points (DSAPs).

✔ Manages the control, sequencing, and acknowledgement of frames being passed up to the Network Layer or down to the Physical Layer.

✔ Bears responsibility for timing and flow control. Flow control monitors the flow of data between devices to ensure that a receiving device, which may not necessarily be operating at the same speed as the transmitting device, is not overwhelmed.

Table 4-3	The IEEE 802 Standards
Standard	*Description*
802.1	Internetworking
802.2	Logical Link Control (LLC)
802.3	Ethernet
802.4	Physical Bus
802.5	Token Ring
802.6	Metropolitan Area Networks (MANs)
802.7	Broadband Technical Advisory Group
802.8	Fiber Optic Technical Advisory Group
802.9	Integrated Voice/Data Networks
802.10	Network Security
802.11	Wireless Networks
802.12	High-speed Networks

The Media Access Control (MAC) sublayer is defined in IEEE standards 802.3 (Ethernet), 802.4 (Physical Bus), 802.5 (Token Ring), and 802.12 (High-speed Networks).

The Logical Link Control (LLC) and Media Access Control (MAC) are sublayers of the Data Link Layer.

The MAC sublayer operates between the LLC sublayer above and the Physical Layer below. It is primarily responsible for framing and performs the following three functions:

✔ **Performs error control:** Error control is performed by using a cyclic redundancy check (CRC). A *CRC* is a simple mathematical calculation or checksum used to create a message profile (analogous to a simple message digest, which I discuss in Chapter 7). The CRC is re-calculated by the receiving device. If the calculated CRC doesn't match the received CRC, the packet is dropped and a request to resend is transmitted.

✔ **Identifies hardware device (or MAC) addresses:** A *MAC address* (also known as a *hardware address* or *physical address)* is a 48-bit address that is encoded on each device by its manufacturer. The first 24 bits identify the manufacturer or vendor. The second 24 bits uniquely identify the device.

✔ **Controls media access:** The three basic types of media access are as follows:

• **Contention:** In contention-based networks, individual devices must vie for control of the physical network medium. This type of network is ideally suited for networks characterized by small, bursty traffic. Ethernet networks use a contention-based method, known as *Carrier-Sense Multiple Access Collision Detect* (CSMA/CD), in which all stations listen for traffic on the physical network medium. If the line is clear, any station can transmit data. However, if another station attempts to transmit data at the same time, a collision occurs, the traffic is dropped, and both stations must wait a random period of time before attempting to re-transmit. Another slight variation of the CSMA/CD method, used in Apple LocalTalk networks, is known as *Carrier-Sense Multiple Access Collision Avoidance* (CSMA/CA).

• **Token passing:** In token-passing networks, individual devices must wait for a special frame, known as a *token,* before transmitting data across the physical network medium. This type of network is considered *deterministic* (transmission delay can be reliably calculated and collisions don't occur) and is ideally suited for networks with large, bandwidth-consuming applications that are delay-sensitive. Token Ring, FDDI, and ARCnet networks all use various token-passing methods for media access control.

• **Polling:** In polling networks, individual devices (secondary hosts) are polled by a primary host to see whether they have data to be transmitted. Secondary hosts can't transmit until permission is granted by the primary host. Polling is typically used in mainframe environments.

The Logical Link Control (LLC) and Media Access Control (MAC) are sublayers of the Data Link Layer.

LAN protocols and transmission methods

Common LAN protocols are defined at the Data Link (and Physical) Layer and include:

- **ARCnet:** The ARCnet protocol is one of the earliest LAN technologies developed. It transports data to the physical LAN medium by using the token-passing media access method that I discuss in the previous section. It is implemented in a star topology by using coaxial cable. ARCnet provides slow but predictable network performance.

- **Ethernet:** The Ethernet protocol transports data to the physical LAN medium using CSMA/CD (which I discuss in the previous section) and is designed for networks characterized by sporadic, sometimes heavy traffic requirements. Ethernet is the most common LAN protocol used today and is implemented in a bus topology over coaxial or twisted pair cabling (which I also discuss in the previous section). Ethernet operates at speeds up to 10 Mbps. Two recent enhancements to the Ethernet protocol include Fast Ethernet (speeds up to 100 Mbps over CAT-5 twisted pair or fiber optic cabling) and Gigabit Ethernet (speeds up to 1000 Mbps over CAT-6 twisted pair or fiber optic cabling).

- **Token-Ring:** The Token-Ring protocol transports data to the physical LAN medium using the token-passing media access method that I discuss in the previous section. Originally developed by IBM, token-ring refers to both IBM Token-Ring and IEEE 802.5. All nodes are attached to a Multistation Access Unit (MSAU) in a logical ring (physical star) topology. One node on the token-ring network is designated as the *active monitor* and ensures that no more than one token is on the network at any given time. (Variations permit more than one token on the network.) If the token is lost, the active monitor is responsible for ensuring that a replacement token is generated. Token-ring networks operate at speeds of 4 and 16 Mbps.

- **Fiber Distributed Data Interface (FDDI):** The FDDI protocol transports data to the physical LAN medium by using the token-passing media access method that I discuss in the previous section. It's implemented as a dual counter-rotating ring over fiber optic cabling at speeds up to 100 Mbps. All stations on a FDDI network are connected to both rings. During normal operation, only one ring is active. In the event of a network break or fault, the ring wraps back through the nearest node onto the second ring. See Figure 4-9.

LAN data transmissions are classified as

- **Unicast:** Packets are sent from the source to a single destination device by using a specific destination IP address.

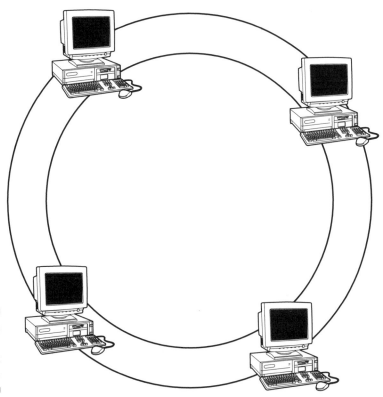

✔ **Multicast:** Packets are copied and sent from the source to multiple destination devices by using a special multicast IP address that the destination stations have been specifically configured to use.

✔ **Broadcast:** Packets are copied and sent from the source to every device on a destination network by using a broadcast IP address.

LAN data transmissions are classified as unicast, multicast, or broadcast.

WAN technologies and protocols

WAN technologies function at the lower three layers of the OSI reference model (the Physical, Data Link, and Network layers), primarily at the Data Link Layer. WAN protocols define how frames are carried across a single data link between two devices. These include

✔ **Point-to-point links:** Provide a single, pre-established WAN communications path from the customer's network, across a carrier network (such as a Public Switched Telephone Network [PSTN]), to a remote network. These include

- **Leased lines:** A transmission line reserved by a communications carrier for the exclusive use of a customer. See Table 4-4 for standard leased line characteristics.

Table 4-4		Standard Leased Lines
Type	Speed	Description
DS0	64 Kbps	Digital Signal Level 0. Framing specification used in transmitting digital signals over a single channel at 64 Kbps on a T1 facility.
DS1	T1 or E1	Digital Signal Level 1. Framing specification used in transmitting digital signals at 1.544 Mbps on a T1 facility (US) or 2.108 Mbps on an E1 facility (EU).
DS3	44.736 Mbps	Digital Signal Level 3. Framing specification used in transmitting digital signals at 44.736 Mbps on a T3 facility.
T1	1.544 Mbps	Digital WAN carrier facility. Transmits DS1-formatted data at 1.544 Mbps.
T3	44.736 Mbps	Digital WAN carrier facility. Transmits DS3-formatted data at 44.736 Mbps.
E1	2.048 Mbps	Wide-area digital transmission scheme used primarily in Europe that carries data at a rate of 2.048 Mbps.
E3	34.368 Mbps	Wide-area digital transmission scheme used primarily in Europe that carries data at a rate of 34.368 Mbps.

- **Serial Line IP (SLIP):** The predecessor of Point-to-Point Protocol (PPP), SLIP was originally developed to support TCP/IP networking over low-speed asynchronous serial lines (such as dial-up modems) for Berkeley Unix computers.

- **Point-to-Point Protocol (PPP):** The successor to SLIP, PPP provides router-to-router and host-to-network connections over synchronous and asynchronous circuits. It is a more robust protocol than SLIP and provides additional built-in security mechanisms. PPP is far more common than SLIP in modern networking environments.

✔ **Circuit-switched networks:** In a circuit-switched network, a dedicated physical circuit path is established, maintained, and terminated between the sender and receiver across a carrier network for each communications session (the *call*). This network type is used extensively in telephone company networks and functions similarly to a regular telephone call. Examples include

- **Integrated Services Digital Network (ISDN):** ISDN is a communications protocol that operates over analog phone lines that have been converted to use digital signaling. ISDN lines are capable of transmitting both voice and data traffic. ISDN defines a *B-channel* for data, voice, and other services, and a *D-channel* for control and signaling information. Table 4-5 describes the two levels of ISDN service that are currently available.

Table 4-5	ISDN Service Levels
Level	*Description*
Basic Rate Interface (BRI)	Two 64 Kbps B-channels and one 16 Kbps D-channel (maximum data rate of 128 Kbps)
Primary Rate Interface (PRI)	23 64 Kbps B-channels (US) or 30 64 Kbps B-channels (EU) and 1 64 Kbps D-channel (maximum data rate of 1.544 Mbps [US] or 2.048 Mbps [EU])

- **Digital Subscriber Lines (xDSL):** xDSL uses existing analog phone lines to deliver high bandwidth connectivity to remote customers. Table 4-6 describes several types of xDSL lines that are currently available.

Table 4-6		xDSL Examples
Type	*Characteristics*	*Description*
ADSL	Downstream rate: 1.5 to 9 Mbps Upstream rate: 16 to 640 Kbps Operating range: up to 14,400 feet	Asymmetric Digital Subscriber Line; designed to deliver higher bandwidth downstream (such as a central office to customer site) than upstream
SDSL	Downstream rate: 1.544 Mbps Upstream rate: 1.544 Mbps Operating range: up to 10,000 feet	Single-Line Digital Subscriber Line; designed to deliver high bandwidth both upstream and downstream over a single copper twisted pair

(continued)

Table 4-6 *(continued)*

Type	Characteristics	Description
HDSL	Downstream rate: 1.544 Mbps Upstream rate: 1.544 Mbps Operating range: up to 12,000 feet	High-rate Digital Subscriber Line; designed to deliver high bandwidth both upstream and downstream over two copper twisted pairs; commonly used to provide local access to T1 services
VDSL	Downstream rate: 13 to 52 Mbps Upstream rate: 1.5 to 2.3 Mbps Operating range: 1000 to 4500 feet	Very-high Data-rate Digital Subscriber Line; designed to deliver extremely high bandwidth over a single copper twisted pair

Circuit-switched networks are ideally suited for always-on connections with constant traffic.

✓ **Packet-switched networks:** In a packet-switched network, devices share bandwidth (by using statistical multiplexing) on communications links to transport packets between a sender and receiver across a carrier network. This type of network is more resilient to error and congestion than circuit-switched networks. I compare packet-switched and circuit-switched networks in Table 4-7. Examples of packet-switched networks include

- **X.25:** The first packet switching network, *X.25* is a CCITT (formerly ITU-T) standard that defines how point-to-point connections between a DTE and DCE (which I discuss in the next section) are established and maintained. X.25 specifies the *Link Access Procedure, Balanced* (LAPB) protocol at the Data Link Layer and the *Packet Level Protocol* (PLP; also known as *X.25 Level 3)* at the Network Layer. X.25 is more common outside of the United States but is being superseded by Frame Relay.

- **Frame Relay:** *Frame Relay* is a packet-switched, standard protocol that handles multiple virtual circuits using High-level Data Link Control (HDLC) encapsulation (which I discuss later in this section) between connected devices. Frame Relay utilizes a simplified framing approach with no error correction and Data Link Connection Identifiers (DLCI) addressing to achieve high speeds across the WAN. Frame Relay can be used on *Switched Virtual Circuits* (SVCs) or *Permanent Virtual Circuits* (PVCs). An *SVC* is a temporary connection that's dynamically created (circuit establishment phase) to transmit data (data transfer phase) and then disconnected (circuit termination phase). PVCs are permanently established connections. Because the connection is permanent, a PVC doesn't require the bandwidth overhead associated with circuit establishment and termination.

- **Switched Multimegabit Data Service (SMDS):** *SMDS* is a high-speed, packet-switched, connectionless-oriented, datagram-based technology available over public switched networks. It's typically used by companies that exchange large amounts of bursty data with other remote networks.

- **Asynchronous Transfer Mode (ATM):** ATM is a very high-speed, low-delay technology that uses switching and multiplexing techniques to rapidly relay fixed-length (53-byte) cells containing voice, video, or data. Cell processing occurs in hardware that reduces transit delays. ATM is ideally suited for fiber optic networks with bursty applications.

- **Voice over IP (VoIP):** *VoIP* transports various data types (such as voice, audio, and video) in IP packets providing major cost, interoperability, and performance benefits.

Table 4-7	Circuit Switching versus Packet Switching
Circuit Switching	*Packet Switching*
Ideal for always-on connections, constant traffic, and voice communications	Ideal for bursty traffic and data communications
Connection-oriented	Connectionless-oriented
Fixed delays	Variable delays

Packet-switched networks are ideally suited for on-demand connections with bursty traffic.

✔ **Other WAN protocols:** Two other important WAN protocols defined at the Data Link Layer include

- **Synchronous Data Link Control (SDLC):** The *SDLC protocol* is a bit-oriented, full-duplex serial protocol that was developed by IBM to facilitate communications between mainframes and remote offices. It defines and implements a polling media-access method, in which the *primary* (front-end) polls the *secondaries* (remote stations) to determine whether communication is required.

- **High-level Data Link Control (HDLC):** The *HDLC protocol* is a bit-oriented, synchronous protocol that was created by the ISO to support point-to-point and multipoint configurations. Derived from SDLC, it specifies a data encapsulation method for synchronous serial links and is the default for serial links on Cisco routers. Unfortunately, various vendor implementations of the HDLC protocol are incompatible.

Asynchronous and synchronous communications

Asynchronous communication transmits data in a serial stream with control data (start and stop bits) embedded in the stream to indicate the beginning and end of characters. Asynchronous devices must communicate at the same speed, which is controlled by the slower of the two communicating devices. Because no internal clocking signal is used, parity bits are used to reduce transmission errors.

Synchronous communications utilize an internal clocking signal to transmit large blocks of data, known as *frames*. Synchronous communication is characterized by very high-speed transmission rates.

Networking equipment at the Data Link Layer

Networking devices that operate at the Data Link layer include bridges, switches, DTEs, and DCEs.

A *bridge* is a semi-intelligent repeater used to connect two or more (similar or dissimilar) network segments. A bridge maintains an Address Resolution Protocol (ARP) cache containing the MAC addresses of individual devices on connected network segments. When a data signal is received by a bridge, it checks its ARP cache to determine whether the destination MAC address is on the local network segment. If it's determined to be local, the data signal isn't forwarded. However, if the MAC address isn't local, the bridge forwards (and amplifies) the data signal to all other connected network segments. A serious networking problem associated with bridges is a *broadcast storm*, in which broadcast traffic is automatically forwarded by a bridge, thus effectively flooding a network.

A *switch* is essentially an intelligent hub that uses MAC addresses to route traffic. Unlike a hub, a switch transmits data only to the port connected to the destination MAC address. This creates separate collision domains (network segments) and effectively increases the data transmission rates available on the individual network segments. Additionally, a switch can be used to implement Virtual LANs (VLANs) to logically segregate a network and limit broadcast domains. Switches are traditionally considered to be Layer 2 (or Data Link Layer) devices, although newer technologies allow switches to function at the upper layers including Layer 3 (the Network Layer) and Layer 7 (the Application Layer).

Data Terminal Equipment (DTE) is a general term used to classify devices at the user end of a user-to-network interface (such as computers). A DTE connects to *Data Communications Equipment* (DCE; also know as a Data Circuit-Terminating Equipment), which consists of devices at the network end of a user-to-network interface. The DCE provides the physical connection to the network, forwards network traffic, and provides a clocking signal to synchronize transmissions between the DCE and DTE. Examples of DCEs include NICs, modems, and CSU/DSUs (Channel Service Unit/Data Service Units).

Network Layer (Layer 3)

The Network Layer (Layer 3) provides routing and related functions that enable data to be transported between systems on the same network or on interconnected networks or *internetworks*. (See Figure 4-10 for an example.) *Routing* protocols, such as the Routing Information Protocol (RIP), Open Shortest Path First (OSPF), and Border Gateway Protocol (BGP) are defined at this layer. Logical addressing of devices on the network is accomplished at this layer by using *routed* protocols, including the Internet Protocol (IP) and Internetwork Packet Exchange (IPX).

The Network Layer is primarily responsible for routing.

Internet Protocol (IP)

Internet Protocol (IP) contains addressing information that enables packets to be routed. IP is documented in RFC 791 and is part of the TCP/IP protocol suite, which is the language of the Internet. IP has two primary responsibilities:

- Connectionless, best-effort delivery of datagrams
- Fragmentation and reassembly of datagrams

IP Version 4 (IPv4; currently the most commonly used) uses a 32-bit logical IP address that's divided into four 8-bit sections (octets) and consists of two main parts: the network number and the host number.

IP addressing supports five different address classes indicated by the high-order (left-most) bits in the IP address, as listed in Table 4-8.

Table 4-8		IP Address Classes		
Class	*Purpose*	*High-Order Bits*	*Address Range*	*Maximum Hosts*
A	Large networks	0	1 to 126	16,777,214 (224-2)
B	Medium networks	10	128 to 191	65,534 (216-2)
C	Small networks	110	192 to 223	254 (28-2)
D	Multicast	1110	224 to 239	N/A
E	Experimental	1111	240 to 254	N/A

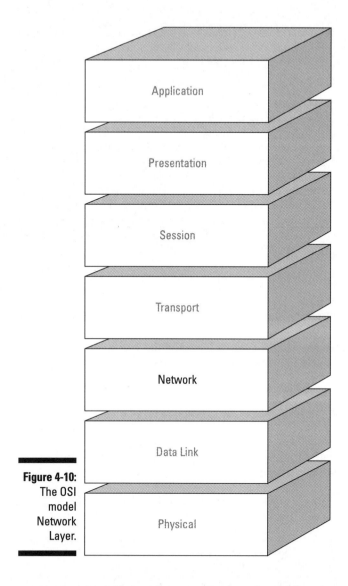

Several IP address ranges are also reserved for use in private networks (for example, 10.x.x.x, 172.16.x.x to 172.31.x.x, and 192.168.x.x). These addresses aren't routable on the Internet and are thus often implemented on firewalls and gateways by using *Network Address Translation* (NAT) to conserve IP addresses, mask the network architecture, and enhance security. NAT translates private, non-routable addresses on internal network devices to registered IP addresses when communication across the Internet is required.

IP Version 6 (IPv6) uses a 128-bit logical IP address and incorporates additional functionality to provide security, multimedia support, plug-and-play compatibility, and backward compatibility with IPv4. IPv6 hasn't yet been widely implemented on the Internet.

Internetwork Packet Exchange (IPX)

Internetwork Packet Exchange (IPX) is a connectionless protocol used primarily in NetWare networks for routing packets across the network. It's part of the IPX/SPX (Internetwork Packet Exchange/Sequenced Packet Exchange) protocol suite, which is analogous to the TCP/IP protocol suite.

The Network layer is also responsible for converting logical addresses into physical addresses. This is accomplished by the Address Resolution Protocol (ARP) and Reverse Address Resolution Protocol (RARP).

Address Resolution Protocol (ARP)

The *Address Resolution Protocol* (ARP), defined in RFC 826, maps Network Layer IP addresses to MAC addresses. ARP discovers physical addresses of attached devices by broadcasting ARP query messages on the network segment. IP address to MAC address translations are then maintained in a dynamic table that is cached on the system.

Reverse Address Resolution Protocol (RARP)

The *Reverse Address Resolution Protocol* (RARP) maps MAC addresses to IP addresses. This is necessary when a system, such as a diskless machine, needs to discover its IP address. The system broadcasts a RARP message providing its MAC address and requests to be informed of its IP address. A RARP server replies with the requested information.

The Network Layer also defines a management protocol for IP known as the *Internet Control Message Protocol (ICMP)*.

Internet Control Message Protocol (ICMP)

The *Internet Control Message Protocol* (ICMP) reports errors and other information back to the source regarding the processing of transmitted IP packets. ICMP is documented in RFC 792.

Common ICMP messages include Destination Unreachable, Echo Request and Reply, Redirect, and Time Exceeded. The Packet Internet Groper (PING) is a popular utility that uses ICMP messages to test the reachability of network device.

Networking equipment at the Network Layer

The primary networking equipment defined at Layer 3 are *routers* and *gateways*.

Routers

Routers are intelligent devices that link dissimilar networks and forward data packets based on logical or physical addresses to the destination network only (or along the network path). Routers consist of both hardware and software components and employ various routing algorithms (for example, RIP, OSPF, and BGP) to determine the best path to a destination based on different variables including bandwidth, cost, delay, and distance.

Gateways

Gateways are created with software running on a PC (workstation or server) or router. Gateways link dissimilar programs and protocols by examining the entire data packet to translate incompatibilities. For example, a gateway can be used to link an IP network to an IPX network or a Microsoft Exchange mail server to a Lotus Notes server (a mail gateway).

Transport Layer (Layer 4)

The Transport Layer (Layer 4) provides transparent, reliable data transport and end-to-end transmission control. The Transport Layer hides the details of the lower layer functions from the upper layers.

Specific Transport Layer functions include

- ✔ **Flow control:** Manages data transmission between devices, ensuring that the transmitting device doesn't send more data than the receiving device can process.

- ✔ **Multiplexing:** Enables data from multiple applications to be transmitted over a single physical link.

- ✔ **Virtual circuit management:** Establishes, maintains, and terminates virtual circuits.

- ✔ **Error checking and recovery:** Implements various mechanisms for detecting transmission errors and taking action to resolve any errors that occur, such as requesting that data be retransmitted.

The Transport Layer is responsible for providing transparent, reliable data transport and end-to-end transmission control.

Two important host-to-host protocols defined at the Transport Layer include

✔ **Transmission Control Protocol (TCP):** TCP is a full-duplex, connection-oriented protocol that provides reliable delivery of packets across a network. A *connection-oriented* protocol requires a direct connection between two communicating devices before any data transfer occurs. In TCP, this is accomplished via a *three-way handshake*. Packets are acknowledged by the receiving device, and packets are re-transmitted if an error occurs. The following characteristics and features are associated with TCP:

- **Connection-oriented:** Establishes and manages a direct virtual connection to the remote device.

- **Reliable:** Guarantees delivery by acknowledging received packets and requesting retransmission of missing or corrupted packets.

- **Slow:** Because of the additional overhead associated with initial handshaking, acknowledging packets, and error correction, TCP is generally slower than other connectionless protocols such as User Datagram Protocol (UDP).

TCP is a connection-oriented protocol.

✔ **User Datagram Protocol (UDP):** *User Datagram Protocol* is a connectionless protocol that provides fast best-effort delivery of datagrams across a network. A connectionless protocol doesn't guarantee delivery of transmitted packets (datagrams) and is thus considered unreliable. It doesn't attempt to establish a connection with the destination network prior to transmitting data, acknowledge received datagrams, perform re-sequencing, and perform error checking or recovery. UDP is ideally suited for data requiring fast delivery, which is not sensitive to packet loss and doesn't need to be fragmented. Examples of applications using UDP include domain name system (DNS), Simple Network Management Protocol (SNMP), and streaming audio or video. The following characteristics and features are associated with UDP:

- **Connectionless:** Doesn't pre-establish a communication circuit with the destination network.

- **Best effort:** Doesn't guarantee delivery and is thus considered unreliable.

- **Fast:** No overhead associated with circuit establishment, acknowledgement, sequencing, or error checking and recovery.

UDP is a connectionless protocol.

Several examples of connection-oriented and connectionless protocols are identified in Table 4-9.

Table 4-9   Connection-oriented and Connectionless Protocols

Protocol	Layer	Type
TCP (Transmission Control Protocol)	4	Connection-oriented
UDP (User Datagram Protocol)	4	Connectionless
IP (Internet Protocol)	3	Connectionless
IPX (Internetwork Packet Exchange)	3	Connectionless
SPX (Sequenced Packet Exchange)	4	Connection-oriented

Transport Layer security protocols include the following:

- ✔ **Secure Shell (SSH and SSH-2):** SSH provides a secure alternative to Telnet for remote access. SSH establishes an encrypted tunnel between the client and server and can also authenticate the client to the server. (For more on this, read Chapter 7.)

- ✔ **Secure Sockets Layer/Transport Layer Security (SSL/TLS):** The SSL protocol, developed by Netscape in 1994, provides session-based encryption and authentication for secure communication between clients and servers on the Internet. SSL provides server authentication with optional client authentication, which I discuss further in Chapter 7.

- ✔ **Simple Key Management for Internet Protocols (SKIP):** SKIP is similar to SSL but doesn't require prior communication to establish a connection or exchange keys.

Session Layer (Layer 5)

The Session Layer (Layer 5) establishes, coordinates, and terminates communication sessions (service requests and service responses) between networked systems.

The Session Layer is responsible for establishing, coordinating, and terminating communication sessions.

A communication session is divided into three distinct phases, as follows:

✔ **Connection establishment:** Initial contact between communicating systems is made, and the end devices agree upon communications parameters and protocols to be used, including the mode of operation:

- **Simplex mode:** In simplex mode, a one-way communications path is established with a transmitter at one end of the connection and a receiver at the other end. An analogy is an AM radio on which a radio station broadcasts music and the radio receiver can only receive the broadcast.

- **Half-duplex mode:** In half-duplex mode, both communicating devices are capable of transmitting and receiving but not at the same time. An analogy is a two-way radio in which a button must be pressed to transmit and then released to receive a signal.

- **Full-duplex mode:** In full-duplex mode, both communicating devices are capable of transmitting and receiving simultaneously. An analogy is a telephone with which you can transmit and receive signals (but not necessarily communicate) at the same time.

✔ **Data transfer:** Information is exchanged between end devices.

✔ **Connection release:** After data transfer is completed, end devices systematically end the session.

Some examples of Session Layer protocols include

✔ **Network File System (NFS):** Developed by Sun Microsystems to facilitate transparent user access to remote resources on a Unix-based network using TCP/IP.

✔ **Structured Query Language (SQL):** Developed by IBM to provide users with a simplified method for defining its data requirements on both local and remote database systems.

✔ **Remote Procedure Call (RPC):** A client/server network redirection tool. Procedures are created on clients and performed on servers.

Presentation Layer (Layer 6)

The Presentation Layer (Layer 6) provides coding and conversion functions that are applied to data being presented to the Application Layer. These functions ensure that data sent from the Application Layer of one system are compatible with the Application Layer of the receiving system.

The Presentation Layer is responsible for coding and conversion functions.

Tasks associated with this layer include

- ✔ **Data representation:** Use of common data representation formats (standard image, sound, and video formats) enable application data to be exchanged between different types of computer systems. Some examples include Graphics Interchange Format (GIF), Musical Instrument Data Interface (MIDI), and Motion Picture Experts Group (MPEG).

- ✔ **Character conversion:** Information is exchanged between different systems using common character conversion schemes, such as Extended Binary-Coded Decimal Interchange Mode (EBCDIC) or American Standard Code for Information Interchange (ASCII).

- ✔ **Data compression:** Common data compression schemes enable compressed data to be properly decompressed at the destination.

- ✔ **Data encryption:** Common data encryption schemes enable encrypted data to be properly decrypted at the destination.

Application Layer (Layer 7)

The Application Layer (Layer 7) is the highest layer of the OSI model. It supports the components that deal with the communication aspects of an application requiring network access and provides an interface to the user. That is, both the Application Layer and end user interact directly with the application.

The Application Layer is responsible for the following:

- ✔ Identifying and establishing availability of communication partners

- ✔ Determining resource availability

- ✔ Synchronizing communication

The Application Layer is responsible for identifying and establishing availability of communication partners, determining resource availability, and synchronizing communication.

Don't confuse the Application Layer with software applications such as Microsoft Word or WordPerfect. Applications that function at the Application Layer include operating systems (such as Windows 2000 Server and NetWare), OSI applications (File Transfer, Access, and Management [FTAM] and Virtual Terminal Protocol [VTP]), and TCP/IP applications, including:

- ✔ **HyperText Transfer Protocol (HTTP):** The language of the World Wide Web (WWW). Attacks typically exploit vulnerabilities in Web browsers or programming languages such as CGI, Java, and ActiveX. HTTP operates on TCP/UDP port 80.

✔ **File Transfer Protocol (FTP):** Used for file transfers between remote systems. Attacks exploit incorrectly configured directory permissions and compromised passwords, which are always sent in clear text. FTP operates on TCP/UDP ports 20 and 21.

✔ **Trivial File Transfer Protocol (TFTP):** A lean, mean version of FTP without directory browsing capabilities or user authentication. Generally considered less secure than FTP. TFTP operates on TCP/UDP port 69.

✔ **Simple Mail Transfer Protocol (SMTP):** Used to send and receive e-mail across the Internet. Inherently insecure protocol with numerous well-known vulnerabilities. SMTP operates on TCP/UDP port 25.

✔ **Simple Network Management Protocol (SNMP):** Used to collect network information by polling stations and sending *traps* (or alerts) to a management station. Many well-known vulnerabilities, including default community strings (passwords), transmitted in clear text. SNMP operates on TCP/UDP port 161.

✔ **Telnet:** Provides terminal emulation for remote access to system resources. Passwords are sent in clear text. Telnet operates on TCP/UDP port 23.

Application Layer security protocols include the following:

✔ **Secure Multipurpose Internet Mail Extensions (S/MIME):** *S/MIME* is a secure method of sending e-mail incorporated into several popular browsers and e-mail applications. I discuss this further in Chapter 7.

✔ **Privacy Enhanced Mail (PEM):** *PEM* is a proposed IETF (Internet Engineering Task Force) standard for providing e-mail confidentiality and authentication. Read more about this in Chapter 7.

✔ **Secure Electronic Transaction (SET):** The *SET* specification was developed by MasterCard and Visa to provide secure e-commerce transactions by implementing authentication mechanisms while protecting the confidentiality and integrity of cardholder data. Find more information on this in Chapter 7.

✔ **Secure HyperText Transfer Protocol (S-HTTP):** *S-HTTP* is an Internet protocol that provides a method for secure communications with a Web server. S-HTTP is a connectionless-oriented protocol that encapsulates data after security properties for the session have been successfully negotiated. I discuss this further in Chapter 7.

✔ **Secure Remote Procedure Call (S-RPC):** *S-RPC* is a secure client-server protocol that's defined at the upper layers of the OSI model, including the Application Layer. RPC is used to request services from another computer on the network. S-RPC provides public and private keys to clients and servers using Diffie-Hellman. (Read more about this in Chapter 7.) After initially authenticating, S-RPC operations are transparent to the end user.

The TCP/IP Model

The Transmission Control Protocol/Internet Protocol (TCP/IP) Model is similar to the OSI Reference Model but consists of only four layers instead of seven.

- ✓ **Application Layer:** Consists of network applications and processes and loosely corresponds to the upper layers of the OSI model (Application, Presentation, and Session layers).
- ✓ **Host-to-Host Transport Layer:** Provides end-to-end delivery and corresponds to the OSI Transport Layer.
- ✓ **Internet Layer:** Defines the IP datagram and routing and corresponds to the OSI Network Layer.
- ✓ **Network Access (or Link) Layer:** Contains routines for accessing physical networks and corresponds to the OSI Data Link and Physical layers.

Network Security

Network security is implemented with various technologies including firewalls, virtual private networks (VPNs), intrusion detection systems (IDSes), and remote access authentication mechanisms.

Firewalls

A *firewall* controls traffic flow between a trusted network (such as a corporate LAN) and an untrusted or public network (such as the Internet). A firewall can comprise hardware, software, or a combination of both hardware and software. The CISSP candidate must understand the various types of firewalls and common firewall architectures.

Firewall types

Currently, the three basic classifications of firewalls are packet-filtering, circuit-level gateway, and application-level gateway.

Three basic types of firewalls are packet-filtering, circuit-level gateway, and application-level gateway.

Packet-filtering

A *packet-filtering* firewall (or *screening router*) is one of the most basic (and inexpensive) types of firewalls and is ideally suited for a low-risk environment. A packet-filtering firewall permits or denies traffic based solely on the TCP, UDP, ICMP, and IP headers of the individual packets. It examines the traffic direction (inbound or outbound), the source and destination IP address, and the source and destination TCP or UDP port numbers. This information is compared with pre-defined rules that have been configured in an Access Control List (ACL) to determine whether a packet should be permitted or denied. A packet-filtering firewall typically operates at the Network or Transport layer of the OSI model. Advantages of a packet-filtering firewall include that it is:

✔ Inexpensive (can be implemented as a router ACL)

✔ Fast and flexible

✔ Transparent to users

Disadvantages of packet-filtering firewalls are that

✔ Access decisions are based only on address and port information.

✔ It has no protection from IP or DNS address spoofing.

✔ It doesn't support strong user authentication.

✔ Configuring and maintaining ACLs can be difficult.

✔ Logging information may be limited.

A more advanced variation of the packet-filtering firewall is the *dynamic packet-filtering firewall*. This type of firewall supports dynamic modification of the firewall rule base using context-based access control (CBAC) or reflexive ACLs, for example.

Circuit-level gateway

A circuit-level gateway controls access by maintaining state information about established connections. When a permitted connection is established between two hosts, a *tunnel* or virtual circuit is created for the session, thus allowing packets to flow freely between the two hosts without the need for further inspecting individual packets. This type of firewall operates at the Session Layer of the OSI model.

Advantages of this type of firewall include are

✔ Speed. (After a connection is established, individual packets aren't analyzed.)

✔ Support for many protocols.

✔ Easy maintenance.

Disadvantages of this type of firewall include

- ✔ Dependence on trustworthiness of the communicating users or hosts. (After a connection is established, individual packets aren't analyzed.)
- ✔ Limited logging information about individual data packets is available after the initial connection is established.

A *stateful inspection firewall* is a type of circuit-level gateway that captures data packets at the Network Layer and then queues and analyzes (examines state and context) these packets at the upper layers of the OSI model.

Application-level gateway

An application-level (or Application Layer) gateway operates at the Application Layer of the OSI model, processing data packets for specific IP applications. This type of firewall is generally considered the most secure and is commonly implemented as a proxy server. In a *proxy server*, no direct communication between two hosts is permitted. Instead, data packets are intercepted by the proxy server, which analyzes the packet's contents and if permitted by the firewall rules, sends a copy of the original packet to the intended host.

Advantages of this type of firewall include

- ✔ Data packets aren't transmitted directly to communicating hosts, thereby masking the internal network's design and preventing direct access to services on internal hosts.
- ✔ It can be used to implement strong user authentication in applications.

Disadvantages of this type of firewall include

- ✔ It reduces network performance because every packet must be passed up to the Application Layer of the OSI model to be analyzed.
- ✔ It must be tailored to specific applications. (This can be difficult to maintain or update for new or changing protocols.)

Firewall architectures

The basic firewall types that I discuss in the previous sections may be implemented in a firewall architecture as I describe next. The four basic types of firewall architectures are screening router, dual-homed gateway, screened-host gateway, and screened-subnet.

Screening router

A *screening router* is the most basic type of firewall architecture employed. An external router is placed between the untrusted and trusted networks, and a security policy is implemented using ACLs. Although a router functions as a choke point between a trusted and untrusted network, an attacker — after being granted access to a host on the trusted network — may potentially be able to compromise the entire network.

Advantages of a screening router architecture include that it's

✔ Completely transparent

✔ Relatively simple and inexpensive

Disadvantages of the screening router architecture include that it

✔ Is difficult to configure and maintain

✔ May have difficulty handling certain traffic

✔ Has limited or no logging available

✔ Uses no user authentication

✔ Is difficult to mask the internal network structure

✔ Has a single point of failure

✔ Doesn't truly implement a firewall choke-point strategy

Still, using a screening router architecture is better than using nothing.

Dual-homed gateways

Another common firewall architecture is the dual-homed gateway. A *dual-homed gateway* (or bastion host) is a system with two network interfaces (NICs) that sits between an untrusted and trusted network. A *bastion host* is a general term often used to refer to proxies, gateways, firewalls, or any server that provides applications or services directly to an untrusted network. Because it's often the target of attackers, a bastion host is sometimes referred to as a *sacrificial lamb*.

However, this term is misleading because a bastion host is typically a hardened system employing robust security mechanisms. A dual-homed gateway is often connected to the untrusted network via an external screening router. The dual-homed gateway functions as a proxy server for the trusted network and may be configured to require user authentication. A dual-homed gateway offers a more fail-safe operation than screening routers because by default, data isn't normally forwarded across the two interfaces. Advantages of the dual-homed gateway architecture include

✔ It operates in a fail-safe mode.

✔ Internal network structure is masked.

Disadvantages of the dual-homed gateway architecture include

- ✔ Its use may inconvenience users.
- ✔ Proxies may not be available for some services.
- ✔ Its use may cause slower network performance.

Screened-host gateways

A *screened-host gateway* architecture employs an external screening router and an internal bastion host. The screening router is configured so that the bastion host is the only host accessible from the untrusted network (such as the Internet). The bastion host provides any required Web services to the untrusted network, such as HTTP and FTP, as permitted by the security policy. Connections to the Internet from the trusted network are routed via an application proxy on the bastion host or directly through the screening router.

Advantages of the screened-host gateway architecture include

- ✔ It provides distributed security between two devices.
- ✔ It has transparent outbound access.
- ✔ It has restricted inbound access.

Disadvantages of the screened-host gateway architecture include

- ✔ It's considered less secure because the screening router can bypass the bastion host for certain trusted services.
- ✔ Masking the internal network structure is difficult.
- ✔ It can have multiple single points of failure (router or bastion host).

Screened-subnet

The screened-subnet is perhaps the most secure of the currently designed firewall architectures. The screened-subnet employs an external screening router, a dual-homed (or multi-homed) host, and a second internal screening router. This implements the concept of a network DMZ (or demilitarized zone). Publicly available services are placed on bastion hosts in the DMZ.

Advantages of the screened-subnet architecture include that

- ✔ It's transparent to end users.
- ✔ It's flexible.
- ✔ Internal network structure can be masked.
- ✔ It provides *defense in depth* rather than relying on a single device to provide security for the entire network.

Disadvantages of a screened-subnet architecture include that it

✔ Is more expensive than other firewall architectures

✔ Is more difficult to configure and maintain

✔ Can be more difficult to troubleshoot

Virtual private networks (VPNs)

A *virtual private network* (VPN) creates a secure tunnel over a public network, such as the Internet. A secure tunnel is created by either encrypting or encapsulating the data as it's transmitted across the VPN. The two ends of a VPN are commonly implemented using one of the following methods:

✔ Client-to-VPN Concentrator (or Device)

✔ Client-to-Firewall

✔ Firewall-to-Firewall

✔ Router-to-Router

Common VPN protocol standards include Point-to-Point Tunneling Protocol (PPTP), Layer 2 Forwarding Protocol (L2F), Layer 2 Tunneling Protocol (L2TP), and Internet Protocol Security (IPSec).

Point-to-Point Tunneling Protocol (PPTP)

The Point-to-Point Tunneling Protocol (PPTP) was developed by Microsoft to enable the Point-to-Point Protocol (PPP) to be tunneled through a public network. PPTP uses native PPP authentication and encryption services (such as PAP, CHAP, EAP), which I discuss later in the section "RAS." It's commonly used for secure dial-up connections using Microsoft Win9*x* or NT/2000 clients. PPTP operates at the Data Link Layer of the OSI model and is designed for individual client-server connections.

Layer 2 Forwarding Protocol (L2F)

The Layer 2 Forwarding Protocol (L2F) was developed by Cisco and provides similar functionality as PPTP. As its name implies, L2F operates at the Data Link Layer of the OSI model and permits tunneling of Layer 2 WAN protocols such as HDLC and SLIP.

Layer 2 Tunneling Protocol (L2TP)

The Layer 2 Tunneling Protocol (L2TP) is an IETF standard that combines Microsoft (and others) PPTP and Cisco L2F protocols. Like PPTP and L2F, L2TP operates at the Data Link Layer of the OSI model to create secure VPN connections for individual client-server connections. The L2TP addresses the following end-user requirements:

✔ **Transparency:** Requires no additional software.

✔ **Robust authentication:** Supports PPP authentication protocols, Remote Authentication Dial-In User Service (RADIUS), Terminal Access Controller Access Control System (TACACS), smart cards, and one-time passwords.

✔ **Local addressing:** IP addresses assigned by the VPN entities rather than the ISP.

✔ **Authorization:** Authorization managed by the VPN server-side similar to direct dial-up connections.

✔ **Accounting:** Accounting performed by both the ISP and user.

IPSec

Internet Protocol Security (IPSec) is an IETF open standard for VPNs that operates at the Network Layer of the OSI model. It's the most popular and robust VPN protocol in use today. IPSec ensures confidentiality, integrity, and authenticity by using Layer 3 encryption and authentication to provide an end-to-end solution. IPSec operates in two modes:

✔ **Transport mode:** Only the data is encrypted.

✔ **Tunnel mode:** The entire packet is encrypted.

The two main protocols used in IPSec are

✔ **Authentication Header (AH):** Provides integrity, authentication, and non-repudiation

✔ **Encapsulating Security Payload (ESP):** Provides confidentiality (encryption) and limited authentication

Each pair of hosts communicating in an IPSec session must establish a security association.

A *security association* (SA) is a one-way connection between two communicating parties; thus, two SAs are required for each pair of communicating hosts. Additionally, each SA only supports a single protocol (AH or ESP). Therefore, if both an AH and ESP are used between two communicating hosts, a total of four SAs is required. An SA has three parameters that uniquely identify it in an IPSec session:

✔ **Security Parameter Index (SPI):** The SPI is a 32-bit string used by the receiving station to differentiate between SAs terminating on that station. The SPI is located within the AH or ESP header.

✔ **Destination IP address:** The destination address could be the end station or an intermediate gateway or firewall, but must be a unicast address.

✔ **Security Protocol ID:** The Security Protocol ID must be either an AH or ESP association.

Key management is provided in IPSec by using the Internet Key Exchange (IKE). *IKE* is actually a combination of three complementary protocols: the Internet Security Association and Key Management Protocol (ISAKMP), the Secure Key Exchange Mechanism (SKEME), and the Oakley Key Exchange Protocol. IKE operates in three modes: Main Mode, Aggressive Mode, and Quick Mode.

Intrusion detection systems (IDSes)

Intrusion detection is defined as real-time monitoring and analysis of network activity and data for potential vulnerabilities and attacks in progress. One major limitation of current IDS technologies is the requirement to filter false alarms lest the operator (system or security administrator) be overwhelmed with data. Intrusion detection systems (IDSes) are classified in many different ways including active and passive, network-based and host-based, and knowledge-based and behavior-based.

Active and passive IDSes

An *active* IDS is a system that's configured to automatically block suspected attacks in progress without any intervention required by an operator. An active IDS has the advantage of providing real-time corrective action in response to an attack but has many disadvantages as well. An active system must be placed in-line along a network boundary; thus, the IDS system itself is susceptible to attack. Also, if false alarms and legitimate traffic haven't been properly identified and filtered, authorized users and applications may be improperly denied access. Finally, the IDS system itself may be used to effect a *Denial of Service* (DoS) attack by intentionally flooding the system with alarms that cause it to block connections until no connections or bandwidth are available.

A *passive* IDS is a system that's configured to only monitor and analyze network traffic activity and alert an operator to potential vulnerabilities and attacks. It's not capable of performing any protective or corrective functions on its own. The major advantages of passive IDSes are that these systems can be easily and rapidly deployed and are not normally susceptible to attack themselves.

Network-based and host-based IDSes

A *network-based* IDS usually consists of a network appliance (or sensor) with a Network Interface Card (NIC) operating in promiscuous mode and a separate management interface. The IDS is placed along a network segment or boundary and monitors all traffic on that segment.

A *host-based* IDS requires small programs (or *agents*) to be installed on individual systems to be monitored. The agents monitor the operating system and write data to log files and/or trigger alarms. A host-based IDS can only monitor the individual host systems on which the agents are installed; it doesn't monitor the entire network.

Knowledge-based and behavior-based IDSes

A *knowledge-based* (or *signature-based*) IDS references a database of previous attack profiles and known system vulnerabilities to identify active intrusion attempts. Knowledge-based IDS is currently more common than behavior-based IDS. Advantages of knowledge-based systems include

- ✔ It has lower false alarm rates than behavior-based IDS.
- ✔ Alarms are more standardized and more easily understood than behavior-based IDS.

Disadvantages of knowledge-based systems include

- ✔ Signature database must be continually updated and maintained.
- ✔ New, unique, or original attacks may not be detected or may be improperly classified.

A *behavior-based* (or *statistical anomaly-based*) IDS references a baseline or learned pattern of normal system activity to identify active intrusion attempts. Deviations from this baseline or pattern cause an alarm to be triggered. Advantages of behavior-based systems include that they

- ✔ Dynamically adapt to new, unique, or original attacks
- ✔ Are less dependent on identifying specific operating system vulnerabilities

Disadvantages of behavior-based systems include

- ✔ Higher false alarm rates than knowledge-based IDS
- ✔ Usage patterns that may change often and may not be static enough to implement an effective behavior-based IDS

Remote access

Remote access is provided through various technologies (such as cable modems and wireless devices) and protocols (such as asynchronous dial-up, ISDN, xDSL), as I discuss in the earlier section "WAN technologies and protocols."

Remote access security is provided through various methods and technologies as I describe in the following sections.

Remote access security methods

Remote access security methods include restricted allowed addresses, caller ID, and callback.

Restricted address

The *restricted address* method restricts access to the network based on allowed IP addresses, essentially performing rudimentary *node* authentication but not *user* authentication.

Caller ID

The *caller ID* method restricts access to the network based on allowed phone numbers, thus performing a slightly more secure form of node authentication because phone numbers are more difficult to spoof than IP addresses. However, this method can be difficult to administer for road warriors that routinely travel to different cities.

Callback

The *callback* method restricts access to the network by requiring a remote user to first authenticate to the remote access service (RAS) server. The RAS server then disconnects and calls the user back at a pre-configured phone number. Like caller ID, this method can be difficult to administer for road warriors.

One limitation of callback can be easily defeated using call forwarding.

Remote access security technologies

Remote access security technologies include RAS servers that utilize various authentication protocols associated with PPP, RADIUS, and TACACS.

RAS

Remote access service (RAS) servers utilize the Point-to-Point Protocol (PPP) to encapsulate IP packets and establish dial-in connections over serial and ISDN links. PPP incorporates the following three authentication protocols:

- ✔ **PAP:** The Password Authentication Protocol (PAP) uses a two-way handshake to authenticate a peer to a server when a link is initially established. PAP transmits passwords in clear text and provides no protection from replay or brute force attacks.

- ✔ **CHAP:** The Challenge Handshake Protocol (CHAP) uses a three-way handshake to authenticate both a peer and server when a link is initially established and, optionally, at regular intervals throughout the session. CHAP requires both the peer and server to be pre-configured with a shared secret that must be stored in plain text. The peer uses the secret to calculate the response to a server challenge using an MD5 one-way hash function. MS-CHAP, a Microsoft enhancement to CHAP, allows the shared secret to be stored in an encrypted form.

- ✔ **EAP:** The Extensible Authentication Protocol (EAP) adds flexibility to PPP authentication by implementing various authentication mechanisms including MD5-challenge, S/Key, generic token card, digital certificates, and so on. EAP is implemented in many wireless networks.

RADIUS

The Remote Authentication Dial-In User Service (RADIUS) protocol is an open-source, UDP-based client-server protocol. Defined in RFC 2058 and RFC 2059, RADIUS provides authentication and accountability. A user provides username/password information to a RADIUS client by using PAP or CHAP.

The RADIUS client encrypts the password and sends the username and encrypted password to the RADIUS server for authentication. *Note:* Passwords exchanged between the RADIUS client and RADIUS server are encrypted, but passwords exchanged between the PC client and the RADIUS client are not necessarily encrypted — if using PAP authentication, for example. However, if the PC client happens to also be the RADIUS client, all password exchanges are encrypted regardless of the authentication protocol being used.

TACACS

The Terminal Access Controller Access Control System (TACACS) is a UDP-based access control protocol, originally developed for the MILNET, which provides authentication, authorization, and accountability (AAA). The original TACACS protocol has been significantly enhanced, primarily by Cisco, as XTACACS (no longer used) and TACACS+ (the most common implementation of TACACS). TACACS+ is TCP-based (port 49) and supports practically any authentication mechanism (PAP, CHAP, MS-CHAP, EAP, token cards, Kerberos, and so on.). The basic operation of TACACS+ is similar to RADIUS, including the caveat about encrypted passwords between client and server. The major advantages of TACACS+ are its wide support of various authentication mechanisms and granular control of authorization parameters.

E-Mail, Facsimile, and Telephone Security

The CISSP candidate should understand common issues associated with e-mail, facsimile, and telephone security.

E-mail security

The Simple Mail Transfer Protocol (SMTP) is used to send and receive e-mail across the Internet. It operates on TCP/UDP port 25 and contains many well-known vulnerabilities.

One of the most common e-mail abuses today — spamming — exploits the default settings of most SMTP mail servers that are configured to forward (or *relay*) all mail regardless of whether the sender's or recipient's address is valid.

Mail servers should always be placed in a DMZ and unnecessary or unused services should be disabled in the operating system.

Several protocols exist for secure e-mail including S/MIME, PEM, and PGP. I discuss several of these protocols in the earlier section "Application Layer (Layer 7)" of this chapter and also in Chapter 7.

Other e-mail security considerations include malicious code contained in attachments, lack of privacy, and lack of authentication. These considerations can be countered by implementing anti-virus scanning software, encryption, and digital signatures, respectively.

Facsimile security

Facsimile transmissions are often taken for granted but definitely present major security issues. A fax transmission, like any other electronic transmission, can be easily intercepted or re-created. General administrative and technical controls for fax security include

- ✔ Using cover pages (with appropriate routing and classification markings)
- ✔ Placing fax machines in secure areas
- ✔ Using secure phone lines
- ✔ Encrypting fax data

PBX fraud and abuse

PBX fraud and abuse is one of the most overlooked and costly aspects of a corporate telecommunications infrastructure. Many employees don't think twice about using a company telephone system for extended personal use, including long distance calls. Personal use of company-supplied mobile phones and pagers is another area of widespread abuse. Perhaps the simplest and most effective countermeasure against internal abuses is to publish and enforce a corporate telephone use policy. Regular auditing of telephone records is also effective for deterring and detecting telephone abuses.

Network Attacks and Countermeasures

Most attacks against networks are Denial of Service (DoS) or Distributed Denial of Service (DDoS) attacks in which the objective is to consume a network's bandwidth to make network services unavailable.

SYN flood

In a SYN flood attack, TCP packets requesting a connection (SYN bit set) are sent to the target network with a spoofed source address. The target responds with a SYN-ACK packet, but the spoofed source never replies (assuming that the spoofed IP address is unreachable). *Half-open connections* are incomplete communication sessions awaiting completion of the TCP three-way handshake. These connections can quickly overwhelm a system's resources while waiting for the connections to time out. This causes the system to crash or otherwise become unusable.

SYN floods are countered on Cisco routers using two features: *TCP Intercept*, which effectively proxies for the half-open connections; and *Committed Access Rate* (CAR), which limits the bandwidth available to certain types of traffic. Checkpoint's FW-1 firewall has a feature known as *SYN Defender* that functions similar to the Cisco TCP Intercept feature. Other defenses include changing the default maximum number of TCP half-open connections and reducing the time-out period on networked systems.

ICMP flood

In an ICMP flood attack, large numbers of ICMP packets (usually Echo Request) are sent to the target network to consume available bandwidth and/or system resources. Because ICMP isn't required for normal network operations, the easiest defense is to drop ICMP packets at the router or filter them at the firewall.

UDP flood

In a UDP flood attack, large numbers of UDP packets are sent to the target network to consume available bandwidth and/or system resources. UDP floods can generally be countered by dropping unnecessary UDP packets at the router. However, if the attack is using a required UDP port (DNS port 53), other countermeasures need to be employed.

Smurf

A Smurf attack is a variation of the ICMP flood attack. (Read the earlier section "ICMP flood.") In a Smurf attack, ICMP Echo Request packets are sent to the broadcast address of a target network by using a spoofed IP address on the target network. The target, or *bounce site*, then transmits the ICMP Echo Request to all hosts on the network. Each host then responds with an Echo

Reply packet, overwhelming the available bandwidth and/or system resources. Countermeasures against Smurf attacks include dropping ICMP packets at the router.

Fraggle

The Fraggle attack is a variant of the Smurf attack (see the previous section) that uses UDP Echo packets (UDP port 7) instead of ICMP packets. Cisco routers can be configured to disable the TCP and UDP services (known as *TCP and UDP small servers*) commonly used in Fraggle attacks.

Teardrop

In a Teardrop attack, the length and fragmentation offset fields of sequential IP packets are modified, causing the target system to become confused and crash.

Session hijacking (Spoofing)

IP spoofing involves altering a TCP packet so that it appears to be coming from a known, trusted source, thus giving the attacker access to the network.

Additional References

Gilster, Ron. *Network+ Certification For Dummies,* Chapters 3–16. Hungry Minds, Inc.

Krutz, Ronald L. and Vines, Russell Dean. *The CISSP Prep Guide: Mastering the Ten Domains of Computer Security*, Chapter 3. John Wiley & Sons, Inc.

Tipton, Harold F. and Krause, Micki. *Information Security Management Handbook,* 4th Edition, Chapters 3–11. Auerbach Publications.

Ford, Merilee and Lew, H. Kim. *Internetworking Technologies Handbook*, Chapters 1–5, 7–13, 15–18, 28–30. Cisco Press.

Carne, E. Bryan. *Telecommunications Primer: Data, Voice, and Video Communications*, Chapters 1, 2, 4–6, 9–12. Prentice Hall.

Zwicky, Elizabeth D., Cooper, Simon, Chapman, D. Brent, and Russell, Deborah. *Building Internet Firewalls*, Chapters 3, 5, 6, 8, 9, 10. O'Reilly and Associates.

Prep Test

1 A data network that operates across a relatively large geographic area defines what type of network?

A ○ LAN

B ○ MAN

C ○ CAN

D ○ WAN

2 The process of wrapping protocol information from one layer in the data section of another layer describes

A ○ Data encryption

B ○ Data encapsulation

C ○ Data hiding

D ○ TCP wrappers

3 The LLC and MAC are sublayers of what OSI model layer?

A ○ Data Link

B ○ Network

C ○ Transport

D ○ Session

4 The Ethernet protocol is defined at what layer of the OSI Model and in which IEEE standard?

A ○ Data Link Layer, 802.3

B ○ Network Layer, 802.3

C ○ Data Link Layer, 802.5

D ○ Network Layer, 802.5

5 All the following are examples of packet-switched WAN protocols, except

A ○ X.25

B ○ Frame Relay

C ○ ISDN

D ○ SMDS

6 Which of the following is an example of a Class B IP address?

A ○ 17.5.5.1

B ○ 127.0.0.1

C ○ 192.167.4.1

D ○ 224.0.0.1

7 **The TCP/IP Protocol Model consists of the following four layers:**

A ○ Application, Presentation, Session, Transport
B ○ Application, Session, Network, Physical
C ○ Application, Session, Host-to-Host Transport, Internet
D ○ Application, Host-to-Host Transport, Internet, Link

8 **Which of the following firewall architectures employs an external and internal router as well as a bastion host?**

A ○ Screening router
B ○ Screened subnet
C ○ Screened host gateway
D ○ Dual-homed gateway

9 **Which of the following is not a common VPN protocol standard?**

A ○ IPSec
B ○ PPTP
C ○ TFTP
D ○ L2TP

10 **A type of network attack in which TCP packets are sent from a spoofed source address with the SYN bit set describes**

A ○ Smurf
B ○ Fraggle
C ○ Teardrop
D ○ SYN Flood

Answers

1 **D.** WAN. A LAN operates across a relatively small geographic area. A MAN and CAN are LAN variations. *Review "Wide area network (WAN)."*

2 **B.** Data encapsulation. Data encapsulation wraps protocol information from one layer in the data section of another layer. The other choices are incorrect. Review *"The OSI Reference Model."*

3 **A.** Data Link. The Data Link Layer is the only layer of the OSI Model that defines sublayers (the Logical Link Control and Media Access Control sublayers). *Review "Data Link Layer (Layer 2)."*

4 **A.** Data Link Layer, 802.3. LAN protocols are defined at the Data Link Layer. IEEE 802.5 defines the Token-Ring standard. *Review "Data Link Layer (Layer 2)."*

5 **C.** ISDN. ISDN is circuit-switched. Packet-switched network technologies include X.25, Frame Relay, SMDS, ATM, and VoIP. *Review "WAN technologies and protocols."*

6 **C.** 192.167.4.1. 17.5.5.1 is a Class A address, 127.0.0.1 is an interface loopback address, and 224.0.0.1 is a multicast address (Class D). *Review "Internet Protocol (IP)."*

7 **D.** Application, Host-to-Host Transport, Internet, Link (or Network). *Review "The TCP/IP Model."*

8 **B.** Screened subnet. The screened subnet employs an external screening router, a dual-homed (or multi-homed) host, and a second internal screening router. *Review "Firewall architectures."*

9 **C.** TFTP. TFTP is the Trivial File Transfer Protocol, a basic variation of the FTP protocol that provides limited file transfer capabilities. It has absolutely nothing to do with VPNs. *Review "Virtual private networks (VPNs)."*

10 **D.** SYN Flood. Smurf attacks exploit vulnerabilities in the ICMP protocol. Fraggle attacks exploit vulnerabilities in the UDP protocol. A Teardrop attack exploits vulnerabilities in the TCP protocol using the length and fragmentation offset fields. *Review "Network Attacks and Countermeasures."*

Telecommunications and Network Security

Chapter 5

Security Management Practices

The Security Management Practices domain introduces many important concepts and overlaps several other domains. Fortunately, it's not an extremely technical domain, and the concepts that I discuss here are fairly straightforward and easy to understand.

Security Management Concepts and Principles

The Certified Information Systems Security Professional (CISSP) candidate must fully understand the three fundamental information security concepts that comprise the C-I-A triad and form the basis of information security (see Figure 5-1):

- ✔ Confidentiality
- ✔ Integrity
- ✔ Availability

All other domains within the CISSP Common Body of Knowledge (CBK) are based on these three important concepts.

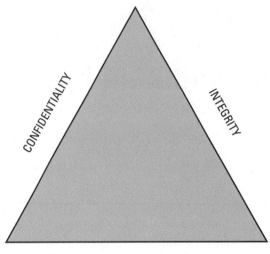

Figure 5-1:
The C-I-A
triad.

Confidentiality

Confidentiality prevents the unauthorized use or disclosure of information, ensuring that information is accessible only to those authorized to have access to the information. Privacy is a closely related concept that's most often associated with personal data. Various US and international laws exist to protect the privacy (confidentiality) of personal data. (Read more on this subject in Chapter 11.)

Privacy ensures the confidentiality of personal data.

Integrity

Integrity safeguards the accuracy and completeness of information and processing methods. It ensures that

- ✔ Modifications to data aren't made by unauthorized users or processes.
- ✔ Unauthorized modifications to data aren't made by authorized users or processes.
- ✔ Data is internally and externally consistent; that is, a given input produces an expected output.

Availability

Availability ensures that authorized users have reliable and timely access to information and associated assets when required.

The opposite of C-I-A is D-A-D: disclosure, alteration, and destruction.

Data Classification

The CISSP candidate must understand the purpose of a data classification scheme, commercial data classification criteria, and the government data classification scheme.

Information and data, in all their various forms, are valuable business assets. As with other more tangible assets, the information's value determines the level of protection required by the organization. Applying a single protection standard uniformly across all an organization's assets is neither practical nor desirable. A data classification scheme helps an organization assign a value to its information assets based on its sensitivity to loss or disclosure as well as to determine the appropriate level of protection. Additionally, data classification schemes may be required for regulatory or other legal compliance.

Commercial data classification

Commercial data classification schemes are typically implemented to protect information that has a monetary value, to comply with applicable laws and protect privacy, and to limit liability. Criteria by which commercial data is classified include

- ✔ **Value:** This is the most common classification criterion in commercial organizations. Classification is based on monetary or some other intrinsic value.

- ✔ **Age/useful life:** Information that loses value over time, becomes obsolete or irrelevant, or becomes common/public knowledge should be classified accordingly.

- ✔ **Regulatory requirements:** Private information, such as medical records subject to HIPAA (Health Insurance Portability and Accountability Act of 1996) regulations and educational records subject to the Privacy Act (see Chapter 11) may have legal requirements for protection. Classification of such information may be based not only on compliance but also liability limits.

Descriptive labels are often applied to company information, such as *Confidential and Proprietary* and *Internal Use Only*. However, the organizational requirements for protecting information labeled as such are often not formally defined or are unknown. Organizations should formally identify standard classification levels as well as specific requirements for labeling, handling, storage, and destruction/disposal.

Government data classification

Government data classification schemes are generally implemented to

- ✔ Protect national interests or security
- ✔ Comply with applicable laws
- ✔ Protect privacy

One of the more common systems, used within the US Department of Defense (DoD), consists of four broad categories for information classification: Unclassified, Sensitive but Unclassified (SBU), Confidential, Secret, Top Secret. (I discuss all these in upcoming sections.)

Within each classification level, certain safeguards are required in the use, handling, reproduction, transport, and destruction of the information. In addition to having an appropriate clearance level at or above the level of information being processed, individuals must have a *need-to-know* in order to have access to the information. The concept of *need-to-know* means that an individual requires the information to perform his or her assigned job function.

Unclassified

The lowest government data classification level is unclassified. *Unclassified* information isn't sensitive, and unauthorized disclosure won't cause any harm to national security. Unclassified information may include information that was once classified at a higher level but has since been declassified by the appropriate authority. Unclassified information isn't automatically releasable to the public and may include additional modifiers such as *For Official Use Only* or *For Internal Use Only*.

Sensitive but Unclassified (SBU)

Sensitive but Unclassified information is one of the more common modifiers of Unclassified information. It generally includes information of a private or personal nature. Examples include test questions, disciplinary proceedings, and medical records.

Confidential

Confidential information is information that, if compromised, could cause damage to national security. Confidential information is the lowest level of "classified" government information.

Secret

Secret information is information that, if compromised, could cause *serious* damage to national security. Secret information must normally be accounted for throughout its life cycle to destruction.

Top Secret

Top Secret information is information that, if compromised, could cause *grave* damage to national security. Top Secret information may require additional safeguards such as special designations and handling restrictions.

Employment Policies and Practices

The CISSP candidate must have a basic understanding of various employment policies and practices, as well as how they achieve information security objectives, and also the various information security roles and responsibilities within an organization. I also discuss various components of this section in Chapter 8.

Background checks/security clearances

Pre- and post-employment background checks can provide an employer with valuable information about an individual being considered for a job or position within an organization. Such checks can give an immediate indication of an individual's integrity and can help screen out unqualified applicants.

Basic background checks should be conducted for all personnel with access to sensitive information or systems within an organization. A basic background check should include

- ✓ **Reference checks:** Personal, professional, and prior employers
- ✓ **Verification of data in employment applications and resumes:** Social Security numbers, education, professional/technical certifications, military records, and previous employment
- ✓ **Other records:** Court, local law enforcement, and motor vehicle records

Personnel who fill more sensitive positions should undergo a more extensive pre-employment screening and background check, possibly including

- ✔ **Credit records**
- ✔ **Drug testing**
- ✔ **Special background investigation:** FBI and INTERPOL records, field interviews with former associates, or a personal interview with a private investigator

Periodic post-employment screenings (such as credit records and drug testing) may also be necessary, particularly for personnel with access to financial data or personnel being considered for promotions to more sensitive or responsible positions.

Employment agreements

Various employment agreements should be signed when an individual joins an organization or is promoted to a more sensitive position within an organization. Typical employment agreements include non-compete/non-disclosure agreements and acceptable use policies.

Hiring and termination practices

Hiring and termination practices should be formalized within an organization to ensure fair and uniform treatment and to protect the organization and its information assets.

Standard hiring practices should include background checks and employment agreements (as I discuss in the earlier section "Background checks/security clearances"), as well as a formal indoctrination and orientation process. This process may include formal introductions to key organizational personnel, creating user accounts and assigning IT resources (PCs and notebook computers), assigning security badges and parking permits, and a general policy discussion with human resources personnel.

Formal termination procedures should be implemented to help protect the organization from potential lawsuits, property theft/destruction, unauthorized access, or workplace violence. Procedures should be developed for various scenarios including resignations, termination, layoffs, accident or death, immediate departures versus prior notification, and hostile situations. Termination procedures may include

✔ Surrendering keys, security badges, and parking permits

✔ Conducting an exit interview

✔ Security escort to desk and/or from premises

✔ Returning company materials (notebook computers, mobile telephones, pagers)

✔ Changing door locks and system passwords

✔ Formal turnover of duties and responsibilities

✔ Removing network/system access and disabling user accounts

✔ Policies regarding retention of e-mail, personal files, and employment records

✔ Notification of customers, partners, vendors, and contractors, as appropriate

Job descriptions

Concise job descriptions that clearly identify an individual's responsibility and authority, particularly on information security issues, help

✔ Reduce confusion and ambiguity

✔ Provide legal basis for an individual's authority or actions

✔ Demonstrate negligence or dereliction in carrying out assigned duties

Roles and responsibilities

The true axiom that information security is everyone's responsibility is too often put into practice as *Everyone is responsible, but no one is accountable.* To avoid this pitfall, specific roles and responsibilities for information security should be defined in an organization's security policy, individual job or position descriptions, and third-party contracts. These roles and responsibilities should apply to employees, consultants, contractors, interns, and vendors. Several broad categories for information security roles and common responsibilities include the following.

Management

Senior-level management is often responsible for information security at several levels, including the role as an information owner, which I discuss in the next section. However, in this context, management has a responsibility to demonstrate a strong commitment to an organization's information security program. This can be achieved through the following actions:

- **Corporate information security policy:** This should include a statement of support from management and should also be signed by the CEO or COO.

- **Lead-by-example:** A CEO who refuses to carry a mandatory identification badge or who bypasses system access controls sets a poor example that others may emulate.

- **Cashola:** Pay exorbitant salaries to your security staff and praise them daily!!

Owner

An *information owner* is normally assigned at an executive or senior-management level within an organization, such as director or vice president. An information owner doesn't legally *own* the information that he's been assigned; the information owner is ultimately *responsible* for the safe-guarding of assigned information assets and may have *fiduciary responsibility* or be held *personally liable* for negligence in protecting these assets under the concept of due care. (For more on due care, read Chapter 11.)

Typical responsibilities of an information owner may include

- Determining information classification levels for assigned information assets

- Maintaining inventories and accounting for assigned information assets

- Periodically reviewing classification levels of assigned information assets for possible downgrading, destruction, or disposal

- Delegating day-to-day responsibility (but not accountability) and functions to a custodian

Custodian

An *information custodian* is the individual with day-to-day responsibility for protecting information assets. IT systems or network administrators often fill this role. Typical responsibilities may include

- Performing regular backups and restoring data when necessary

- Ensuring that directory and file permissions are properly implemented and provide sufficient protection

- Assigning new users to appropriate permission groups and revoking user privileges, when required

The distinction between owners and custodians, particularly regarding their different responsibilities, is an important concept in information security management. The information owner is the individual that has ultimate responsibility for the security of the information, whereas the information custodian is the individual responsible for the day-to-day security administration.

Users

An *end-user* (or user) includes just about everyone within an organization. Users aren't specifically designated. They can be broadly defined as anyone with authorized access to an organization's internal information or information systems. Typical user responsibilities include

- Complying with all security requirements defined in organizational policies, standards, and procedures, applicable legislative or regulatory requirements, and contractual requirements (such as non-disclosure agreements and service-level agreements)
- Exercising due care in safeguarding organizational information and information assets
- Participating in information security training and awareness efforts
- Reporting any suspicious activity, security violations, security problems, or security concerns to appropriate personnel

Separation of duties and responsibilities

The concept of *separation* (or *segregation*) *of duties and responsibilities* ensures that no single individual has complete authority and control of a critical system or process. This practice promotes security in the following ways:

- Reduces opportunity for waste, fraud, or abuse
- Provides two-man control (or dual-control, two-person integrity)
- Reduces dependence on individuals

In smaller organizations, this practice can sometimes be difficult to implement because of limited personnel and resources.

Job rotations

Job rotations (or rotation of duties) are another effective security control with many benefits to an organization. Similar to the concept of separation of duties and responsibilities, job rotations involve regularly transferring key personnel into different positions or departments within an organization. Job rotations benefit an organization in the following ways:

- ✔ Reduce opportunity for waste, fraud, or abuse
- ✔ Reduce dependence, through cross-training opportunities, on individuals; also promotes professional growth
- ✔ Reduce monotony and/or fatigue for individuals

As with the practice of separation of duties, job rotations can be difficult to implement in smaller organizations.

Policies, Standards, Guidelines, and Procedures

The CISSP candidate must understand the differences and relationships between policies, standards, guidelines, and procedures, and also recognize the different types of policies and their applications.

Policies, standards, guidelines, and procedures are the blueprints for a successful information security program. They

- ✔ Present governing rules and regulations
- ✔ Provide valuable guidance and decision support
- ✔ Help establish legal authority

Too often, technical security solutions are implemented without first creating the necessary policies, standards, guidelines, and procedures. This results in often expensive and ineffective controls that aren't uniformly applied and don't support an overall security strategy.

Policies

A *security policy* forms the basis of an organization's information security program. RFC 2196, *The Site Security Handbook*, defines a security policy as "a formal statement of rules by which people who are given access to an organization's technology and information assets must abide."

The four main types of policies are

- ✔ **Senior Management:** A high-level management statement of an organization's security objectives, organizational and individual responsibilities, ethics and beliefs, and general requirements and controls.

- ✔ **Regulatory:** Highly detailed and concise policies usually mandated by federal, state, industry, or other legal requirements.

- ✔ **Advisory:** Not mandatory, but highly recommended, often with specific penalties or consequences for failure to comply. Most policies are considered to be in this category.

- ✔ **Informative:** Purpose is only to inform with no explicit requirements for compliance.

Standards, guidelines, and procedures are supporting elements of a policy and provide specific implementation details of the policy.

Standards

Standards are specific, mandatory requirements that further define and support higher-level policies. For example, a standard may require the use of a specific technology, such as a minimum requirement for encryption of sensitive data using 3DES, without specifying the exact product to be implemented.

Baselines are similar to and related to standards. A baseline can be useful for identifying a consistent basis for an organization's security architecture, taking into account system-specific parameters, such as different operating systems. After consistent baselines are established, appropriate standards can be defined across the organization.

Guidelines

Guidelines are similar to standards but are recommendations rather than compulsory requirements. For example, a guideline may provide tips or recommendations for determining the sensitivity of a file and whether encryption is required.

Procedures

Procedures provide detailed instructions on how to implement specific policies and meet the criteria defined in standards. Procedures may include Standard

Operating Procedures (SOPs), run books, and user guides. For example, a procedure may be a step-by-step guide for encrypting sensitive files using a specific software encryption product.

Principles of Risk Management

Beyond basic security fundamentals, the principles of risk management are perhaps the most important and complex part of the security management domain. The CISSP candidate must fully understand the risk management triple, quantitative compared with qualitative risk assessment methodologies, risk calculations, and safeguard selection criteria and objectives.

The business of information security is all about risk management. A *risk* comprises a threat and a vulnerability, defined as follows:

- **Threat:** Any natural or man-made circumstance or event that could have an adverse or undesirable impact, minor or major, on an organizational asset.
- **Vulnerability:** The absence or weakness of a safeguard in an asset that makes a threat potentially more harmful or costly, more likely to occur, or likely to occur more frequently.

Threat + Vulnerability = Risk

An *asset* is a resource, process, product, or system that has some value to an organization and must therefore be protected. Assets may be *tangible* (computers, data, software, records) or *intangible* (privacy, access, public image, ethics), and may likewise have a *tangible value* (purchase price) or *intangible value* (competitive advantage).

The risk management triple consists of an asset, threat, and vulnerability.

Risk can never be completely eliminated. Given sufficient time, resources, motivation, and money, any system or environment, no matter how secure, can eventually be compromised. Some threats or events, such as natural disasters, are entirely beyond our control and are largely unpredictable. Therefore, the main goal of risk management is *risk mitigation:* reducing risk to a level that's acceptable to an organization. Risk management comprises the following three main elements:

- Identification
- Analysis
- Control

Risk identification

A preliminary step in risk management is risk identification. Risk identification involves identifying specific elements of the three components of risk: assets, threats, and vulnerabilities.

Asset valuation

Identifying an organization's assets and determining its value is a critical step in determining the appropriate level of security required for an asset. The value of an asset to an organization can be both *quantitative* (cost) and *qualitative* (importance). An inaccurate or hastily conducted asset valuation process can have the following consequences for controls:

- Poorly chosen or improperly implemented
- Not cost-effective
- Protect the wrong asset

A properly conducted asset valuation process has several benefits to an organization:

- Supports quantitative and qualitative risk assessments, business impact assessments, and security auditing
- Facilitates cost/benefit analysis and supports management decisions regarding selection of appropriate safeguards
- Can be used to determine insurance requirements, budgeting, and replacement costs
- Helps demonstrate due care and limit personal liability

Three basic elements used to determine the value of an asset are

- **Initial and maintenance costs:** This is most often a tangible dollar value and may include purchasing, licensing, development, maintenance, and support costs.
- **Organizational (or internal) value:** This is often a difficult and intangible value. It may include the cost of creating, acquiring, and re-creating information, and the business impact or loss if the information is lost or compromised. It can also include liability costs associated with privacy issues, personal injury, and death.
- **Public (or external) value:** Another difficult and often intangible cost, it can include loss of proprietary information or processes and loss of business reputation.

Threat analysis

Threat analysis involves the following four steps:

1. **Define the actual threat.**

2. **Identify possible consequences to the organization if the threat is realized.**

3. **Determine the probable frequency of a threat.**

4. **Assess the probability that a threat will actually materialize.**

For example, a company with a major distribution center located along the Gulf Coast of the United States may be concerned about hurricanes. Possible consequences may include power outages, wind damage, and flooding. Based on climatology, the company can determine that an annual average of three hurricanes pass within 50 miles of its location between June and September and that a high probability exists of a hurricane actually affecting the company's operations during this period. During the remainder of the year, the threat of hurricanes is a low probability.

The number and types of threats that an organization must consider can be overwhelming but can generally be categorized as

- ✔ **Natural:** Earthquakes, floods, hurricanes, lightning, fire, and so on

- ✔ **Man-made:** Unauthorized access, data entry errors, strikes/labor disputes, theft, terrorism, social engineering, malicious code and viruses, and so forth

Not all threats can be easily or rigidly classified. For example, fires and utility losses can be both natural and man-made. See Chapter 10 for more on disaster recovery.

Vulnerability assessment

A *vulnerability assessment* provides a valuable baseline for determining appropriate and necessary safeguards. For example, a denial-of-service threat may exist based on a vulnerability found in Microsoft's implementation of Domain Name System (DNS). However, if an organization's DNS servers have been properly patched or the organization uses a Unix-based BIND (Berkeley Internet Name Domain) server, the specific vulnerability may already have been adequately addressed, and no additional safeguards may be necessary for that threat.

Risk analysis

The next element in risk management is risk analysis. A *risk analysis* brings together all the elements of risk management (identification, analysis, and control) and is critical to an organization for developing an effective risk management strategy. A risk analysis involves the following four steps:

1. **Identify the assets to be protected, including their relative value, sensitivity, or importance to the organization.** This is a component of risk identification (asset valuation).

2. **Define specific threats, including threat frequency and impact data.** Again, this is a component of risk identification (threat analysis).

3. **Calculate Annualized Loss Expectancy (ALE).** ALE calculation is a fundamental concept in risk analysis; I discuss this in further detail later in this section.

4. **Select appropriate safeguards.** This is a component of both risk identification (vulnerability assessment) and risk control (which I discuss in the following section).

The *Annualized Loss Expectancy (ALE)* provides a standard, quantifiable measure of the impact that a realized threat has on an organization's assets. The estimated annual loss for a threat or event, expressed in dollars, ALE is particularly useful for determining the cost-benefit ratio of a safeguard or control. ALE is determined by this formula:

SLE x ARO = ALE

where

- ✔ **Single Loss Expectancy** (SLE) is a measure of the loss incurred from a single realized threat or event, expressed in dollars. It is calculated as Asset Value ($) x Exposure Factor (EF).

- ✔ **Exposure Factor** (EF) is a measure of the negative effect or impact that a realized threat or event would have on a specific asset, expressed as a percentage.

- ✔ **Annualized Rate of Occurrence** (ARO) is the estimated annual frequency of occurrence for a threat or event.

The two major types of risk analysis are *quantitative* and *qualitative*.

Quantitative risk analysis

A *quantitative risk analysis* attempts to assign an objective numeric value (cost) to the components (assets and threats) of the risk analysis.

A fully quantitative risk analysis requires all elements of the process, including asset value, impact, threat frequency, safeguard effectiveness, safeguard costs, and uncertainty and probability, to be measured and assigned a numeric value. However, assigning a value to every component associated with a risk (safeguard effectiveness and uncertainty) is not possible, and some qualitative measures must be applied.

Achieving a purely quantitative risk analysis is impossible.

Advantages of a quantitative compared with qualitative risk analysis include the following:

- ✔ Financial costs are defined; therefore, cost/benefit analysis is possible.
- ✔ More concise, specific data supports analysis; thus, fewer assumptions and less guesswork are required.
- ✔ Analysis and calculations can often be automated.
- ✔ Specific quantifiable results are easier to communicate to executives and senior-level management.

Disadvantages of a quantitative compared with qualitative risk analysis include the following:

- ✔ Many complex calculations are usually required.
- ✔ Time and work effort involved is relatively high.
- ✔ Volume of input data required is relatively high.
- ✔ Some assumptions are required. Purely quantitative risk analysis is generally not possible.

Qualitative risk analysis

A *qualitative risk analysis* is scenario-driven and doesn't attempt to assign numeric values to the components (assets and threats) of the risk analysis.

Qualitative risk analysis is more subjective than a quantitative risk analysis; and, unlike a quantitative risk analysis, it's possible to conduct a purely qualitative risk analysis. The challenge of a qualitative risk analysis is developing real scenarios that describe a threat and potential losses to organizational assets.

Advantages of a qualitative compared with quantitative risk analysis include

- ✔ No complex calculations are required.
- ✔ Time and work effort involved is relatively low.
- ✔ Volume of input data required is relatively low.

Disadvantages of a qualitative compared with quantitative risk analysis include

- ✔ No financial costs are defined; therefore, cost/benefit analysis isn't possible.
- ✔ Because qualitative risk analysis is less concise, it naturally relies more on assumptions and guesswork.

✔ Generally, qualitative risk analysis can't be automated.

✔ Qualitative risk analysis is less easily communicated. (Executives seem to understand *This will cost us 3 million dollars* better than *This will cause a cataclysmic collapse of the universe!*)

Risk control

A properly conducted risk analysis provides the basis for selecting appropriate safeguards and countermeasures. A *safeguard* is a control or countermeasure that reduces risk associated with a specific threat. The absence of a safeguard against a threat creates a vulnerability and increases the risk.

Safeguards counter risks through one of three general remedies:

✔ **Risk reduction:** Mitigating risk by implementing the necessary security controls, policies, and procedures to protect an asset. This can be achieved by altering, reducing, or eliminating the threat and/or vulnerability associated with the risk.

This is the most common risk control remedy.

✔ **Risk assignment (or transference):** Transferring the potential loss associated with a risk to a third party, such as an insurance company.

✔ **Risk acceptance:** Accepting the loss associated with a potential risk. This is sometimes done for convenience (not prudent) but more appropriately when the cost of other countermeasures is prohibitive and the potential risk probability is low.

Several criteria for selecting safeguards include cost effectiveness, legal liability, operational impact, and technical factors.

Cost effectiveness

The most common criterion for safeguard selection is *cost effectiveness*, which is determined through *cost/benefit analysis*. Cost/benefit analysis for a given safeguard or collection of safeguards can be computed as follows:

ALE before safeguard – ALE after safeguard – cost of safeguard = value of safeguard to the organization

For example, if: the ALE associated with a specific threat (data loss) is $1,000,000; the ALE after a safeguard (enterprise tape backup) has been implemented is $10,000 (recovery time); and the cost of the safeguard (purchase, installation, training, and maintenance) is $140,000; then the value of the safeguard to the organization is $850,000.

When calculating the cost of the safeguard, you should consider the *total cost of ownership,* including

- ✔ Purchase, development, and licensing
- ✔ Testing and installation
- ✔ Normal operating costs
- ✔ Resource allocation
- ✔ Maintenance and repair
- ✔ Production or service disruptions

The total cost of a safeguard is normally stated as an annualized amount.

Legal liability

An organization that fails to implement a safeguard against a threat is exposed to *legal liability* if the cost to implement a safeguard is less than the loss resulting from a realized threat. A cost/benefit analysis is a useful tool for determining legal liability.

Operational impact

The operational impact of a safeguard must also be considered. If a safeguard is too difficult to implement and operate, or interferes excessively with normal operations or production, it will be circumvented or ignored and thus not be effective.

Technical factors

The safeguard itself should not introduce new vulnerabilities. This may include improper placement, configuration, or operation; lack of fail-safe capabilities; insufficient auditing and accounting features; and improper reset causing asset damage or destruction, covert channel access, or otherwise unsafe conditions.

Security Awareness

The CISSP candidate should be familiar with the tools and objectives of awareness, training, and education programs that compose security awareness.

Security awareness is an often-overlooked factor in an information security program. Although security is the focus of security practitioners in their day-to-day functions, it's often taken for granted that common users possess this same level of security awareness. As a result, users can unwittingly become the weakest link in an information security program. Several key factors are critical to the success of a security awareness program:

✔ **Senior-level management support.** Under ideal circumstances, senior management is seen attending and actively participating in training efforts.

✔ **Clear demonstration of how security supports the organization's business objectives.**

✔ **Clear demonstration of how security is important to all individuals and their job functions.**

✔ **Current levels of training and understanding of the intended audience taken into account.** Training that's too basic will be ignored; training that's too technical will not be understood.

✔ **Action and follow-up.** A glitzy presentation that's forgotten as soon as the audience leaves the room is useless. Find ways to incorporate the lessons with day-to-day activities and follow-up plans.

The three main components of an effective security awareness program are a *general awareness program, formal training,* and *education.*

Awareness

A *general awareness program* provides basic security information and ensures that everyone understands the importance of security. Awareness programs may include the following elements:

✔ **Indoctrination and orientation:** New employees and contractors should receive a basic indoctrination and orientation. During the indoctrination, they may receive a copy of the corporate information security policy, be required to acknowledge and sign acceptable use statements and non-disclosure agreements, and meet immediate supervisors and pertinent members of the security and IT staff.

✔ **Presentations:** Lectures, video presentations, and interactive computer-based training (CBTs) are excellent tools for disseminating security training and information. Employee bonuses and performance reviews are sometimes tied to participation in these types of security awareness programs.

✔ **Printed materials:** Security posters, corporate newsletters, and periodic bulletins are useful for disseminating basic information such as security tips and promoting awareness of security.

Training

Formal training programs provide more in-depth information than an awareness program and may focus on specific security-related skills or tasks. Such training programs may include

✓ **Classroom training:** Instructor-led or other formally facilitated training, possibly at corporate headquarters or a company training facility.

✓ **On-the-job training:** May include one-on-one mentoring with a peer or immediate supervisor.

✓ **Technical or vendor training:** Training on a specific product or technology provided by a third-party.

✓ **Apprenticeship or qualification programs:** Formal probationary status or qualification standards that must be satisfactorily completed within a specified time period.

Education

An *education program* provides the deepest level of security training focusing on underlying principles, methodologies, and concepts.

An education program may include

✓ **Continuing education requirements:** Continuing Education Units (CEUs) are becoming popular for maintaining high-level technical or professional certifications such as the CISSP or Cisco Certified Internetworking Expert (CCIE).

✓ **Certificate programs:** Many colleges and universities offer adult education programs with classes on current and relevant subjects for working professionals.

✓ **Formal education or degree requirements:** Many companies offer tuition assistance or scholarships for employees enrolled in classes that are relevant to their profession.

Additional References

Krutz, Ronald L. and Vines, Russell Dean. *The CISSP Prep Guide: Mastering the Ten Domains of Computer Security,* Chapter 1. John A. Wiley & Sons, Inc.

Tipton, Harold F. and Krause, Micki. *Information Security Management Handbook,* 4th Edition, Chapters 12 and 15. Auerbach Publications.

Pipkin, Donald. *Information Security, Protecting the Global Enterprise*, Chapters 1, 2, 5, 7, 14, and Phase II. Prentice Hall PTR.

Wood, Charles Cresson. *Information Security Policies Made Easy,* Version 8. PentaSafe.

Prep Test

1 The three elements of the C-I-A triad include

- **A** ○ Confidentiality, Integrity, Authentication
- **B** ○ Confidentiality, Integrity, Availability
- **C** ○ Confidentiality, Integrity, Authorization
- **D** ○ Confidentiality, Integrity, Accountability

2 Which of the following government data classification levels describes information that, if compromised, could cause serious damage to national security?

- **A** ○ Top Secret
- **B** ○ Secret
- **C** ○ Confidential
- **D** ○ Sensitive but Unclassified

3 The practice of regularly transferring personnel into different positions or departments within an organization is

- **A** ○ Separation of duties
- **B** ○ Re-assignment
- **C** ○ Lateral transfers
- **D** ○ Job rotations

4 The individual responsible for assigning information classification levels for assigned information assets is

- **A** ○ Management
- **B** ○ Owner
- **C** ○ Custodian
- **D** ○ User

5 Most security policies are categorized as

- **A** ○ Informative
- **B** ○ Regulatory
- **C** ○ Mandatory
- **D** ○ Advisory

6 A baseline is a type of

- **A** ○ Policy
- **B** ○ Guideline
- **C** ○ Procedure
- **D** ○ Standard

7 **ALE is calculated by using the following formula:**

A ○ SLE x ARO x EF = ALE

B ○ SLE x ARO = ALE

C ○ SLE + ARO = ALE

D ○ SLE – ARO = ALE

8 **Which of the following is not considered a general remedy for risk management?**

A ○ Risk reduction

B ○ Risk acceptance

C ○ Risk assignment

D ○ Risk avoidance

9 **Failure to implement a safeguard may result in legal liability if**

A ○ The cost to implement the safeguard is less than the cost of the associated loss.

B ○ The cost to implement the safeguard is more than the cost of the associated loss.

C ○ An alternate but equally effective and less expensive safeguard is implemented.

D ○ An alternate but equally effective and more expensive safeguard is implemented.

10 **A cost-benefit analysis is useful in safeguard selection for determining**

A ○ Safeguard effectiveness

B ○ Technical feasibility

C ○ Cost effectiveness

D ○ Operational impact

Answers

1 **B.** Confidentiality, Integrity, Availability. Confidentiality, integrity, and availability are the three elements of the C-I-A triad. Authentication, authorization, and accountability are access control concepts. *Review "Security Management Concepts and Principles."*

2 **B.** Secret. Top Secret information leaks could cause *grave damage*. Confidential information breaches could cause *damage*. Sensitive but Unclassified information doesn't have a direct impact on national security. *Review "Government data classification."*

3 **D.** Job rotations. Separation of duties is related to job rotations but is distinctly different. Re-assignment and lateral transfers are functionally equivalent to job rotations but aren't necessarily done for the same reasons and aren't considered security employment practices. *Review "Job rotations."*

4 **B.** Owner. Although an information owner may be in a management position and is also considered a user, the information owner role has the responsibility for assigning information classification levels. An information custodian is responsible for day-to-day security tasks. *Review "Roles and responsibilities."*

5 **D.** Advisory. Although not mandatory, advisory policies are highly recommended and may provide penalties for failure to comply. *Review "Policies."*

6 **D.** Standard. A baseline takes into account system-specific parameters to help an organization identify appropriate standards. *Review "Standards."*

7 **B.** SLE x ARO = ALE. SLE x ARO = ALE is the correct formula for calculating ALE, where SLE is the Single Loss Expectancy, ARO is the Annualized Rate of Occurrence, and ALE is the Annualized Loss Expectancy expressed in dollars. *Review "Risk analysis."*

8 **D.** Risk avoidance. Although risk avoidance is a valid concept, it's impossible to achieve and therefore not considered a general remedy for risk management. *Review "Risk control."*

9 **A.** The cost to implement the safeguard is less than the cost of the associated loss. This basic legal liability test determines whether the cost of the safeguard is less than the cost of the associated loss if a threat is realized. *Review "Legal liability."*

10 **C.** Cost effectiveness. A cost-benefit analysis won't help an organization determine the effectiveness of a safeguard, its technical feasibility, or its operational impact. *Review "Cost effectiveness."*

Chapter 6

Applications and Systems Development Security

● ●

In This Chapter

▶ Distributed environments

▶ Object-oriented environments

▶ Databases and data warehousing

▶ Knowledge-based systems

▶ Systems development lifecycle

▶ Application security controls

▶ Malicious code

▶ System attack methods

▶ Perpetrators

● ●

*T*he Applications and Systems Development Security domain introduces many important concepts, overlapping several other domains.

The Certified Information Systems Security Professional (CISSP) candidate must fully understand the principles of applications, application development, and databases. Applications and data are the foundation of information processing; applications can't exist apart from application development. One can see the importance of the application development discipline if software is to be reliable and secure.

Additionally, the CISSP candidate must also understand how malicious code works, how it can be stopped, and how hackers attack systems. Security professionals should be familiar with these potential problems so that they can guide application developers towards development practices that will help to strengthen systems against such attacks.

Distributed Applications

Applications escaped the computer room in the early 1980s with the advent of personal computers (PCs). Perhaps it was the computer operator's white lab coats, the pocket protectors, or the horn-rimmed glasses, but applications couldn't take it any more. They wanted a life.

I've seen smart terminals with field editing capabilities (cough . . . most of you readers weren't yet born when these were prevalent), and later on, two-tier and three-tier client-server applications in which some of the application logic ran on a server and some of it ran on a PC. Client-server looked really good on paper (and on those fancy new white boards), but it was terrible in practice.

But in 1992, Eric Bina, Marc Andresson, and Al Gore (Father of the Internet) developed the first popular Web browser called *Mosaic*, which sported such features as hyperlinks and Web pages that contained pictures *and* text. Thousands of people downloaded Mosaic, which was available for PCs, Macs, and UNIX, and soon the modern World Wide Web (WWW) was born. The Web was cool and really fast until the general public found out about it and ruined it. Seriously, though, a lot of neat and relevant technologies were born out of the Web, many of which I discuss in this chapter.

The Web was the death knell for client-server applications for reasons that are irrelevant to the CISSP Common Body of Knowledge (CBK). Read the side-bar "WWW 3, client-server 0" elsewhere in this chapter for a little more background on this.

Security in distributed systems

Securing distributed systems is anything but easy, and it boils down to two distinct issues: software integrity and access control.

Software integrity is a challenge because in a distributed system, the application may consist of software components located on various systems possibly in different physical locations. Keeping track of the versions of all these separate components can be a nightmare, particularly when the various hardware platforms are supported by different parts of the organization (or even different companies!). Imagine for a moment that after a new release of an application is recently installed on all the systems, a few days later one of the systems suffers a catastrophic failure that requires that it be rebuilt from back-up tapes.

What if those back-up tapes were made before the application upgrade? Now suddenly you have a hardware platform running an older version of some part of the application. Perhaps the changes in the application were subtle, but the older application component restored onto that system that died a few days earlier didn't work quite right and resulted in every customer's middle name being changed to *Celine*. (Royalty checks not included.)

The other problem with distributed systems is access control. All those distributed components need to talk with each other, presumably over networks. The easy thing to do here is to have the systems just talk with each other with full and complete trust. Well, Microsoft taught us that trusting everybody isn't such a great idea, so the best approach is for the various components in a distributed environment to prove their identity to one another. This means setting up some sort of authentication, access control, or maybe even a full-blown Kerberos environment so that the various parts of a distributed application know that the other parts that they're talking to are the real deal and not script kiddies looking for credit card numbers to steal.

It's enough for the over-fifty set to wish for mainframes again.

WWW 3, client-server 0

So what was it about the Web that sent client-server down for the count? The Web had three distinct advantages over client-server.

First, client-server brought with it a tremendous software distribution problem. Client-server was supposed to scale in big organizations, the kind with thousands or even tens of thousands of client systems. Who was supposed to make sure that the software components on all those clients were up-to-date? And in a 24x7 environment, how were those tens of thousands of PCs all over the world supposed to get simultaneously upgraded? The Web solved this by moving the application software back to the server. What we have instead is *the universal client*, as Web browsers have been called, which seldom needs updating. However, the business application can change frequently because the code only needs updated on the one (or two, or three) server(s).

Second, client-server exacted a large performance penalty. The truth is, it didn't scale because of two reasons. One, too much network traffic existed between just a single client and the server. For instance, if the client wanted

to do a *join* of two tables, depending upon how the application was written, those two tables might have had to be sent in their entirety to the client for processing. Not good if the tables are large. Also, whenever there was a change made in the application, the new version of the application had to be distributed to all clients. This probably doesn't sound like a big deal, but imagine tens of thousands of these clients all over the world. Many times the nature of the application change necessitated that all clients be upgraded simultaneously — by no means an easy task.

Third, PCs running in client-server environments also needed to have very fast CPUs and lots of memory, which made them very expensive. Client-server was supposed to save businesses a lot of money by moving some of the business logic to the desktop where it was performed, thus preventing those companies from having to upgrade to bigger and bigger servers. This was a laudable goal, but it turned out that PCs didn't have the processing power necessary to do a very good job of holding up the client end of the bargain.

Agents

An *agent* is a component in a distributed system that performs a particular service. An example of an agent might be a system that takes a credit card number (with expiration date, customer name, purchase amount, and so forth) and builds a merchant transaction to send to a bank. The agent then processes the result and gives a yea or nay response back to the main application, which then gets to give the customer ordering books on the Web the good news or bad news.

An agent is a component in a distributed system that performs a particular function.

Applets

An *applet* is a component in a distributed environment that's downloaded and executed by a Web browser. Web browsers, which are designed to display text and graphics and also accept data input on forms, aren't very good at processing information locally on the client system, so applets were invented to solve this problem.

The neat thing about applets is that they run seamlessly right in a Web browser, and you can't even tell that an applet is running or whether you're just dealing with straight HTML. Those among you who develop Web applications for food can tell the difference because you know a lot more about what applets can do compared with what plain HTML can do. The rest of us are clueless, and that's fine by me.

The two most popular environments for applets are Java and ActiveX. Java code runs in something called a *sandbox*, which is to say that the Java code can only communicate with the host that it was downloaded from. Java is also permitted to display things on the screen and accept keyboard or mouse input. However, Java applets aren't permitted to access a PC's hard drive, memory, or any other devices. Web browsers today get a lot of practice saying to Java applets, "Go play in your sandbox and leave my hard drive alone!," and rarely do Java applets escape from their sandboxes.

ActiveX, which is really just a cool name for *OLE over the Internet*, is Microsoft's response to Java. ActiveX uses a completely different security philosophy than Java, and it goes something like this: People running Web browsers get to decide whether they trust all ActiveX applets that come from a particular server. Digital certificates are used to enforce this trust relationship. But the primary weakness with ActiveX is that a rogue developer can write some pretty nasty ActiveX code to melt your hard drive and play old Perry Como songs through your PC's speakers.

This kind of thing is possible because ActiveX has no concept of a sandbox like Java does. If you trust the server that the ActiveX applet comes from, then you're basically saying that you give all control of your PC over to the ActiveX applet, and it can do whatever it wants. This is all fine and good in an ideal world (for a three-mile radius around Redmond, Washington) where everyone is trustworthy. In the real world, though, programmers with an attitude — or even honest and ethical programmers who make a mistake — can make those bad things happen to your system. Always turn down your speaker volume before running ActiveX applets unless you're in a closed room or you really like Perry Como.

Firewalls and proxy servers can be configured to filter out ActiveX applets. Most firewall administrators will put in extra hours to do this. Web browsers can also be configured to not run Java or ActiveX applets, but the last time that I checked, users could still just change this back so that they can see their stock ticker or the cool picture at www.time.gov. Enterprises that are serious about protecting themselves really need to block applets at the firewall or proxy server.

Applets are also known as *mobile code* because they're downloaded from a server and run on a client.

Object-Oriented Environments

Object-oriented applications have their foundation based in a completely different approach to information systems and process — of *objects* and *reusability*. Object orientation is an entire universe comprising object-oriented analysis, design, programming, and even databases.

The object-oriented religion is based upon a fundamental principle: Objects, after they're written, can be reused again and again, thereby making the enterprise's entire software development effort more and more efficient over time.

Object orientation is known as *OO*, pronounced *oh oh*.

As I mention above, the *object* is the primary, er, object of OO. An object is *encapsulated*, which means that the inner workings of an object are hidden and can remain so. Objects communicate with each other by using *messages*. When an object receives a message, it performs whatever function it was designed to do, which is its *method*.

An object that's running is an *instance*. The process of starting an instance is *instantiation*. But an *instance* can also refer to an object that's a member of a *class* of objects.

As you can see, OO has quite a vocabulary, and you haven't seen half of it yet. But now you can be sure than when you hear a couple of guys talking about someone's objects, you've got the secret decoder ring to know that they're computer science types, probably even hip Web developers.

Because you might be tiring of reading about OO terms buried in paragraphs, here they are in a little glossary.

Behavior: The results of an *object* having been sent a *message*.

Class: In his book, *Business Engineering with Object Technology*, author David Taylor describes this as "a template that defines the methods and variables to be included in a particular type of object." The class itself contains the common *methods* and *variables*, and *objects* in the class contain only those characteristics that make them unique. There are also *subclasses* (parts of a class) and *superclasses* (collections of *classes*).

Class hierarchy: The tree structure of a collection of *objects* and *classes*.

Delegation: What happens when an *object* receives a *message* requesting a *method* that it doesn't have. The *object* will *delegate* the *message* to the *object* that does contain the requested *method*.

Encapsulation: The packaging of an *object*. Everything inside the *object* is hidden, or *encapsulated*.

Inheritance: An *object* that gets some of its characteristics from a *class*. An *object* inherits characteristics from the *class* when it's *instantiated*. It doesn't have to wait for the *class* to grow old and die.

Instance: A particular *object* that's a member of a *class*.

Message: How objects communicate with one another. A message contains the name of an *object* that it wants to communicate to, the *method* it should perform, and usually one or more *parameters*. The object sending the message is the *sender*; the object receiving it is the *receiver*.

Method: The *procedure* (code) contained in an object.

Multiple inheritance: When an *object* or *class* inherits characteristics from more than one *class*.

Object: The basic unit in OO.

Polyinstantiation: The process of developing one *object* from another *object* but with different values in the new *object*.

Polymorphism: Taylor describes this as "the ability to hide implementation details behind a common message interface." This permits new objects to be added to a system without having to rewrite existing procedures.

Objective trivia

Object orientation has its roots in two programming languages: Simula and Smalltalk. Simula was developed in the 1960s, and Smalltalk in the early 1970s. C++ was developed at AT&T Bell Laboratories in the early 1980s as an add-on to the popular C language, which was also developed at Bell Labs.

Data and Information Storage

I describe common terms and methods for storing information in this section. The "Computer Architecture" section in Chapter 8 covers the other components.

Primary storage

Primary storage is a computer's main memory, usually known as *main memory* or RAM (Random Access Memory). Primary storage is the fastest memory in a computer system. It stores the information used most often. Computers have hundreds or thousands of megabytes of primary storage. Primary storage is *random access* storage — any memory location can be read from or written to in any random order. Primary storage is *volatile* or not. Volatility determines whether the data remains without power. Generally, primary storage in RAM is volatile: when power is removed from the computer, the contents of primary storage are lost.

Some technologies for semiconductor memory are not volatile, such as PROM (Programmable Read-Only Memory), EPROM (Erasable Programmable Read-Only Memory), EEPROM (Electrically Erasable Programmable Read-Only Memory), and Flash memory. These types require no power to hold data.

Secondary storage

Secondary storage usually is a magnetic disk, often referred to as *hard drives* or *hard disks*. Secondary storage holds the operating system, programs, and data files. Secondary memory is slower than primary memory, but a computer can have as much as several terabytes of secondary storage. *Magnetic tapes* are most often used to make backups of data.

Hard disks, like primary storage, are *random access* devices. Any locations on the disk can be read or written in any order. Magnetic tapes are *sequential* access devices: you must read through the tape until you reach the location.

Real and virtual

The terms *real* and *virtual* have everything to do with the representation of memory more than the memory itself.

Real memory refers to actually-present physical memory, whether primary storage (RAM) or secondary storage (disks). Such memory is directly addressable — if you want to read the nth cluster from a disk or the nth byte from memory, that's what you get.

Virtual memory refers to an abstract memory-addressing scheme that is used to present a virtual memory space that usually differs from the physical memory. I'll describe two different examples of virtual memory.

First example — a computer system has 64MB of physical main memory, but 128MB of virtual main memory. How does the computer fit 128MB of virtual memory into 64MB of physical memory? It *pages out* the least-used memory to a *swap file* on the system's secondary storage. When a program wishes to read from or write to an address in virtual memory that has been paged out, a *page fault* occurs, and the computer copies the location back into main memory.

In olden times, computers used a simpler virtual memory scheme called *swapping*. The computer would *swap out* the entire memory for a program to make room to *swap in* another program. Paging allows the computer to page out only unused portions of an active program's memory space.

Second example — a computer system has a large number of relatively small disk drives, say 100GB apiece. The system administrator wishes to build a 500GB filesystem. The administrator builds a *virtual filesystem* that spans multiple physical disks. The filesystem uses a virtual addressing scheme.

Databases

A *database* is used to define, store, and manipulate data. In modern information systems as database management systems (DBMSs), which exist apart from application software, a database contains the data and a programming and command interface to create, manage, and administer data.

DBMSs generally contain an access-control mechanism used to protect data and permit certain users, or classes of users, to view or modify portions of the database. I describe access-control mechanisms in databases in Chapter 3.

Database security

The *granularity* of access control is a description of how finely you can control who can see which tables, rows, and fields. An example of low granularity is read or read/write access to all rows and fields in a table. High granularity restricts access to certain fields and even certain rows.

Views can simplify security issues. A view is a virtual table of the rows and fields from tables in the database. You give access to these views, not the actual tables.

Aggregation refers to the process of combining low-sensitivity data items resulting in high-sensitivity data. By themselves, dates of birth or a home address don't mean a lot, but together, you've got something. That's aggregation. If you get Ed McMahon's home address from one database, his Social Security number from another, his driver's license from another, and his date of birth from yet another, then you've got something potentially damaging . . . or valuable. That's *identity theft*.

Aggregation is the process of combining low-sensitivity data items to produce a high-sensitivity data item.

Inference is the ability to deduce or infer sensitive information that's beyond normal reach because of its sensitivity level.

Data dictionaries

A *data dictionary* is a database of databases. In a large application with many tables, a data dictionary could be a database containing all the information about all the tables and fields in an application. A data dictionary is used by the DBMS, the application, and security tools such as access control. A data dictionary can be used to create or recreate tables, manage security access, and as a control point for managing the schema of the application's database.

Data warehouses

A *data warehouse* is a special purpose database for business research, decision support, and planning; typical databases support daily operations. For instance, a bank executive may want a list of customers with more than $35,000 in their checking accounts who haven't made any deposits in the past month and who also live in the 94027 Zip code. The company's main production databases isn't the place for such activity. You can tune the database for *inserts and updates* (the activities typical in regular production databases) or large queries (activities typical of data warehouses) but not both. These two activities require opposite tuning settings in the database.

The respectable term for the activity that the what-iffers play is *decision support*. These folks try to figure out trends to support strategic decisions. The new term for decision support is *data mining*.

Another application of data mining is *fraud detection*. Banks and credit card companies sift records for spending trends associated with stolen credit cards.

Data warehouses use *metadata*. Metadata describes how data was collected and how it is formatted.

The type of database used for decision support is called a data warehouse.

Knowledge-Based Systems

Also known as *artificial intelligence*, knowledge-based systems accumulate knowledge and make decisions or predictions based upon historical data.

Expert systems

Expert systems build a database of past events in order to develop the ability to predict outcomes in future situations. An *inference engine* analyzes the past events to see whether a match between a past event and the current problem can be found. For instance, if a stock-picking program knows that IBM always goes up 2 points when the Mets are in town under a full moon, then it tells you to buy IBM when the Mets are in town and the moon is full.

Expert systems are designed to work with degrees of uncertainty, and they do so in one of two ways: fuzzy logic and certainty factors.

Fuzzy logic breaks the factors of a decision or outcome into components, evaluates each component, and recombines the individual evaluations to arrive at the yes/no or true/false conclusion for the big question.

Certainty factors operate on the numeric probability of yes/no, true/false, rain/snow, or whatever the expert system is working on. The individual probabilities are aggregated, and the final conclusion is reached.

Fuzzy logic is the component of an expert system that produces a quantitative result based upon uncertainties.

Neural networks

Neural networks mimic the biological function of the brain: A neural network accumulates knowledge by observing events; it measures their inputs and outcome. Over time, the neural network becomes proficient because it has observed repetitions of the circumstances and is also told the outcome each time. Then, when confronted with a fresh set of inputs for a new situation, the neural network predicts outcomes with increasing reliability over time.

Neural networks learn that input components are weighted, which is to say that their degree of influence on the outcome is calculated. Neural network decisions are only as good as what it has learned from past experiences.

Systems Development Lifecycle

The system development lifecycle refers to the steps required to develop a system from conception through implementation.

The lifecycle is a *development process* designed to achieve two objectives: a system that performs its intended function correctly and securely, and a development project that's completed on time and on budget.

A typical system development model contains all the steps required to take a project from conception to completion. See an illustration of this in Figure 6-1.

Read on as I take a look at each of these steps in detail to understand what happens in each.

Conceptual definition

Conceptual definition is a high-level description of the system. It generally contains no details — it's the sort of description that you want to give to the Finance people. You know, those folks who fund your projects and keep you employed. You don't want to scare them with details.

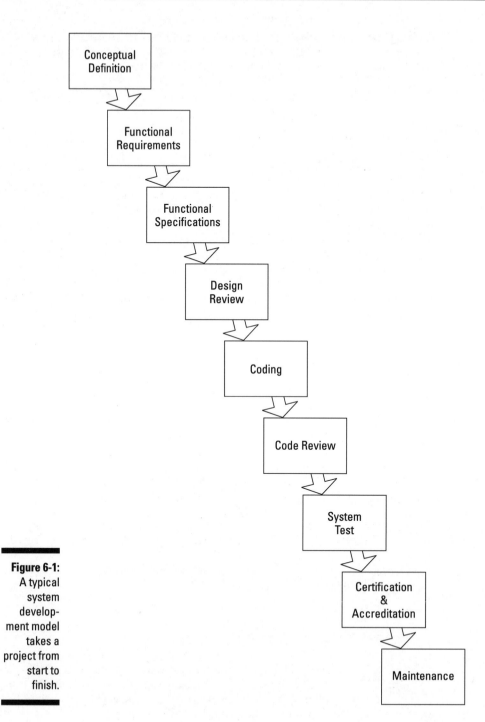

Figure 6-1:
A typical
system
develop-
ment model
takes a
project from
start to
finish.

A typical conceptual definition for the Segway Human Transporter would read something like this: "Lightweight, electric powered, side-by-side two-wheeled one-person vehicle. Intuitive controls — just lean forward to move forward, straight up to stop, back to reverse, and left/right to turn. User stands on a small platform and holds waist-high handgrips."

No detail here is too specific. Conceptual is just that.

Functional requirements

Here is a list of required characteristics of the system. It's not a design but a collection of things that the system must do. Continuing the Segway example, some functional requirements would include

- **Weight:** No more than 75 lbs
- **Turning radius:** Zero
- **Range:** 7–15 miles
- **Top speed:** 70 mph
- **Width:** No wider than a typical person

Still, this isn't design-level material, but it contains more details than the conceptual definition. This is a document that Marketing or Product Concept people would come up with.

Functional requirements usually includes a *test plan*, which is a detailed list of characteristics of the system that must be tested. The test plan describes how each test should be performed and also what the expected results should be. Generally you have at least one test in the test plan for each requirement in the functional requirements.

Functional requirements must contain security requirements that the system is expected to have.

A proposed system's list of desired features is its *functional requirements*.

Functional specifications

You could call this the Engineering version of functional requirements. Instead of a list of *have-to-have* and *nice-to-have* items, the functional specification is more of a *what-it-will-be (we hope)* or a *what-we-think-we-can-build* statement. Continuing my example:

- ✔ **Weight:** 95 lbs
- ✔ **Power supply:** 4 LiIon type 67 batteries, rechargeable
- ✔ **Wheels:** 7.5" x 1.5" forged magnesium alloy
- ✔ **Tires:** Dunlop A520, light gray
- ✔ **Motors:** General Electric 290wh, 12v, industrial package
- ✔ **Top speed:** 14 mph

This is still not quite a design rather but a list of characteristics that Engineering thinks is *real-world*. Note the compromises on weight and top speed: Marketing didn't get what they wanted (70 mph), but then those folks never do.

From a security perspective, the functional specifications for an operating system or application should contain all the details about authentication, authorization, access control, confidentiality, audit, integrity, and availability.

Design

Design is the process of developing highest-detail designs. In the application software world, this would comprise entity-relationship diagrams, data flow diagrams, and so forth.

An example, were I to show you one, would consist of engineering drawings, bills of materials (a list of all the components required to build one Segway HT), and building instructions.

The *design review* is the last step in the design process, where the detailed designs are examined by a group of experts, some of whom are on the design team and some of whom are not. Those not on the design team give the design a set of fresh eyes and a chance to maybe catch a design flaw or two.

Coding

Coding is the phase that the software developers yearn for. Most of them would just as soon skip all previous steps and start coding right away even before the product people have a chance to develop formal requirements. It's scary to think about how much of the world's software was created in which coding was the first activity. (Would you fly in an airplane that the machinists built before the designers could produce engineering drawings?)

Coding usually includes *unit testing*, which is the process of verifying all the modules that are built in this phase.

Software developers had better be following secure coding practices!

Code review

Just as in the design phase, the coding phase ends with a code review where a bunch of prima donna engineers examine each other's program code and get into religious arguments about levels of indenting and the correct use of curly braces.

System test

System test occurs when all the components of the entire system have been assembled, and the entire system is tested *end to end*. The test plan that was developed back in the functional requirements step is carried out here.

Of course, the system test includes testing all the system's security functions because they were included in the test plan.

Certification

Certification is the formal evaluation of the system. The system is declared fully functional. Every intended feature performs as planned.

Accreditation

Accreditation is a five-dollar word that means the people in the mahogany offices have said that it's okay to put the system into production. That could be to offer it for sale, build and ship, or whatever *put into production* means, depending upon what kind of a product it is.

Maintenance

At this point, the system is in production, and now its customers start putting in *change requests* because of a bunch of bone-headed mistakes made while developing requirements. Here's where maintenance comes alive. The Change Management and Configuration Management processes kick into play in order to maintain control of and document all changes to the system over its lifetime.

Good documentation in the form of those specification and design documents is important because the developers who wrote this system have probably moved on to some other cool project . . . and the new guys who don't know any better are left to maintain it.

Notes about the lifecycle

Larger organizations implement the lifecycle with a complex, formal process. Each step in the process contains its own steps, actions, deliverables, and reviews. A formal process dictates knowing what step a project is in (product concept, functional requirements, functional specs, design, and so on), as well as whether a project is allowed to pass from one step to the next.

Because of unexpected events, frequently a project must back up one step to make corrections. For instance, in the example above, the marketing people wanted the Segway to go 70 mph, but the Engineering folks could only eke out 14 mph. Such a discrepancy would trigger a return to the functional requirements step to get the marketing people back to earth and get the functional requirements to align with realistic functional specifications. After they settle their differences, they move on.

Change Management

Change Management is the formal business process that ensures that all changes made to a system receive formal review and approval from all stakeholders. Change Management gives everyone a chance to voice their opinions, concerns, and impacts from any proposed change so that the change will go as smoothly as possible, with no surprises or interruptions in service.

Change Management is usually performed by a Change Review Board, which has members from departments such as Development, Operations, and Customer, as well as other stakeholders in the company.

The process of approving modifications to a production environment is called Change Management.

Configuration Management

Often confused with Change Management (and vice versa), Configuration Management has little to do with approvals but everything to do with recording all the facts about the change. Configuration Management is the mechanism that captures actual changes to software code, end-user documentation, operations documentation, disaster recovery planning documentation, and anything else that's affected by the change.

Change Management and Configuration Management address two different aspects of change in a system's maintenance mode. Change Management is the *what*, and Configuration Management is the *how*.

Application Security Controls

Up to this point, my discussion has centered on system architectures and development processes. Hopefully, you've begun to wonder how applications are made to be secure in the first place. I discuss several techniques, characteristics, and mechanisms in this section.

Process isolation

With *process isolation*, running processes aren't allowed to view or modify memory and cache that's assigned to another process. For instance, if a user can see that a payroll program is running on the system, he won't be able to read the memory space used by the payroll program.

Process isolation is a service that's provided by the operating system. The system developer doesn't have to build a wall around his application to prevent others from snooping on it.

Hardware segmentation

Hardware segmentation refers to the practice of isolating functions to separate platforms as required to ensure the integrity and security of system functions. This can also refer to keeping developers off of production systems and vice versa.

Hardware segmentation is used to keep application developers off of production systems.

Separation of privilege

Also known as *least privilege*, *separation of privilege* assures that no individuals have excessive functions on a system. For instance, in a finance application, you'd have at least three people involved in payments to others: those who *request* the payment, those who *approve* the payment, and those who *perform* the payment. Each of these functions should have privileges that permit them to perform only their approved function.

Accountability

Accountability refers to an application's ability to record every auditable event by describing the event: who made the change and when the change was made. This feature makes it impossible (you hope) for an individual to make any change to data without the application capturing the details about the change.

Accountability is only as strong as the underlying authentication mechanism. If employees habitually share passwords or use each other's accounts, then it's very difficult to associate any inappropriate data tampering with a specific individual.

Defense in depth

Also known as *layering*, *defense in depth* is a security architecture concept wherein assets requiring protection are protected with multiple mechanisms that form protective layers around the assets. For example, a company may have a firewall but additionally implement host-based access control and other mechanisms in the unlikely event that the firewall fails.

The practice of protecting a system or network with several concurrent mechanisms is *defense in depth*.

Abstraction

Abstraction is a process of viewing an application from its highest-level functions, which makes all lower-level functions into abstractions.

Data hiding

Data hiding is an Object Orientation term that refers to the practice of encapsulating an object within another in order to hide the first object's functioning details.

System high mode

System high mode refers to a system that operates at the highest level of information classification. Any user who wishes to access such a system must have clearance at or above the information classification level.

Security kernel

The *security kernel* is a part of the *protection rings* model in which the operating system kernel occupies the innermost ring, and rings further away from the innermost ring represent fewer access rights. The security kernel is the innermost ring and has full access to all system hardware and data.

Reference monitor

Reference monitor is the operating system component that enforces access controls on data and devices on a system. In other words, when a user tries to access a file, the reference monitor ultimately performs the *Is this person allowed to access this file?* test.

Access controls on a system are enforced by the system's reference monitor.

Supervisor and user modes

Modern operating systems use the concept of privilege that's associated to user accounts. For instance, UNIX has the `root` account, and NT has the Domain Administrator and Local Administrator roles. These accounts and roles are intended to be used only by system or network administrators for operating system and utility management functions.

Now and again you may hear of administrators who grant `root` or administrator privileges to normal applications. This is a serious mistake because applications that run in supervisor mode bypass some or all security controls, which could lead to unexpected application behavior. For instance, any user of a payroll application could view or change anyone's data because the application running in supervisor mode was never told *no* by the operating system.

Supervisor mode is for system administration purposes only. Business applications should always be run in *user mode*.

Service Level Agreements

In the real world, users of any business application need to know whether their application is going to be functioning when they need it. Users need to know more than "Is it up?" or "Is it down AGAIN?" The users of an application are held accountable to their customers and/or superiors for getting a certain amount of work performed, so consequently they need to know whether they can depend upon their application to help them get there.

The Service Level Agreement (SLA) is a quasi-legal document (a real legal document when the application service provider is a different company than the user[s] using it) that is a pledge made by the operations group or service provider that they will perform to a set of minimum standards, such as:

- **Hours of availability:** This refers to the *wall clock hours* that the application will be available for users. This could be 24x7 (24 hours per day, seven days per week) or something more limited, like daily from 4 a.m.–12 p.m.

- **Average and peak number of concurrent users:** This is the maximum number of users who can log on to the application at once.

- **Transaction throughput:** This is the number of transactions that the application can perform in a given time period.

- **Data storage capacity:** This determines the amount of data that the users can store in the application.

- **Application response times:** This refers to the maximum period of time (in seconds) that key transactions take. Similarly, it's the amount of time that longer processes (nightly runs, and so on) take should be in an SLA.

- **Escalation process during times of failure:** When things go wrong, this describes how quickly the service provider will contact the customer as well as what steps will be taken to restore service.

Because the SLA is a quantified statement, the service provider and the user alike can take measurements to see how well the service provider is meeting the SLA's standards. This measurement, which is sometimes accompanied by analysis, is frequently called a *scorecard*.

Malicious Code

As soon as data found a way to move easily from computer to computer, a creative individual with a bad attitude figured out that he could include something that would play a not-so-practical joke, like delete files from someone else's computer.

Unfortunately, several types of malicious code are out there; I define the most interesting ones here.

Virus

The main purpose of a computer *virus,* a (usually) small program, is to replicate itself. Early computer viruses would attach themselves to floppy disk boot sectors or to executable (such as COM or EXE files). Boot sector viruses would spread if the PC were booted with an infected diskette. Viruses attached to executable files would spread when those executable files were run. Multipartite viruses spread using both the boot sector and executable files.

Today, viruses spread in some new ways, including macros found in Microsoft Word and Excel documents.

Strictly speaking, a virus spreads by making (usually) identical copies of itself on files that are likely to be transported to other computers. Other types of malicious code such as worms and Trojan horses are often mistakenly called viruses.

Worm

A *worm* is very similar to a virus: Both are designed to replicate quickly, but worms don't attach themselves to programs like viruses do. Instead, worms propagate by attacking known weaknesses on computer systems. On those systems where a weakness is found, the worm is able to successfully break in and enter. Whatever the weakness happens to be, the result is the same: The worm is able to assume enough control of the system (or just of the application whose weakness it exploited) to use that system as a base to launch attacks against other systems. And in the meantime, the worm may also have some destructive characteristics as well: It could change or delete data on the system.

A brief history of viruses

The term *virus* in the context of computers was first coined by Dr. Fred Cohen in 1983. He used the term appropriately because a computer virus shares many characteristics with biological viruses.

The first viruses appeared in the early 1980s. The first one in the wild (researchers are still trying to get them to mate in captivity) was written for the Apple II. The first IBM PC virus, called *Brain*, was first found in 1986. By the late 1980s, viruses in the wild were attacking Atari, Amiga, PC, and Macintosh computers. The Atari and Amiga viruses were so effective that they successfully drove their hosts into extinction.

Viruses have become increasingly complex and difficult to detect and eradicate. *Cascade*, which appeared in 1987, was the first encrypted virus. So-called Stealth viruses appeared in 1989; these were engineered to avoid detection. In 1990, self-modifying viruses appeared.

Many people have asked why viruses on PCs are so common when viruses for UNIX are almost nonexistent. Here are two reasons: PC users historically were more apt to exchange data and programs on floppy disks. Also, PCs historically have lacked any form of access control or distinction between user mode and supervisor mode. The fact that the PC user has read/write privileges on all files on the computer (not just the user's file, but also the entire operating system) makes PCs particularly vulnerable. UNIX systems, on the other hand, have always had a strong distinction between user mode and supervisor mode: A virus can't attach itself to a system executable file because ordinary users don't have permission to change system files including executable programs.

Some of the most successful malicious code events (NIMDA and Code Red) were worms.

Trojan horse

A *Trojan horse*, like its storybook namesake, is an object that claims to be something but turns out to be something far different (and not very nice).

Trojan horses generally don't spread by replicating themselves, but they can be equally damaging nonetheless. Trojan horses became prevalent with the rise of the Internet and e-mail. A typical Trojan horse arrives in the payload of an e-mail message, usually an attached executable file or a file with macros. The text portion of the e-mail message may read something like *Viagra without a prescription, click here* or *See Britney Spears naked!!* or some other enticing message designed to lure people into executing the Trojan horse and aiding in its sword-wielding propagation through Cyberspace.

Hoaxes

As the popularity of e-mail increased, viruses rode the rails and propagated themselves via e-mail. Conscientious people everywhere, learning of real viruses, would write up warning messages and send them to their friends and colleagues. But chip-on-their-shoulder virus writers decided to attack on another front: creating phony virus warning messages in order to instill panic and occasionally to get naive users to unwittingly do harmful things.

Computer scientists must have a name for everything, and *hoax* is the term they came up with to describe these false warning messages.

Would it help if I explained this with an example? Okay. . . .

Suppose that someone writes up a message and sends it out to a lot of acquaintances. The message says something like this:

> Please watch your inbox and DO NOT OPEN any message that has "Pictures for you" in the subject line. Whatever you do, do not open the message or your entire hard disk will be reformatted. I know — it happened to me two weeks ago, and I just got my computer back today.

Sounds convincing, right? (Play along with me.) The kicker is that this is a complete hoax. But still, even hoaxes serve a purpose: They can account for millions of productivity hours lost in companies around the world. Sometimes these hoax messages clog e-mail systems, which is usually one of the intentions of the perpetrator of the hoax.

Logic bombs

A *logic bomb* is a program designed to cause damage when some event has occurred. For instance, a logic bomb could destroy files when the user invokes a certain program such as a text editor. Logic bombs don't replicate themselves, but they can be left behind by viruses or worms.

Malicious applets

ActiveX and Java applets have been known to carry malicious code and wreak havoc on users' computers. Strictly speaking, writing destructive ActiveX applets is easier because they have access to the entire computer. Destructive Java applets are far more difficult to write because they must exploit some weakness in the Java sandbox in order to break out of it and do whatever damaging deed it was designed to do. For more, read the earlier section "Applets."

Trap doors

A *trap door* is a part of a program that performs an undocumented function when certain conditions are met. Generally these functions are designed to bypass security mechanisms. An example trap door that I saw many years ago was planted in the */bin/login* program on a UNIX system. When any ordinary user logged in to the system, the login program performed by the book. But when a special password was typed in (the publisher won't let me tell you what it is), the login program would log the person in as `root`; further, the login program, which usually logs the session to an audit file, would conveniently forget to log the trap door session. The login program was hard to detect because its date, size, and checksum were the same as the original login program.

Anti-virus software

Anti-virus software has understandably become very popular, so much so that nearly every organization requires its use on all its desktop systems, and many manufacturers and integrators of personal computers sold at retail include an anti-virus program as standard equipment.

Anti-virus software (commonly known as *AV software*) operates by intercepting operating system routines that store files and open files. The AV software compares the contents of the file being opened or stored against a list of virus signatures. If the AV software detects a virus, it prevents the file from being opened or saved, alerts the user usually via a pop-up window (which is like a jack-in-the-box). Enterprise versions of the AV software will send an alert to a central monitoring console so that the company's Anti-Virus Division is alerted and can take evasive action if needed.

As the number of viruses grew, the anti-virus software vendors designed a way for users to update their AV software's list of signatures so that they could defend against the latest viruses. In early versions, users would log onto the vendor's Bulletin Board System (BBS) to download new signature files. Later, users could send signature files via FTP (File Transfer Protocol) or go to the vendor's Web site to check for new files. More recently, AV software can automatically contact the AV vendor's central computer and download a new signature file if the vendor's version is newer than the user's. Enterprise versions of AV software now have the ability to push new signature files to all desktop systems and even invoke scans in real-time.

AV software's new problem is that more than 70,000 known viruses exist, and the rate of introduction of new viruses is increasing each year. This has led AV software vendors to consider a new approach to defending against viruses called *heuristics*. With heuristics, the AV software detects certain kinds of anomalous behavior (for instance, the replacement of an .exe file with a newer version) rather than the brute force method of checking against all the virus signatures. Most AV products today use both the signature method and the heuristics method for detecting viruses; everyone (except the virus writers) hopes that someday heuristics will become the primary method for virus detection.

Heuristics solves a number of problems. First, as the number of viruses grows, signature files grow ever larger, taking more time to download and consuming more space on systems. This isn't much of an issue when PC hard drives cost under $5 per gigabyte, but AV software is making its way onto resource-limited personal digital assistants (PDAs) and other lightweight devices. Also, the rate of virus creation means that signature files need to be downloaded more and more frequently. Pretty soon the Internet will only have enough capacity to support AV signature file downloads, Dilbert, and porn sites.

Another nice feature found in enterprise-class AV software is that the software can't be defeated or reconfigured by the user. Automatic virus scan slowing you down, buddy? Tough beans.

Anti-virus software is found on more than just PC desktops. It's also found on e-mail servers that scan attachments, as well as on Web proxy servers, file servers, and application servers.

I say *viruses*, you say *virii*

What exactly is the plural of the word *virus*? Viruses or virii? Both uses are common. If you take a look in a dictionary, you'll find that the plural of *virus* is *viruses*. So why is it that so many people use *virii* instead? Is it because *virus* ends in *us*, which often takes the *i* suffix in the plural form, like *cacti*? Is *viruses* preferred because no one knows how to pronounce *virii*? Is it because *virii* sounds too academic?

The big AV vendors (Symantec and McAfee) use the plural *viruses* on their Web sites. Poor highbrow virii is nowhere to be found.

Anti-virus software is available for UNIX systems, too, but ironically the UNIX versions aren't checking for UNIX viruses but PC viruses.

System Attack Methods

Now I take a look at the methods that are used to break in to computer systems. Attackers develop new methods as fast as new products and technologies are introduced. It seems as though as soon as something new and cool comes out, only days later we learn that someone has found a way to attack it.

Denial of service

The *denial of service* (DOS) attack is an interesting one because the attacker never does gain entry into the targeted computer system — then again, he isn't trying to get in. Instead, he floods the victim system with such a large number of network packets that legitimate users of the system are unable to reach it. The most successful DOS attacks not only slow down the system but actually cause it to hang or crash. This is because some methods of DOS attacks, such as the *SYN attack*, exhaust the system's resources to the point that it can no longer function. For the skinny on a SYN attack, read the sidebar elsewhere in this chapter, "Anatomy of a SYN attack."

A new form of DOS attack, called *distributed denial of service* (DDOS), occurs when an attacker uses dozens, or even hundreds, of systems all attacking a target simultaneously. There are even tools available for hackers so that they can discover, penetrate, and recruit new DDOS attack drones that attack a specified target at a time of their choosing. These tools come in the form of Trojan horses that install a DDOS slave program on a PC, which then listens in on an IRC (Internet Relay Chat), awaiting attack instructions from the hacker.

Dictionary attack

The *dictionary attack* is a method used to crack computer account passwords by using common words found in a dictionary.

Most commonly, a dictionary attack tool requires a copy of the UNIX *password* or *shadow* file, or the NT *SAM* file. The hacker then will load the file on his local system and run a password-cracking program to attempt to discover account passwords by guessing dictionary words and combinations of dictionary words and numbers: for example, 4food.

Anatomy of a SYN attack

When two computers wish to talk with one another, most often they do so via a TCP connection. This is a technical term that means they will exchange packets over the network (or the Internet) and set up a session that may last a few minutes or possibly hours.

The TCP/IP protocol uses something called a *three-way handshake* when initiating one of these sessions. First, the computer that wishes to initiate a session sends a SYN packet to the destination computer. This packet in effect says, "I would like to start a conversation with you." If the destination computer is in the mood, it will reply with an ACK packet, saying "Sure, let's talk." The first computer replies to this reply with another packet, "I received your acknowledgement; let's start talking now." Then the two computers communicate over this session until one of them decides enough is enough, at which time they negotiate a shutdown of the session.

Now that you have the necessary background . . . a *SYN attack* consists of one or more computers sending those session-requesting SYN packets — thousands to millions — to a victim computer. The computer being attacked, thinking that it's suddenly very popular (a problem many of us would like to have), must allocate resources for each of these new conversations. It builds what's called a *half-open connection* — a chunk of memory space holding information about the new session it expects to establish. The problem is, the system(s) sending the SYN packets have no intention of starting real sessions; they only send more SYN packets. The attacked system soon exhausts its memory resources to the point that it may hang or crash.

Most operating systems are able to "tune" their way out of being vulnerable to SYN attacks, and it goes like this: The operating system will have a setting that specifies how long it should keep one of these half-open connections open before giving up. In the old days, a system might wait a minute or more before giving up, but nowadays that setting can be tuned down to just a few seconds. A SYN attack can still consume resources, but rarely to the point of crashing the system.

This type of attack has prompted companies to require their employees and customers to pick *good* passwords — that is, passwords that aren't just ordinary dictionary words, but rather words or even random letters interspersed with numbers and special characters: !@#)(*&^%;[]{}:'"><. So instead of an easily guessed password like *Alexis*, a user would use a more difficult-to-guess password like *Al3x1s**.

Spoofing

In a *spoofing* attack, the attacker is using some way to change the network identity of a computer or program in order to trick the targeted system into granting access to the attacker. For instance, a targeted computer may only accept Telnet requests from systems with specific IP addresses. Knowing this, the attacker can send spoofed TCP/IP packets to the system in an attempt to break in. The target system may let the attacker in if it thinks that he's one of the systems that it's configured to permit.

Hidden code

If the attacker is able to modify or replace programs on the target system, he may elect to install hidden code. *Hidden code* is a set of computer instructions hiding inside another program that carries out some usually malicious act. An example of hidden code might be an application's reporting program that also happens to erase certain audit trail entries.

An *alteration of authorized code* is an attack similar to a trap door, in which a program with specified privileges (for instance, the system's administrator account or an application's master user account) is modified to carry out some illicit functions of the attacker's choosing.

Social engineering

Social engineering is an attack against people as a way of getting access to targeted systems. The classic case of social engineering occurs when a hacker makes a number of telephone calls to various people in an organization and gets a tidbit of information from each one. For instance, he can get modem access numbers from one person, IP addresses and system names from another, and get a password reset from a helpdesk employee. And voilà, the attacker puts these pieces together to log into the company's system using its established remote access facilities.

Another common social engineering ploy is one where the attacker, posing as the system or security administrator, tells people to change their passwords to a specified value. The attacker then tries to log into the system using that account to see whether any suckers did what he asked them to.

Pseudo flaw

A *pseudo flaw* attack is a special form of social engineering in which an attacker, posing as a system or security administrator or vendor, tells unsuspecting users that a security flaw has been discovered on their system and that they should install a certain *patch*, which is usually a Trojan horse.

Remote maintenance

Organizations need to be especially wary of vendors who need to connect, via modem or the Internet, to one's systems or networks in order to troubleshoot a problem or perform maintenance. If the vendor's employee is dishonest, he may perform any number of acts that would constitute abuse at best and hacking at worst. He may steal information or services, insert trap doors or logic bombs, or use his customer's system to attack other systems in the enterprise.

In all fairness, most vendors have honest intentions when they have a legitimate need to connect to a customer's computer in order to try and fix a problem. But a few dishonest employees in these vendor organizations have made this an activity that you should think twice about.

Sniffing and eavesdropping

An intruder (or employee) may devise some means for listening to traffic on the organization's internal network using a *sniffer* program. His sniffer program can listen for and capture login sessions, in which he will have recorded a userid and password. Systems that encrypt the login password on the wire aren't necessarily much better off. Hacking tools are available that can capture the encrypted password and later on perform a *dictionary* or *brute force* attack against it to discover the password. This can, however, take months or even years, so you should think of encrypted passwords over the network as being substantially safer than cleartext.

Eavesdropping isn't limited to the high-tech approach. One can listen in on conversations in airports, restaurants, and other public places. An intruder can install listening devices in conference rooms, telephone lines, or in gifts given to the intended victim. "Here, have this large attractive lapel pin."

Traffic analysis and inference

An attacker can analyze network traffic patterns and other types of transmissions in order to make inferences about something that he wants to know more about. In this type of attack, the attacker doesn't have access to the *contents* of the transmissions but only their patterns. For instance, he could be in a position to know the workload on a network, and thus infer that the network's high utilization from 10 p.m.–1 a.m. is the organization performing backups over the network. He can use this information to his advantage by attempting to sabotage systems shortly before 10 p.m. in order to prevent a backup from occurring, which may be part of a bigger plan.

Brute force

The *brute force* attack is the most time consuming and is used as a last resort when more clever methods fail. Whatever the target, in a brute force attack the perpetrator repeatedly hits his target, making small changes each time, hoping that he'll eventually get in.

Brute force attacks are most often seen in the form of an attacker trying to log in with some userid and trying every possible password until the right one is found. Most newer computer systems are designed to repel this sort of attack by locking out accounts that have had too many unsuccessful login attempts. Honest users see this sometimes when they try to log into their account at work, only to be locked out until they remember that they changed their password the day before . . . um, they were using the *old* password trying to log in. D'oh!

Perpetrators

You often hear the nomenclature of hacker, intruder, script kiddie, virus writer, and phreaker. Just what sorts of people are these, anyway?

Hackers

Calling someone a *hacker* is a broad-brush term implicating almost any person of ill will, but actually the *real* hacker is a rare breed indeed. The genuine hacker is extremely knowledgeable, patient, creative, and resourceful. He is determined to find a new exploit in some particular system, protocol, or program. He studies the architecture and design of his target in order to find a weakness and exploit it.

Hackers are often employees with day jobs who experiment after hours. Most hackers are socially responsible and want to discover weaknesses and help get them fixed before persons of ill will discover them and cause real damage.

Script kiddies

Script kiddies are individuals with nowhere near the technical acumen of real hackers. Instead, they acquire programs, tools, and scripts developed by hackers in order to carry out attacks. Frequently script kiddies don't even know how their attack tool does what it does.

Don't underestimate the power of script kiddies, however. If they choose, they can cause significant damage to systems and networks if they're determined to attack them.

Virus writers

Like hackers and script kiddies, *virus writers* can span a broad range of expertise. Some virus writers are highly skilled and creative, quite able to engineer a good virus on their own. But like script kiddies, many virus writers rely upon templates and cookbooks to create subtle variations of existing viruses.

Phreakers

The original *phreakers* were people who cracked telephone networks in order to get free long distance. Improvements in telephone networks have rendered the original techniques useless, and some resorted to outright criminal acts such as stealing long-distance calling cards.

The term *phreakers* is sometimes used to describe hackers who try to break into systems and services in order to get free services.

Additional References

Krutz, Ronald L. and Vines, Russell Dean. *The CISSP Prep Guide: Mastering the Ten Domains of Computer Security,* Chapter 5. John Wiley & Sons, Inc.

Taylor, David A. *Object-Oriented Technology: A Manager's Guide.* Addison-Wesley.

McClure, Stuart. *Hacking Exposed: Network Security Secrets & Solutions.* McGraw Hill.

Pipkin, Donald L. *Halting the Hacker: A Practical Guide to Computer Security.* Prentice Hall Professional Technical Reference.

Grimes, Roger A. *Malicious Mobile Code: Virus Protection for Windows.* O'Reilly & Associates.

Anderson, Ross J. *Security Engineering: A Guide to Building Dependable Distributed Systems*. John Wiley & Sons, Inc.

Prep Test

1 Masquerading as another person in order to illicitly obtain information is known as

A ○ Hacking
B ○ Social engineering
C ○ Extortion
D ○ Exhumation

2 Viruses, worms, and Trojan horses are known as

A ○ Maniacal code
B ○ Fractured code
C ○ Infectious code
D ○ Malicious code

3 Anti-virus software that detects viruses by watching for anomalous behavior uses what technique?

A ○ Signature matching
B ○ Fleuristics
C ○ Heroistics
D ○ Heuristics

4 A developer, suspecting that he may be fired soon, modifies an important program that will corrupt payroll files long after he is gone. The developer has created a(n)

A ○ Delayed virus
B ○ Time bomb
C ○ Applet bomb
D ○ Signal bomb

5 A SYN flood is an example of a

A ○ Dictionary attack.
B ○ High Watermark attack
C ○ Buffer Overflow attack
D ○ Denial of Service attack

6 The process of recording changes made to systems is known as

A ○ Change Review Board
B ○ System Maintenance
C ○ Change Management
D ○ Configuration Management

7 A system that accumulates knowledge by observing events' inputs and outcomes is known as a(n)

A ○ Expert system
B ○ Neural network
C ○ Synaptic network
D ○ Neural array

8 The business logic present in an object is known as

A ○ Encapsulation
B ○ Personality
C ○ Behavior
D ○ Method

9 The restricted environment that Java applets occupy is known as

A ○ Sandbox
B ○ Restricted Zone
C ○ Capability Zone
D ○ Instantiation

10 Using several concurrent methods to protect a resource is called

A ○ Abstraction
B ○ Polymorphism
C ○ Defense in depth
D ○ Service Level Agreement

Answers

1 **B.** Social engineering. *Social engineering* is the process of obtaining information from people by tricking them into giving up an important piece of information such as a modem access number. *Review "System Attack Methods."*

2 **D.** Malicious code. *Malicious code* is the generic term used to describe computer codes used to inflict damage on a computer system. *Review "Malicious Code."*

3 **D.** Heuristics. *Heuristics* is the technique used to detect viruses by recognizing anomalous behavior. *Review "Malicious Code."*

4 **B.** Time bomb. A *time bomb* is a type of malicious code that is designed to cause damage at a predetermined date in the future. *Review "Malicious Code."*

5 **D.** Denial of Service attack. These attacks are designed to incapacitate a system by flooding it with traffic. *Review "Denial of service."*

6 **D.** Configuration Management. This is the process used to record all configuration changes to hardware and software. *Review "Configuration Management."*

7 **B.** Neural network. Neural networks become proficient at predicting outcomes by making large numbers of observations, noting inputs and results of each. *Review "Neural networks."*

8 **D.** Method. A *method* is the formal name given to business logic — also known as *code* — present in an object. *Review "Object-Oriented Environments."*

9 **A.** Sandbox. This is the name given to the restricted environment that Java applets reside in. *Review "Applets."*

10 **C.** Defense in depth. Defense in depth uses several concurrent mechanisms to protect a resource. Even if one of the mechanisms fails, others still protect the resource. *Review "Defense in depth."*

Chapter 7

Cryptography

● ●

In This Chapter

▶ Cryptography roles in information security

▶ Basic cryptography concepts

▶ Symmetric and asymmetric key systems

▶ Components and operation of a Public Key Infrastructure (PKI) and related issues

▶ Cryptography technologies and applications

▶ Cryptanalysis and attack methods against cryptosystems

● ●

*T*his is the part where *Good Will Hunting* meets *Rain Man*. You'll probably want to read this chapter slowly and carefully (sounding out the words), read it again, and then possibly delve into some additional resources — which I conveniently list at the end of this chapter.

Cryptography (from the Greek, *kryptos* meaning *hidden* and *graphia* meaning *writing*) is the science of encrypting and decrypting communications to make them unintelligible for all but the intended recipient.

The Certified Information Systems Security Professional (CISSP) candidate must have a thorough understanding of the fundamental concepts of cryptography, the basic operation of cryptographic systems, common uses and applications, and methods of attack. The CISSP exam tests the candidate's ability to apply general cryptographic concepts to real-world issues and problems. You won't be required to memorize mathematical formulas or the step-by-step operation of various cryptographic systems. However, you should have a firm grasp of cryptographic concepts and technologies as well as their specific strengths, weaknesses, uses, and applications.

The Role of Cryptography in Information Security

Cryptography can be used to achieve several goals of information security, including confidentiality, integrity, and authentication.

- ✔ **Confidentiality:** First, cryptography protects the confidentiality (or secrecy) of information. Even when the transmission or storage medium has been compromised, the encrypted information is practically useless to unauthorized persons without the proper keys for decryption.

- ✔ **Integrity:** Cryptography can also be used to ensure the integrity (or accuracy) of information through the use of hashing algorithms and message digests.

- ✔ **Authentication:** Finally, cryptography can be used for authentication (and non-repudiation) services through digital signatures, digital certificates, or a Public Key Infrastructure (PKI).

A brief history of cryptography

Cryptography dates back over 4,000 years to the ancient Egyptians when hieroglyphs were used not to protect messages but to add mystique.

Around 400 B.C., the Spartans began using a military cryptography system known as the *scytale*. This consisted of a strip of parchment wrapped around a wooden rod of a specified secret length and diameter. The message to be encoded was written on the strip of parchment vertically down the rod and then unwrapped and sent by messenger to the intended recipient. The recipient had an identical rod to wrap the strip of parchment around and decode the message.

Around 50 B.C., Julius Caesar used a substitution cipher to transmit secret messages. This system involved substituting letters of the message with other letters from the same alphabet. For example, a simple encryption scheme may have required the sender to shift each letter three spaces to the right: that is, A=D, B=E, C=F, and so on. The recipient would then shift the letters three spaces to the left to obtain the message.

This system, which used only a single alphabet to encrypt and decrypt an entire message, is known as a *monoalphabetic substitution*. This system was particularly effective because most of the population was illiterate at the time.

In the 15th century, a cryptographic system utilizing concentric disks to provide substitution was used in Italy. In 1790, Thomas Jefferson invented an encryption device using a stack of 26 individually rotating disks. The Japanese Purple Machine and German Enigma Machine are two examples of cryptographic devices used successfully during World War II — at least, until the codes were cracked. More recently, Quaker Oats developed the Cap'n Crunch Magic Decoder Ring for encrypting and decrypting simple messages.

Don't confuse these three points this with the C-I-A triad, which I discuss in Chapter 5: The C-I-A triad deals with confidentiality, integrity, and *availability*; cryptography does nothing to ensure availability.

Cryptography Basics

Cryptography today has evolved into a complex science (some say an art) presenting many great promises and challenges in the field of information security. The basics of cryptography include classes and types of ciphers, various terms and concepts, and the individual components of the cryptosystem.

Classes of ciphers

Ciphers are cryptographic transformations. The two main classes of ciphers are *block* and *stream*, which describes how the cipher operates on input data.

The two main classes of ciphers are block ciphers and stream ciphers.

Block ciphers

Block ciphers operate on a single fixed block (typically 64 bits) of plaintext to produce the corresponding ciphertext. (To read more about these, jump to the later section "Plaintext and ciphertext.") Advantages of block ciphers compared with stream ciphers are

- ✔ **Reusable keys:** Key management is much easier.
- ✔ **Interoperability:** Block ciphers are more widely supported.

Block ciphers are typically implemented in software.

Stream ciphers

Stream ciphers operate in real-time on a continuous stream of data, typically bit-by-bit. Stream ciphers are generally faster than block ciphers and require less code to implement. However, the keys in a stream cipher are generally used only once (see the later section "A Disposable Cipher: The One-time Pad") and then discarded. Key management becomes a serious problem. Stream ciphers are typically implemented in hardware.

Types of ciphers

The two basic types of ciphers are *substitution* and *transposition,* which describes how the cipher transforms plaintext into ciphertext.

Substitution ciphers

Substitution ciphers replace bits, characters, or character blocks in plaintext with alternate bits, characters, or character blocks to produce ciphertext. A classic example of a substitution cipher is one that Julius Caesar used: He substituted letters of the message with other letters from the same alphabet. (Read more about this in the sidebar "A brief history of cryptography," elsewhere in this chapter.) In a simple substitution cipher using the standard English alphabet, a cryptovariable (key) is added modulo 26 to the plaintext message. In modulo 26 addition, the remainder is the final result for any sum equal to or greater than 26. For example, a basic substitution cipher in which the word *BOY* is encrypted by adding three characters using modulo 26 math produces the following result:

```
    B    O    Y      PLAINTEXT
    2   15   25      NUMERIC VALUE
+   3    3    3      SUBSTITUTION VALUE

    5   18    2      MODULO 26 RESULT
    E    R    B      CIPHERTEXT
```

A substitution cipher may be monoalphabetic or polyalphabetic. In a monoalphabetic substitution, a single alphabet is used to encrypt the entire plaintext message.

A more complex substitution cipher might use a polyalphabetic substitution, which uses a different alphabet to encrypt each bit, character, or character block of a plaintext message.

A more modern example of a substitution cipher is the S-boxes (Substitution boxes) employed in the Data Encryption Standard (DES) algorithm. The S-boxes in DES produce a non-linear substitution (6 bits in, 4 bits out). ***Note:*** DO NOT attempt to sing this to the tune "Shave and a Haircut" to improve the strength of the encryption by hiding any statistical relationship between the plaintext and ciphertext characters.

Transposition (or permutation) ciphers

Transposition ciphers rearrange bits, characters, or character blocks in plaintext to produce ciphertext. In a simple columnar transposition cipher, a message might be read horizontally but written vertically to produce the ciphertext as in the following example:

THE QUICK BROWN FOX JUMPED OVER THE LAZY DOG

written in 9 columns as

THEQUICKB
ROWNFOXJU
MPEDOVERT
HELAZYDOG

then transposed (encrypted) vertically as

TRMHHOPEEWELQNDAUFOZIOVYCXEDKJROBUTG

The original letters of the plaintext message are the same; only the order has been changed to achieve encryption.

DES performs permutations through the use of P-boxes (Permutation boxes) to spread the influence of a plaintext character over many characters so that they're not easily traced back to the S-boxes used in the substitution cipher.

Other types of ciphers include

- **Codes:** Includes words and phrases. For example:
  - Ciphertext = "Did you order the Code Red!?"
  - Plaintext = "Did you tell them to beat the !#@% out of that guy!?"
- **Running (or book) ciphers:** For example, the key is page 137 of _The Catcher in The Rye_, and text on that page is added modulo 26 to perform encryption/decryption.
- **Vernam ciphers:** Also known as _one-time pads_, which are keystreams that can only be used once. I discuss these more in the upcoming section "A disposable cipher: The one-time pad."
- **Concealment ciphers:** These include steganography, which I discuss further in the upcoming section "Steganography: A picture is worth a thousand (hidden) words."

Most modern cryptosystems use both substitution and permutation to achieve encryption.

Key clustering

Key clustering (or clustering) occurs when identical ciphertext messages are generated from a plaintext message by using the same encryption algorithm but different encryption keys.

The science of crypto: Cryptanalysis, cryptography, and cryptology

Cryptanalysis is the science of deciphering ciphertext without the cryptographic key.

Cryptography is the science of encrypting and decrypting information, such as a private message, to protect its confidentiality, integrity, and/or authenticity.

Cryptology is the science that encompasses both cryptography and cryptanalysis.

Putting it all together: The cryptosystem

A *cryptosystem* is the hardware or software implementation that transforms plaintext into ciphertext (encryption) and back into plaintext (decryption).

An effective cryptosystem must have the following properties:

- ✔ The encryption and decryption process is efficient for all possible keys within the cryptosystem's keyspace.
- ✔ The cryptosystem is easy to use.
- ✔ The strength of the cryptosystem is dependent on the secrecy of the cryptovariables (or keys) rather than the secrecy of the algorithm. (Most cryptographic algorithms are public anyway.)

Cryptosystems typically comprise two elements:

- ✔ **Cryptographic algorithm:** This details the step-by-step procedures used to produce
  - Ciphertext (encipher)
  - Plaintext (decipher)
- ✔ **Cryptovariable:** The key to the cryptographic algorithm, the *cryptovariable* is a secret value applied to the algorithm. The strength and effectiveness of the cryptosystem is largely dependent upon the secrecy and strength of the cryptovariable.

A *cryptosystem* consists of two elements: the cryptographic algorithm and the cryptovariable (key).

An analogy of a cryptosystem is a deadbolt lock. A deadbolt lock can be easily identified, and its inner working mechanisms aren't closely guarded state secrets. What makes a deadbolt lock effective is the individual key that controls a specific lock on a specific door. However, if the key is weak (imagine only one or two notches on a flat key) or not well protected (left under your doormat), the lock won't protect your belongings. Similarly, if an attacker is able to determine what cryptographic algorithm (lock) was used to encrypt a message, it should still be protected because you're using a strong key (128 bit) that you have kept secret rather than a 6-character password written on a scrap of paper left under your mousepad.

Encryption and decryption

Encryption (or enciphering) is the process of converting plaintext communications into ciphertext. *Decryption* (or deciphering) reverses that process, converting ciphertext into plaintext. Traffic on a network can be encrypted by using either *end-to-end* or *link encryption*.

End-to-end encryption

With *end-to-end encryption*, packets are encrypted once at the original encryption source and then decrypted only at the final decryption destination. The advantages of end-to-end encryption are its speed and overall security. However, in order for the packets to be properly routed, only the data is encrypted, not the routing information.

Link encryption

Link encryption requires that each node (for example, a router) has separate key pairs for its upstream and downstream neighbors. Packets are encrypted and decrypted at every node along the network path.

The following example in Lab 7-1 illustrates link encryption:

Lab 7-1   Link Encryption

1. **Computer 1 encrypts a message by using Secret Key A and then transmits the message to Router 1.**

2. **Router 1 decrypts the message by using Secret Key A, re-encrypts the message by using Secret Key B, and then transmits the message to Router 2.**

3. **Router 2 decrypts the message by using Secret Key B, re-encrypts the message by using Secret Key C, and then transmits the message to Computer 2.**

4. **Computer 2 decrypts the message by using Secret Key C.**

The advantage of using link encryption is that the entire packet (including routing information) is encrypted. However, link encryption has the following two disadvantages:

- ✔ **Latency:** Packets must be encrypted/decrypted at every node.
- ✔ **Inherent vulnerability:** If a node is compromised or a packet's decrypted contents are cached in a node, the message can be compromised.

He said, she said: The concept of non-repudiation

To *repudiate* is to deny; *non-repudiation* means that an action (such as an online transaction, e-mail communication, and so on) or occurrence can't be easily denied. Non-repudiation is a related function of identification and authentication (I&A) and accountability. For example, it's difficult for a user to deny sending an e-mail message that was digitally signed with that user's private key. Likewise, it's difficult to deny responsibility for an enterprise-wide outage if the accounting logs positively identify you (from username and strong authentication) as the poor soul who inadvertently issued the write-erase command on the core routers two seconds before everything dropped. Gulp.

A disposable cipher: The one-time pad

A *one-time pad* (key) is a keystream that can only be used once. Considered unbreakable because it's completely random and is used only once and then destroyed, it consists of a pad of the same length as the message to which it's applied. Both the sender and receiver have an identical pad, which is used by the sender to encrypt the message and by the receiver to decrypt the message. This type of cipher is very effective for short messages but is impractical for larger (several megabytes) messages. One-time pads are typically implemented as stream ciphers.

A one-time pad is an example of a stream cipher.

Plaintext and ciphertext

A *plaintext* message is a message in its original readable format or a ciphertext message that has been properly decrypted (unscrambled) to produce the original readable plaintext message.

A *ciphertext* message is a plaintext message that has been transformed (encrypted) into a scrambled message that's unintelligible. This concept doesn't apply to messages from your boss that may also happen to be unintelligible!

Steganography: A picture is worth a thousand (hidden) words

Steganography is the art of hiding the very existence of a message. It is related to but different from cryptography. Like cryptography, one purpose of steganography is to protect the contents of a message. However, unlike cryptography, the contents of the message aren't encrypted. Instead, the existence of the message is hidden in some other communications medium. For example, a message may be hidden in a graphic or sound file, slack space on storage media, traffic noise over a network, or in a digital image. By using the example of a digital image, the least significant bit of each byte in the image could be used to transmit a hidden message without noticeably altering the image. However, because the message itself isn't encrypted, if it is discovered, its contents can be easily compromised.

Work factor: Force x effort = work!

Work factor describes the difficulty — in terms of time, effort, and resources — that are required to break a cryptosystem. Given enough time, effort, and resources, any cryptosystem can be broken. The goal of all cryptosystems, then, is to achieve a work factor that sufficiently protects the encrypted information against a reasonable estimate of available time, effort, and resources. However, *reasonable* can be difficult to estimate with the rapid improvements in technology today.

Moore's Law is based on an observation by Gordan Moore, one of the founders of Intel, that processing power seems to double about every 18 months. To compensate for Moore's Law, some *really* hard encryption algorithms are used. Today, encrypted information is valuable for perhaps only three months with encryption algorithms that will theoretically take several hundred millennia to break, confident in the knowledge that tomorrow it will be mere child's play.

Not Quite the Metric System: Symmetric and Asymmetric Key Systems

Cryptographic algorithms are broadly classified as either symmetric or asymmetric key systems.

Symmetric key cryptography

Symmetric key cryptography, also known as *symmetric algorithm*, *secret key*, *single key*, and *private key*), uses a single key to both encrypt and decrypt information. Two parties (Thomas and Richard) can exchange an encrypted message by using the following procedure in Lab 7-2:

Lab 7-2   Exchanging an Encrypted Message with Symmetric Key Cryptography

1. **The sender (Thomas) encrypts the plaintext message with a secret key known only to the intended recipient (Richard).**

2. **The sender then transmits the encrypted message to the intended recipient.**

3. **The recipient decrypts the message with the same secret key to obtain the plaintext message.**

In order for an attacker (Harold) to read the message, he must guess the secret key (for example, a brute-force attack) or intercept the secret key during the initial exchange.

The following are the main disadvantages of symmetric systems:

- ✔ **Distribution:** Secure distribution of secret keys is absolutely required either through out-of-band methods or by using asymmetric systems.

- ✔ **Scalability:** A different key is required for each pair of communicating parties.

- ✔ **Limited functionality:** Symmetric systems can't provide authentication or non-repudiation.

Of course, symmetric systems do have many advantages:

- ✔ **Speed:** Symmetric systems are much faster than asymmetric systems.

- ✔ **Strength:** Strength is gained when used with a large key.

- ✔ **Availability:** Many algorithms are available.

Symmetric key algorithms include DES, Triple DES, Advanced Encryption Standard (AES), International Data Encryption Algorithm (IDEA), and RC5.

Symmetric key systems use a shared secret key.

Data Encryption Standard (DES)

In the early 1970s, the National Institute of Standards and Technology (NIST) solicited vendors to submit encryption algorithm proposals to be evaluated by the National Security Agency (NSA) in support of a national cryptographic standard. This new encryption standard was used for private-sector and sensitive but unclassified (SBU) government data. In 1974, IBM submitted a 128-bit algorithm originally known as *Lucifer*. After some modifications (the algorithm was shortened to 56 bits and the S-boxes were changed), the IBM proposal was endorsed by the NSA and formally adopted as the Data Encryption Standard. It was published in *Federal Information Processing Standards* (FIPS) PUB 46 in 1977 (updated and revised in 1988 as FIPS PUB 46-1) and *American National Standards Institute* (ANSI) X3.92 in 1981.

DES is the most common symmetric key algorithm used today. It is a block cipher that uses a 56-bit key.

The DES algorithm is a symmetric (or private) key cipher consisting of an algorithm and a key. The algorithm is a 64-bit block cipher based on a 56-bit symmetric key. (It comprises 56 key bits + 8 parity bits . . . or think of it as 8 bytes with each byte containing 7 key bits and 1 parity bit.) During encryption, the original message (plaintext) is divided into 64-bit blocks. Operating on a single block at a time, each 64-bit plaintext block is split into two 32-bit blocks. Under control of the 56-bit key, 16 rounds of transpositions and substitutions are performed on each individual character to produce the resulting ciphertext output.

The four distinct modes of operation (the mode of operation defines how the plaintext/ciphertext blocks are processed) in DES are Electronic Code Book, Cipher Block Chaining, Cipher Feedback, and Output Feedback.

Electronic Code Book (ECB)

Electronic Code Book (ECB) mode is the native mode for DES operation and normally produces the highest throughput. It is best used for encrypting keys or small amounts of data. ECB mode operates on 64-bit blocks of plaintext independently and produces 64-bit blocks of ciphertext. One significant disadvantage of ECB is that the same plaintext, encrypted with the same key, will always produce the same ciphertext. If used for large amounts of data, it's susceptible to Chosen-Text Attacks (CTA) because certain patterns may be revealed.

Cipher Block Chaining (CBC)

Cipher Block Chaining (CBC) mode is the most common mode of DES operation. Like ECB mode, CBC mode operates on 64-bit blocks of plaintext to produce 64-bit blocks of ciphertext. However, in CBC mode, each block is XORed (see the sidebar "The XORcist" elsewhere in this chapter) with the ciphertext of the preceding block to create a dependency or *chain*, thereby producing a more random ciphertext result. The first block is encrypted with a random block known as the *initialization vector* (IV). One disadvantage of CBC mode is that errors propagate. However, this problem is limited to the block in which the error occurs and the block that immediately follows, after which the decryption will re-synchronize.

The XORcist

The *Exclusive Or (XOR) function* is a binary operation applied to two input bits: for example, a plaintext bit and a key bit. If the two bits are equal, the result is 0 (zero). If the two bits aren't equal, the result is 1.

Input A (Plaintext)	Input B (Key)	Output C (Ciphertext)
0	0	0
0	1	1
1	0	1
1	1	0

Cipher Feedback (CFB)

Cipher Feedback (CFB) mode is a stream cipher most often used to encrypt individual characters. In this mode, previously generated ciphertext is used as feedback for key generation in the next key stream. The resulting ciphertext is chained together, which causes errors to be multiplied throughout the encryption process.

Output Feedback (OFB)

Output Feedback (OFB) mode is also a stream cipher very similar to CFB. It is often used to encrypt satellite communications. In this mode, previous plaintext is used as feedback for key generation in the next key stream. The resulting ciphertext is not chained together; therefore, errors don't spread throughout the encryption process.

The four modes of DES are ECB, CBC, CFB, and OFB. ECB and CBC are the most commonly used.

The original goal of the DES standard was to develop an encryption standard that would be viable for 10–15 years. Although DES far exceeded this goal, in 1999 the Electronic Frontier Foundation achieved the inevitable, breaking a DES key in only 23 hours.

Triple DES (3DES)

Triple DES (3DES) has effectively extended the life of the DES algorithm. In Triple DES implementations, a message is encrypted by using one key, encrypted by using a second key, and then again encrypted by using either the first key or a third key.

The use of three separate 56-bit encryption keys produces an effective key length of 168 bits. But Triple DES doesn't just triple the work factor required to crack the DES algorithm. Because the attacker doesn't know whether he successfully cracked even the first 56-bit key (pick a number between 0 and 72 quadrillion!) until all three keys are cracked and the correct plaintext is produced, the workforce is more like 2^{56} x 2^{56} x 2^{56}, or 72 quadrillion x 72 quadrillion x 72 quadrillion. (Don't try this on a calculator; just trust me on this one.)

Double DES wasn't a significant improvement to DES. In fact, by using a meet-in-the-middle attack, it has been shown that the work factor required to crack Double DES is only slightly greater than for DES. For this reason, Double DES isn't commonly used.

Using Triple DES would seem enough to protect even the most sensitive data for at least a few lifetimes, but a few problems exist with Triple DES. First, the performance cost is significant. Although Triple DES is faster than many other symmetric encryption algorithms, it's still unacceptably slow and won't work with many applications requiring high-speed throughput of large volumes of data.

Secondly, a weakness exists in the implementation that allows a cryptanalyst to reduce the effective key size to 108 bits in a brute force attack. Although a 108-bit key size still requires a significant amount of time to crack (theoretically several million millennia), it's still a weakness.

You say *To-may-to*, and I say *To-mah-to*: 3DES variations

The several variations of Triple DES (3DES) are as follows:

- ✔ DES-EEE2 (Encrypt-Encrypt-Encrypt) using 1st key, 2nd key, 1st key

- ✔ DES-EDE2 (Encrypt-Decrypt-Encrypt) using 1st key, 2nd key, 1st key

- ✔ DES-EEE3 (Encrypt-Encrypt-Encrypt) using 1st key, 2nd key, 3rd key

- ✔ DES-EDE3 (Encrypt-Decrypt-Encrypt) using 1st key, 2nd key, 3rd key

The basic function of Triple DES is sometimes explained like this: The message is encrypted using one key, decrypted using a second key, and again encrypted using the first key. The differences in syntax (and operation) are subtle but important: The second key (in an EDE implementation) doesn't truly decrypt the original message because the output is still gibberish (ciphertext). This variation was developed for backwards compatibility with single DES cryptosystems. Also, you should understand that use of the first key twice (in EDE2 and EEE2) is one common implementation, but use of a third distinct key is also possible (in EDE3 and EEE3).

Advanced Encryption Standard (AES)

The *Advanced Encryption Standard (AES)* is a block cipher that will eventually replace DES. In October 2000, NIST announced selection of the Rijndael Block Cipher to implement AES.

AES is based on the Rijndael Block Cipher.

Rijndael Block Cipher

The *Rijndael Block Cipher*, developed by Dr. Joan Daemen and Dr. Vincent Rijmen, has variable block and key lengths (128, 192, or 256 bits). It was designed to be simple, resistant to known attacks, and fast.

Twofish Algorithm

The *Twofish Algorithm* was a finalist in the AES selection process. It is a symmetric block cipher that operates on 128-bit (vice 64-bit) blocks, employing 16 rounds with key lengths up to 256 bits.

IDEA Cipher

The *International Data Encryption Algorithm (IDEA) Cipher* evolved from the Proposed Encryption Standard and the Improved Proposed Encryption Standard originally developed in 1990. IDEA is a block cipher that operates on 64-bit plaintext blocks using a 128-bit key. IDEA performs eight rounds on 16-bit sub-blocks and can operate in four distinct modes similar to DES. The IDEA cipher provides stronger encryption than RC4 and Triple DES, but because it's patented, it's not widely used. It is, however, used in the Pretty Good Privacy (PGP) e-mail encryption system. For more on RC4, read the following section. For more on PGP, read "Pretty Good Privacy (PGP)."

RC5

RC5 (Rivest Cipher No. 5) is part of a series of symmetric algorithms developed by RSA Data Security. RC2 is a block mode cipher that encrypts 64-bit blocks of data by using a variable-length key. RC4 is a stream cipher (data is encrypted in real time) that uses a variable-length key (128 bits is standard). RC5 is similar to RC2 but includes a variable-length key (0 to 2048 bits), variable block size (32, 64, or 128 bits) and variable number of processing rounds (0 to 255).

Asymmetric key cryptography

Asymmetric key cryptography (also known as *asymmetric algorithm*, or *public key*) uses two separate keys: one key to encrypt and a different key to decrypt information. These keys are known as *public* and *private* key pairs. When two parties want to exchange an encrypted message by using asymmetric key cryptography, they follow these steps, as in Lab 7-3.

Lab 7-3   Exchanging an Encrypted Message with Asymmetric Key Cryptography

1. **The sender (Thomas) encrypts the plaintext message with the intended recipient's (Richard) public key.**

2. **This produces a ciphertext message that can then be transmitted to the intended recipient (Richard).**

3. **The recipient (Richard) then decrypts the message with his private key, known only to him.**

Only the private key can decrypt the message; thus, an attacker (Harold) possessing only the public key can't decrypt the message. This also means that not even the original sender can decrypt the message. This use of an asymmetric key system is known as a *secure message*. A secure message guarantees the confidentiality of the message.

Asymmetric key systems use a public key and private key.

Secure Message Format uses the recipient's private key to protect confidentiality.

If the sender wants to guarantee the authenticity of a message (or, more correctly, the authenticity of the sender), he can sign the message by using the following procedure in Lab 7-4:

Lab 7-4   Signing a Message to Guarantee Authenticity

1. **The sender (Thomas) encrypts the plaintext message with his own private key.**

2. **This produces a ciphertext message that can then be transmitted to the intended recipient (Richard).**

3. **To verify that the message is in fact from the purported sender, the recipient (Richard) applies the sender's (Thomas's) public key (which is known to everyone — every Tom, Dick, and Harry).**

Of course, this means that an attacker can also verify the authenticity of the message. This use of an asymmetric key system is known as an *open message format* because only the authenticity, not the confidentiality, is guaranteed.

Open message format uses the sender's private key to protect authenticity.

If the sender wants to guarantee both the confidentiality and authenticity of a message, he can do so by using the following procedure in Lab 7-5:

Lab 7-5   Guaranteeing Confidentiality and Authenticity of a Message

1. **The sender (Thomas) encrypts the message first with the intended recipient's (Richard's) public key and then with his own private key.**

2. **This produces a ciphertext message that can then be transmitted to the intended recipient (Richard).**

3. **The recipient (Richard) uses the sender's (Thomas's) public key to verify the authenticity of the message, and then uses his own private key to decrypt the message's contents.**

If an attacker intercepts the message, he can apply the sender's public key but will then have an encrypted message that can't be decrypted without the intended recipient's private key. Thus, both confidentiality and authenticity are both assured. This use of an asymmetric key system is known as a *secure and signed message format*.

A secure and signed message format uses the sender's private key and the recipient's public key to protect confidentiality and authenticity.

A public and a private key are mathematically related but theoretically, the private key can't be computed or derived from the public key. This property of asymmetric systems is based on the concept of a one-way function. A *one-way function* is a problem that's easy to compute in one direction but not in the reverse direction. In asymmetric key systems, a *trapdoor* (private key) resolves the reverse operation of the one-way function.

Because of the complexity of asymmetric key systems, they are more commonly used for key management or digital signatures than for encryption of bulk information. Often, a *hybrid* system is employed, using an asymmetric system to securely distribute the secret keys of a symmetric key system that's used to encrypt the data.

The main disadvantage of asymmetric systems is speed. Because of the types of algorithms that are used to achieve the one-way hash functions, very large keys are required. (A 128-bit symmetric key has the equivalent strength of a 2,304-bit asymmetric key.) This, in turn, requires more computational power, causing a significant loss of speed (up to 10,000 times slower than a comparable symmetric key system).

However, many significant advantages to asymmetric systems exist, including

- ✔ **Extended functionality:** Asymmetric key systems can provide both confidentiality and authentication; symmetric systems can only provide confidentiality.

- ✔ **Scalability:** This resolves key management issues associated with symmetric key systems.

Asymmetric key algorithms include RSA, Diffie-Hellman, El Gamal, Merkle-Hellman (Trapdoor) Knapsack, and Elliptic Curve.

RSA

In 1978, Drs. Ron Rivest, Adi Shamir, and Len Adleman published the RSA algorithm, which is a *key transport* algorithm based on the difficulty of factoring a number that is the product of two large prime numbers (typically 512 bits). Two users (Thomas and Richard) can securely transport symmetric keys by using RSA as follows in Lab 7-6:

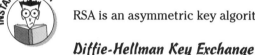

Lab 7-6   Securely Transporting Symmetric keys with RSA

1. **Thomas creates a symmetric key, encrypts it with Richard's public key, and then transmits it to Richard.**

2. **Richard decrypts the symmetric key by using his own private key.**

RSA is an asymmetric key algorithm based on factoring prime numbers.

Diffie-Hellman Key Exchange

In 1976, Drs. Whitfield Diffie and Martin Hellman published a paper entitled "New Directions in Cryptography" detailing a new paradigm for secure key exchange based on discrete logarithms. Diffie-Hellman is described as a *key agreement* algorithm. Two users (Thomas and Richard) can exchange symmetric keys by using Diffie-Hellman as follows in Lab 7-7:

Lab 7-7   Exchanging Symmetric Keys with Diffie-Hellman

1. **Thomas and Richard obtain each other's public keys.**

2. **Thomas and Richard then combine their own private key with the public key of the other person, producing a symmetric key that's known only to the two users involved in the exchange.**

Diffie-Hellman key exchange is vulnerable to man-in-the-middle attacks in which an attacker (Harold) intercepts the public keys during the initial exchange and substitutes his own private key to create a session key that will decrypt the session. A separate authentication mechanism is necessary to protect against this type of attack, ensuring that the two parties communicating in the session are, in fact, the legitimate parties.

Diffie-Hellman is an asymmetric key algorithm based on discrete logarithms.

El Gamal

El Gamal is an unpatented, asymmetric key algorithm based on the discrete logarithm problem used in Diffie-Hellman. It extends the functionality of Diffie-Hellman to include encryption and digital signatures.

Merkle-Hellman (Trapdoor) Knapsack

The Merkle-Hellman (Trapdoor) Knapsack, published in 1978, employs a unique approach to asymmetric cryptography. It's based on the problem of determining what items, in a set of items with fixed weights, can be added to in order to obtain a given total weight. Knapsack was broken in 1982.

Knapsack is an asymmetric key algorithm based on fixed weights.

Elliptic Curve (EC)

In 1985, Neal Koblitz and Victor Miller proposed a new model for asymmetric algorithms based on elliptic curves (EC). Elliptic curves are far more difficult to compute than conventional discrete logarithm problems or factoring prime numbers. (A 160-bit EC key is equivalent to a 1,024-bit RSA key.) The use of smaller keys means that EC is significantly faster than other asymmetric algorithms and many symmetric algorithms and can be widely implemented in various hardware applications including wireless devices and smart cards.

Elliptic Curve is more efficient than other asymmetric key systems and many symmetric key systems because it can use a smaller key.

Message Authentication

Message authentication guarantees the authenticity and integrity of a message by ensuring that:

- ✔ A message hasn't been altered (either maliciously or accidentally) during transmission.
- ✔ A message isn't a replay of a previous message.
- ✔ The message was sent from the origin stated (not a forgery).
- ✔ The message is sent to the intended recipient.

Checksums, CRC-values, and parity checks are examples of basic message authentication and integrity controls. More advanced message authentication is performed by using digital signatures and message digests.

Digital signatures and message digests are used for message authentication.

Digital signatures

The *Digital Signature Standard* (DSS), published by NIST in Federal Information Processing Standard (FIPS) 186-1, specifies two acceptable algorithms in its standard: the RSA Digital Signature Algorithm and the Digital Signature

Algorithm (DSA, which is based on a modified El Gamal algorithm). Both algorithms use the SHA-1 Secure Hash Algorithm, which I discuss in the upcoming section "SHA-1."

A *digital signature* is a simple way to verify the authenticity (and integrity) of a message. Instead of encrypting a message with the intended receiver's public key, the sender encrypts it with his own private key. The sender's public key properly decrypts the message, authenticating the originator of the message. This is known as an *open message format* in asymmetric key systems, which I discuss earlier in the section "Asymmetric key cryptography."

However, it's often impractical to encrypt a message with the receiver's public key to protect confidentiality, and then encrypt the entire message again by using the sender's private key to protect authenticity and integrity. Instead, a representation of the encrypted message is encrypted with the sender's private key to produce a digital signature. The intended recipient decrypts this representation by using the sender's public key, and then independently calculates the expected results of the decrypted representation by using the same, known one-way hashing algorithm. Read more about this in the upcoming section "Message digests." If the results are the same, the integrity of the original message is assured. This representation of the entire message is known as a *message digest*.

Message digests

To *digest* means to reduce or condense something, and this is precisely what a message digest does. (Conversely, *indigestion* means to expand, as in gases . . . how do you spell *relief*?). A message digest is a condensed representation of a message; think *Reader's Digest*. Ideally, a message digest has the following properties:

- The original message can't be re-created from the message digest.
- Finding a message that produces a particular digest shouldn't be computationally feasible.
- No two messages should produce the same message digest.
- The message digest should be calculated by using the entire contents of the original message — it shouldn't be a representation of a representation.

Message digests are produced by using a one-way hash function. There are several types of one-way hashing algorithms (digest algorithms), including MD5, SHA-1, and HMAC.

A *collision* results when two messages produce the same digest or when a second message produces the same digest as a previous message. Seriously!

A *one-way function* ensures that the same key can't encrypt and decrypt a message in an asymmetric key system. One key encrypts the message (produces ciphertext), and a second key (the trapdoor) decrypts the message (produces plaintext), effectively reversing the one-way function. Its purpose is to ensure confidentiality.

A *one-way hashing algorithm* produces a hashing value (or message digest) that can't be reversed; that is, it can't be decrypted. In other words, no trapdoor exists for a one-way hashing algorithm. The purpose of a one-way hashing algorithm is to ensure integrity and authentication.

MD5

MD5 is a one-way hash algorithm developed by Ronald Rivest in 1991. It is actually part of a family (like the Jackson Family of pop music fame) of digest algorithms developed by Ronald Rivest beginning with MD (Jermaine). After some limited success with MD, individual variations were created beginning with MD2 (Michael). MD2 produced a 128-bit digest and was used extensively for many years, but eventually flaws were found and a new replacement was needed. MD3 (Tito) was never taken seriously, and after a very short period in the limelight, MD4 (LaToya) was quickly exploited. However, unlike any of its predecessors, MD5 (Janet) is strong, fast, resilient, and sexy (ooops!) and is one of the most popular hashing algorithms in use today. MD5 takes a variable size input (message) and produces a fixed-size output (128-bit message digest). Messages are processed in 512-bit blocks using four rounds of transformation.

SHA-1

SHA-1 (Secure Hash Algorithm) functions very similar to MD5. In fact, Ronald Rivest was instrumental in its design. Like MD5, SHA-1 takes a variable size input (message) and produces a fixed-size (160-bit message digest versus MD5's 128-bit message digest). SHA-1 processes messages in 512-bit blocks and adds padding to a message length, if necessary, to produce a total message length that's a multiple of 512.

HMAC

The Hashed Message Authentication Code (or Checksum) (HMAC) further extends the security of the MD5 and SHA-1 algorithms through the concept of a *keyed digest*. HMAC incorporates a previously shared secret key and the original into a single message digest. Thus, even if an attacker intercepts a message, modifies its contents, and calculates a new message digest, the result won't match the receiver's hash calculation because the modified message's hash doesn't include the secret key.

MD5, SHA-1, and HMAC are all examples of message authentication algorithms.

Public Key Infrastructure (PKI)

A Public Key Infrastructure (PKI) enables secure e-commerce through the integration of digital signatures, digital certificates, and other services necessary to ensure confidentiality, integrity, authentication, non-repudiation, and access control.

The four basic components of a PKI are the Certification Authority, Registration Authority, Repository, and Archive.

Certification Authority (CA)

The Certification Authority (CA) comprises hardware, software, and the personnel administering the PKI. The CA issues certificates, maintains and publishes status information and Certificate Revocation Lists (CRLs), and maintains archives.

Registration Authority (RA)

The Registration Authority (RA) also comprises hardware, software, and the personnel administering the PKI. It's responsible for verifying certificate contents for the CA.

Repository

A *repository* is a system that accepts certificates and CRLs from a CA and distributes them to authorized parties.

Archive

An *archive* is responsible for long-term storage of archived information from the CA.

The four components of a PKI are the CA, RA, Repository, and Archive.

Key Management Functions

Like physical keys, encryption keys must be safeguarded. Most successful attacks against encryption exploit vulnerability in key management functions rather than some inherent weakness in the encryption algorithm. The following are the major functions associated with key management.

Key generation

Keys must be generated randomly on a secure system, and the generation sequence itself shouldn't provide potential clues regarding the contents of the keyspace. Generated keys shouldn't be displayed in the clear.

Key distribution

Keys must be securely distributed. This is a major vulnerability in symmetric key systems. Using an asymmetric system to securely distribute secret keys is one solution.

Key installation

Key installation is often a manual process. This process should ensure that the key isn't compromised during installation, incorrectly entered, or too difficult to be used readily.

Key storage

Keys must be stored on protected or encrypted storage media, or the application using the keys should include safeguards that prevent extraction of the keys.

Key change

Keys, like passwords, should be changed regularly relative to the value of the information being protected and the frequency of use. Frequently used keys are more likely to be compromised through interception and statistical analysis. However, like a changing of the guard, vulnerabilities inherent to any change must be addressed.

Key control

Key control addresses the proper use of keys. Different keys have different functions and may only be approved for certain levels of classification.

Key disposal

Keys (and any distribution media) must be properly disposed of, erased, or destroyed so that the key's contents are not disclosed, possibly providing an attacker insight into the key management system.

The seven key management issues are generation, distribution, installation, storage, change, control, and disposal.

Key Escrow and Key Recovery

Law enforcement has always been concerned about the potential use of encryption for criminal purposes. To counter this threat, the Escrowed Encryption Standard (EES) was published by NIST in FIPS PUB 185 (1994). The premise of the EES is to divide a secret key into two parts and place those two parts into escrow with two separate, trusted organizations. With a court order, the two parts can be obtained by law enforcement officials, the secret key recovered, and the suspected communications decrypted. One implementation of the EES is the Clipper Chip proposed by the US government. The Clipper Chip uses the Skipjack Secret Key algorithm for encryption and an 80-bit secret key.

E-Mail Security Applications

Several applications employing various cryptographic techniques have been developed to provide confidentiality, integrity, authentication, non-repudiation, and access control for e-mail communications.

Secure Multipurpose Internet Mail Extensions (S/MIME)

Secure Multipurpose Internet Mail Extensions (S/MIME) is a secure method of sending e-mail incorporated into several popular browsers and e-mail applications. S/MIME provides confidentiality and authentication by using the RSA asymmetric key system, digital signatures, and X.509 digital certificates. S/MIME complies with the Public Key Cryptography Standard (PKCS) #7 format and has been proposed as a standard to the Internet Engineering Task Force (IETF).

MIME Object Security Services (MOSS)

MIME Object Security Services (MOSS) provides confidentiality, integrity, identification and authentication, and non-repudiation by using MD2 or MD5, RSA asymmetric keys, and DES. MOSS has not been widely implemented on the Internet.

Privacy Enhanced Mail (PEM)

Privacy Enhanced Mail (PEM) was proposed as a PKCS-compliant standard by the IETF but hasn't been widely implemented on the Internet. It provides confidentiality and authentication by using 3DES for encryption, MD2 or MD5 message digests, X.509 digital certificates, and the RSA asymmetric system for digital signatures and secure key distribution.

Pretty Good Privacy (PGP)

Pretty Good Privacy (PGP) is freely available, open source e-mail software developed by Phil Zimmerman. It provides confidentiality and authentication by using the IDEA Cipher for encryption and the RSA asymmetric system for digital signatures and secure key distribution. Instead of a central Certificate Authority (CA), PGP uses a trust model, which is ideally suited to smaller groups for validation of user identity.

PGP is a freeware e-mail security application that uses the IDEA algorithm (symmetric) for encryption and the RSA algorithm (asymmetric) for key distribution and digital signatures.

Internet Security Applications

As with e-mail applications, several protocols, standards, and applications have been developed to provide security for Internet communications and transactions.

Secure Electronic Transaction (SET)

The *Secure Electronic Transaction* (SET) specification was developed by MasterCard and Visa to provide secure e-commerce transactions by implementing authentication mechanisms while protecting the confidentiality and integrity of cardholder data. SET defines the following features:

- ✔ **Confidentiality** (using DES)
- ✔ **Integrity** (using digital signatures and RSA asymmetric system)
- ✔ **Cardholder authentication** (using digital signatures and X.509 digital certificates)
- ✔ **Merchant authentication** (using digital signatures and X.509 digital certificates)
- ✔ **Interoperability** (between different hardware and software manufacturers)

SET utilizes dual signatures by allowing two pieces of data to be linked and sent to two different entities.

SET is an Internet security application developed jointly by MasterCard and Visa for secure e-commerce.

Secure Sockets Layer (SSL)/Transport Layer Security (TLS)

The *Secure Sockets Layer* (SSL) protocol, developed by Netscape in 1994, provides session-based encryption and authentication for secure communication between clients and servers on the Internet. SSL operates at the Transport Layer, is independent of the application protocol, and provides server authentication with optional client authentication. SSL uses the RSA asymmetric key system; IDEA, DES, and 3DES symmetric key systems; and the MD5 hash function. The current version is SSL 3.0. SSL 3.0 was standardized by the IETF in TLS 1.0 and released in 1999 with only minor modifications to the original SSL 3.0 specification.

Secure Hypertext Transfer Protocol (S-HTTP)

Secure Hypertext Transfer Protocol (S-HTTP) is an Internet protocol that provides a method for secure communications with a Web server. S-HTTP is a connectionless-oriented protocol that encapsulates data after security properties for the session have been successfully negotiated. It uses symmetric encryption (for confidentiality), message digests (for integrity), and public key encryption (for client-server authentication and non-repudiation). Rather than encrypting an entire session as in SSL, S-HTTP can be applied to individual Web documents.

IPSec

Internet Protocol Security (IPSec) is an IETF open standard for secure communications over public IP-based networks, such as the Internet. IPSec ensures confidentiality, integrity, and authenticity by using Layer 3 (Network) encryption and authentication to provide an end-to-end solution. IPSec operates in two modes:

- ✔ **Transport Mode:** Only the data is encrypted.
- ✔ **Tunnel Mode:** The entire packet is encrypted.

The two modes of IPSec are Transport Mode and Tunnel Mode.

The two main protocols used in IPSec are

- ✔ **Authentication Header (AH):** Provides integrity, authentication, and non-repudiation
- ✔ **Encapsulating Security Payload (ESP):** Provides confidentiality (encryption) and limited authentication

Each pair of hosts communicating in an IPSec session must establish a security association (SA).

An *SA* is a one-way connection between two communicating parties, meaning that two SAs are required for each pair of communicating hosts. Additionally, each SA only supports a single protocol (AH or ESP). Thus, if both AH and ESP are used between two communicating hosts, a total of four SAs is required. An SA has three parameters that uniquely identify it in an IPSec session:

- ✔ **Security Parameter Index (SPI):** The SPI is a 32-bit string used by the receiving station to differentiate between SAs terminating on that station. The SPI is located within the AH or ESP header.
- ✔ **Destination IP Address:** The destination address could be the end station or an intermediate gateway or firewall but must be a unicast address.
- ✔ **Security Protocol ID:** This is either an AH or ESP association.

In IPSec, a Security Association (SA) is a one-way connection. A minimum of two SAs is required for two-way communications.

Key management is provided in IPSec by using the Internet Key Exchange (IKE). *IKE* is actually a combination of three complementary protocols: The Internet Security Association and Key Management Protocol (ISAKMP), the Secure Key Exchange Mechanism (SKEME), and the Oakley Key Exchange Protocol. IKE operates in three modes: Main Mode, Aggressive Mode, and Quick Mode.

Multi-Protocol Label Switching (MPLS)

Multi-Protocol Label Switching (MPLS) is an extremely fast method for forwarding packets through a network by using labels inserted between Layer 2 and Layer 3 headers in the packet. It is protocol independent and highly scalable, providing Quality of Service (QoS) with multiple Classes of Service (CoS) and secure Layer 3 Virtual Private Network (VPN) tunneling.

Secure Shell (SSH-2)

Secure Shell (SSH-2, or version 2) is used for secure remote access as one alternative to Telnet. It can be used to provide confidentiality, integrity, and authentication. SSH-2 establishes an encrypted tunnel between the SSH client and SSH server and can also authenticate the client to the server. SSH version 1 is also widely used but has inherent vulnerabilities that are easily exploited.

SSH-2 (or simply SSH) is an Internet security application that provides secure remote access.

Wireless Transport Layer Security (WTLS)

The *Wireless Transport Layer Security* (WTLS) protocol provides security services for the Wireless Application Protocol (WAP) commonly used for Internet connectivity by mobile devices. WTLS provides three classes of security as follows:

- ✔ **Class 1:** Anonymous Authentication
- ✔ **Class 2:** Server Authentication Only
- ✔ **Class 3:** Client-Server Authentication

Additional (but somewhat limited) security is provided in WAP through the use of Service Set Identifiers (SSID) and Wired Equivalent Privacy (WEP) Keys. A significant improvement in wireless security incorporates the Extensible Authentication Protocol (EAP), which uses a Remote Authentication Dial-In User Service (RADIUS) server for authentication.

Methods of Attack

Attempts to crack a cryptosystem can be generally classified into four classes of attack methods: analytic, brute force, implementation, and statistical.

Analytic attacks

An *analytic attack* uses algebraic manipulation in an attempt to reduce the complexity of the algorithm.

Brute force attacks

In a *brute force* (or *exhaustion*) *attack*, the cryptanalyst attempts every possible combination of key patterns. This type of attack can be very time (up to several hundred million years) and resource intensive, depending on the length of the key . . . and the life span of the attacker.

Implementation attacks

Implementation attacks attempt to exploit some weakness in the cryptosystem such as a vulnerability in a protocol or algorithm.

Statistical attacks

A *statistical attack* attempts to exploit some statistical weakness in the cryptosystem such as a lack of randomness in key generation.

Specific methods of attack

The following specific attack methods employ various elements of the above classes.

The Birthday Attack

The *Birthday Attack* attempts to exploit the probability of two messages by using the same hash function and producing the same message digest. It's based on the statistical probability (greater than 50 percent) that 2 people in a room will have the same birthday if there are 23 or more people in the room. However, for 2 people in a room to share a *given* birthday, there must be 253 or more people in the room to have a statistical probability of greater than 50 percent.

Ciphertext Only Attack (COA)

In a *Ciphertext Only Attack* (COA), the cryptanalyst obtains the ciphertext of several messages, all encrypted by using the same encryption algorithm but without the associated plaintext. The cryptanalyst then attempts to decrypt the data by searching for repeating patterns and through statistical analysis. For example, certain words in the English language such as *the* and *or* occur frequently. This type of attack is generally difficult and requires a large sample of ciphertext.

Chosen Text Attack (CTA)

In a *Chosen Text Attack* (CTA), the cryptanalyst selects a sample of plaintext and obtains the corresponding ciphertext. Several types of Chosen Text Attacks exist, including Chosen Plaintext, Adaptive Chosen Plaintext, Chosen Ciphertext, and Adaptive Chosen Ciphertext.

- **Chosen Plaintext Attack (CPA):** The cryptanalyst chooses plaintext to be encrypted, and the corresponding ciphertext is obtained.

- **Adaptive Chosen Plaintext Attack (ACPA):** The cryptanalyst chooses plaintext to be encrypted; then, based on the resulting ciphertext, he chooses another sample to be encrypted.

- **Chosen Ciphertext Attack (CCA):** The cryptanalyst chooses ciphertext to be decrypted, and the corresponding plaintext is obtained.

- **Adaptive Chosen Ciphertext Attack (ACCA):** The cryptanalyst chooses ciphertext to be decrypted; then, based on the resulting ciphertext, he chooses another sample to be decrypted.

Known Plaintext Attack (KPA)

In a *Known Plaintext Attack* (KPA), the cryptanalyst has obtained the ciphertext and corresponding plaintext of several past messages.

Man-in-the-Middle

A *Man-in-the-Middle Attack* involves an attacker intercepting messages between two parties on a network and potentially modifying the original message.

Meet-in-the-Middle

A *Meet-in-the-Middle Attack* involves an attacker encrypting known plaintext with each possible key on one end, decrypting the corresponding ciphertext with each possible key, and then comparing the results *in the middle*. This might also be considered an Analytic Attack because it does involve some differential analysis.

Replay Attack

A *Replay Attack* occurs when a session key is intercepted and used against a later encrypted session between the same two parties. Replay attacks can be countered by incorporating a time stamp in the session key.

Additional References

Burnett, Steve and Paine, Stephen. *RSA Security's Official Guide to Cryptography*, Chapters 1–8, 10. RSA Press.

Krutz, Ronald L. and Vines, Russell Dean. *The CISSP Prep Guide: Mastering the Ten Domains of Computer Security*, Chapter 4. John Wiley & Sons, Inc.

Housley, Russ and Polk, Tim. *Planning for PKI: Best Practices Guide for Deploying Public Key Infrastructure*, Chapters 2–5. John Wiley & Sons, Inc.

Russell, Deborah and Gangemi Sr, G.T. *Computer Security Basics,* Chapter 7. O'Reilly and Associates.

Tipton, Harold F. and Krause, Micki. *Information Security Management Handbook,* 4th Edition, Chapters 19–22. Auerbach Publications.

Prep Test

1 The four modes of DES include all the following except

- **A** ○ ECB
- **B** ○ ECC
- **C** ○ CFB
- **D** ○ CBC

2 A type of cipher that replaces bits, characters, or character blocks with alternate bits, characters, or character blocks to produce ciphertext is known as a

- **A** ○ Permutation Cipher
- **B** ○ Block Cipher
- **C** ○ Transposition Cipher
- **D** ○ Substitution Cipher

3 Which of the following is not an advantage of symmetric key systems?

- **A** ○ Scalability
- **B** ○ Speed
- **C** ○ Strength
- **D** ○ Availability

4 The Advanced Encryption Standard (AES) is based on what symmetric key algorithm?

- **A** ○ Twofish
- **B** ○ Knapsack
- **C** ○ Diffie-Hellman
- **D** ○ Rijndael

5 A message that's encrypted with the sender's private key only, for the purpose of authentication, is known as a(n)

- **A** ○ Secure message format
- **B** ○ Signed and secure message format
- **C** ○ Open message format
- **D** ○ Message digest

6 All the following are examples of asymmetric key systems based on discrete logarithms except

- **A** ○ Diffie-Hellman
- **B** ○ Elliptic Curve
- **C** ○ RSA
- **D** ○ El Gamal

7 The four main components of a Public Key Infrastructure (PKI) include all the following except

A ○ Directory Service

B ○ Certificate Authority

C ○ Repository

D ○ Archive

8 Which of the following Internet specifications provides secure e-commerce by using symmetric key systems, asymmetric key systems, and dual signatures?

A ○ Public Key Infrastructure (PKI)

B ○ Secure Electronic Transaction (SET)

C ○ Secure Sockets Layer (SSL)

D ○ Secure Hypertext Transfer Protocol (S-HTTP)

9 The minimum number of SAs required for a two-way IPSec session between two communicating hosts using both AH and ESP is

A ○ 1

B ○ 2

C ○ 4

D ○ 8

10 An IPSec SA consists of the following parameters that uniquely identify it in an IPSec session, except:

A ○ Source IP Address

B ○ Destination IP Address

C ○ Security Protocol ID

D ○ Security Parameter Index (SPI)

Answers

1 **B.** ECC. ECC is the Elliptic Curve Cryptosystem, an asymmetric algorithm. ECB (Electronic Code Book), CFB (Cipher Feedback), CBC (Cipher Block Chaining), and OFB (Output Feedback) are all valid DES modes of operation. *Review "Data Encryption Standard (DES)."*

2 **D.** Substitution Cipher. Transposition Ciphers and Permutation Ciphers rearrange data to produce ciphertext. A Block Cipher is a type of cipher that operates on a block of data. *Review "Types of ciphers."*

3 **A.** Scalability. Symmetric key systems aren't scalable because of the difficulty of key management between individual pairs of communicating parties. *Review "Symmetric key cryptography."*

4 **D.** Rijndael. The Rijndael Block Cipher has been selected as the AES. Twofish was a finalist for the AES standard but wasn't selected. Knapsack and Diffie-Hellman are asymmetric key systems. *Review "Rijndael Block Cipher."*

5 **C.** Open message format. A secure message is encrypted with the receiver's public key to achieve confidentiality. A signed and secure message is encrypted with both the receiver's public key and the sender's private key. A message digest is produced by a one-way hashing function to digitally sign a message for authentication. *Review "Asymmetric key cryptography."*

6 **C.** RSA. RSA is based on factoring large prime numbers. *Review "RSA."*

7 **A.** Directory Service. The four basic components of a PKI are the Certificate Authority (CA), Registration Authority (RA), Repository, and Archive. *Review "PKI pieces."*

8 **B.** Secure Electronic Transaction (SET). Only SET implements the concept of dual signatures for authentication. *Review "Internet Security Applications."*

9 **C.** 4. Four Security Associations (SAs) are required because SAs are simplex (one-way) and an SA is required for each protocol. *Review "IPSec."*

10 **A.** Source IP Address. The Source IP Address isn't included in an SA. *Review "IPSec."*

Chapter 8

Security Architecture and Models

• •

In This Chapter

▶ Computer architecture, including hardware, firmware, and software

▶ Security architecture basic concepts

▶ Access control models

▶ Evaluation criteria and certification/accreditation

• •

*W*hereas Domains 2 and 4 address network and applications development security, respectively, the primary focus of the Security Architecture and Models domain is *systems* security.

In this chapter, I discuss basic computer architecture (if you're already CompTIA A+ certified, this will be a simple, quick review), security architectures (including important concepts like the Trusted Computing Base [TCB], open and closed systems, and security modes), access control models, evaluation criteria, and certification and accreditation.

Computer Architecture

A basic computer (system) architecture refers to the structure of a computer system and comprises hardware, firmware, and software.

The CompTIA A+ certification exam covers computer architecture in depth and is an excellent way to prepare for this portion of the CISSP examination.

Hardware

Hardware consists of the physical components in a computer architecture. This broad definition of hardware can include keyboards, monitors, printers, and other peripherals. However, in this context, only concern yourself with the main components of the computer architecture itself, which include the CPU, memory, and bus.

CPU

The *CPU* (Central Processing Unit) or microprocessor is the electronic circuitry that performs a computer's arithmetic, logic, and computing functions. As shown in Figure 8-1, the main components of a CPU include

- **Arithmetic Logic Unit (ALU):** Performs numerical calculations and comparative logic functions, such as ADD, SUBTRACT, DIVIDE, and MULTIPLY
- **Bus Interface Unit (BIU):** Supervises data transfers over the bus system between the CPU and I/O devices
- **Control Unit:** Coordinates activities of the other CPU components during program execution
- **Decode Unit:** Converts incoming instructions into individual CPU commands
- **Floating Point Unit (FPU):** Handles higher math operations for the ALU and control unit
- **Memory Management Unit (MMU):** Handles addressing and cataloging of data stored in memory and translates logical addressing into physical addressing
- **Pre-Fetch Unit:** Preloads instructions into CPU registers
- **Protection Test Unit (PTU):** Monitors all CPU functions to ensure that they're properly executed
- **Registers:** Buffers used to temporarily hold CPU data, addresses, and instructions

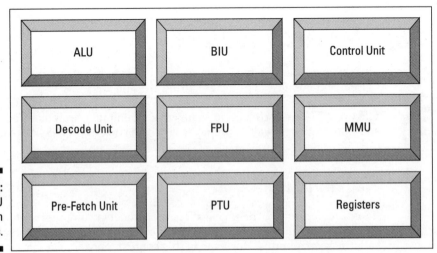

Figure 8-1:
The CPU main components.

The basic operation of a microprocessor consists of two distinct phases: fetch and execute. During the fetch phase, the CPU locates and retrieves a required instruction from memory. During the execute phase, the CPU decodes and executes the instruction. These two phases comprise a basic machine cycle that's controlled by the CPU clock signals. Many complex instructions require more than a single machine cycle to execute.

The four operating states for a computer (CPU) are

- **Operating (or run) state:** The CPU executes an instruction or instructions.

- **Problem (or application) state:** The CPU calculates a solution to an application-based problem. During this state, only a limited subset of instructions (*non-privileged* instructions) is available.

- **Supervisory state:** The CPU executes a *privileged* instruction: that is available only to a system administrator or other authorized user/process.

- **Wait state:** The CPU hasn't yet completed execution of an instruction and must extend the cycle.

The two basic types of CPU designs used in modern computer systems are

- **Complex-Instruction-Set-Computing (CISC):** Can perform multiple operations per single instruction. Optimized for systems in which the fetch phase is the longest part of the instruction execution cycle.

- **Reduced-Instruction-Set-Computing (RISC):** Uses fewer, simpler instructions than CISC architecture, requiring less clock cycles to execute. Optimized for systems in which the fetch and execute phases are approximately equal.

Microprocessors are also often described as scalar or superscalar. A *scalar* processor executes a single instruction at a time. A *superscalar* processor can execute multiple instructions concurrently.

Finally, many systems (microprocessors) are classified according to additional functionality as follows (must be supported by the installed operating system):

- **Multitasking:** Alternates execution of multiple subprograms or tasks on a single processor

- **Multiprogramming:** Alternates execution of multiple programs on a single processor

- **Multiprocessing:** Executes multiple programs on multiple processors simultaneously

Two related concepts are multi-state and multi-user systems that, more correctly, refer to operating system capabilities:

- **Multi-state:** The operating system supports multiple operating states, such as *single-user* and *multi-user* modes in the Unix/Linux world and *Normal* and *Safe* mode in the Windows world.

- **Multi-user:** This refers to the ability of the operating system to differentiate between users: for example, providing different shell environments, profiles, or privilege levels.

An important security issue in multi-user systems is privileged accounts and programs or processes that run in a privileged state. Programs such as *su* (Unix/Linux) and *RunAs* (Windows) allow a user to switch to a different account, such as root or administrator, and execute privileged commands in this context. Many programs rely on privileged service accounts to function properly. Utilities such as *Superzap* (developed by IBM) are used to install fixes to the operating system or other applications.

Bus

The *bus* is a group of electronic conductors that interconnect the various components of the computer, transmitting signals, addresses, and data between these components. Bus structures are organized as follows:

- **Data bus:** Transmits data between the CPU, memory, and peripheral devices

- **Address bus:** Transmits addresses of data and instructions between the CPU and memory

- **Control bus:** Transmits control information (device status) between the CPU and other devices

Memory

Memory is used to store programs, instructions, and data. The two basic types of physical (or real) memory are

- **Random Access Memory (RAM):** Volatile memory (data is lost if power is removed) that can be directly addressed and stored data can be altered. RAM is typically implemented in a computer architecture as cache memory and primary memory. The two main types of RAM are

  - **Dynamic RAM (DRAM)** must be refreshed (contents re-written) every two milliseconds because of capacitance decay. This is accomplished using multiple clock signals known as *multi-phase clock signals.*

  - **Static RAM (SRAM)** is faster than DRAM and uses circuit latches to represent data; that is, it doesn't need to be refreshed. Because SRAM doesn't need to be refreshed, a *single-phase clock signal* is used.

✔ **Read-Only Memory (ROM):** Non-volatile memory (data is retained even if power is removed) that can be directly addressed but stored data can't be easily altered. ROM is typically implemented in a computer architecture as firmware (as I discuss later in the section "Firmware"). Variations of ROM include

- Erasable Programmable Read-Only Memory (EPROM)

- Electrically Erasable Programmable Read-Only Memory (EEPROM)

- Electrically Alterable Read-Only Memory (EAROM)

- Programmable Logic Device (PLD)

- Flash Memory

Secondary memory is a variation of these two basic types of physical memory. It provides dynamic storage on non-volatile magnetic media, such as a hard disk drive or tape drive (considered *sequential memory* because data cannot be directly accessed — instead, you must search from the beginning of the tape media). *Virtual memory* (such as a paging file, swap space, or swap partition) is a type of secondary memory that uses both installed physical memory and available hard drive space to present a larger, apparent memory space to the CPU.

Two important security concepts associated with memory are the protection domain (or *protected memory*) and memory addressing.

A *protection domain* prevents other programs or processes from accessing and modifying the contents of address space that's already been assigned to an active program or process. This can be accomplished by the operating system or implemented in hardware.

Memory space describes the amount of memory available in a computer system (for example, 256MB), whereas *address space* specifies where memory is located in a computer system (a memory address). *Memory addressing* describes the method used by the CPU to access the contents of memory. A *physical* memory address is a hard-coded address assigned to physically installed memory. It can only be accessed by the operating system that maps physical addresses to virtual addresses. A *virtual* (or symbolic) memory address is the address used by applications (and programmers) to specify a desired location in memory. Common virtual memory addressing modes include

✔ **Base addressing:** An address used as the origin for calculating other addresses.

✔ **Absolute addressing:** An address that identifies a location without reference to a base address — or it may be a base address itself.

✔ **Indexed addressing:** Specifies an address relative to an index register. (If the index register changes, the resulting memory location changes.)

✔ **Indirect addressing:** The specified address contains the address to the final desired location in memory.

✔ **Direct addressing:** Specifies the address of the final desired memory location.

Don't confuse the concepts of virtual memory and virtual addressing. *Virtual memory* combines physical memory and hard drive space to create more apparent memory (memory space). *Virtual addressing* is the method used by applications and programmers to specify a desired location in memory (address space).

Firmware

Firmware is a program or code that is programmed into ROM memory. These types of programs are typically changed infrequently or not at all. A computer's BIOS is a common example of firmware.

Software

Software includes the operating system and programs or applications that are installed on a computer system. I cover applications security in Chapter 6. The focus on software in this domain is the operating system.

The *operating system* (OS) controls a computer's resources. The four main functions of the operating system are

✔ Process management

✔ I/O device management

✔ Memory management

✔ File management

Security Architecture

Basic concepts related to security architecture include the Trusted Computing Base (TCB), open and closed systems, protection rings, security modes, and recovery procedures.

Trusted Computing Base (TCB)

A *Trusted Computing Base* (TCB) is the total combination of protection mechanisms within a computer system, including hardware, firmware, and software, which is responsible for enforcing a security policy. A *security perimeter* is the boundary that separates the TCB from the rest of the system.

A Trusted Computing Base (TCB) is the total combination of protection mechanisms within a computer system, including hardware, firmware, and software, which is responsible for enforcing a security policy.

Access control is the ability to permit or deny the use of an *object* (a passive entity such as a system or file) by a *subject* (an active entity such as individual or process).

Access control is the ability to permit or deny the use of an object (system or file) by a subject (individual or process).

A *reference monitor* is a system component that enforces access controls on an object. Stated another way, a reference monitor is an abstract machine that mediates all access to an object by a subject.

A reference monitor is a system component that enforces access controls on an object.

A *security kernel* is the combination of hardware, firmware, and software elements in a Trusted Computing Base that implements the reference monitor concept. Three requirements of a security kernel are that it must

- ✔ Mediate all accesses
- ✔ Be protected from modification
- ✔ Be verified as correct

A security kernel is the combination of hardware, firmware, and software elements in a Trusted Computing Base (TCB) that implements the reference monitor concept.

Open and closed systems

An *open system* is a vendor-independent system that complies with an accepted standard. This promotes interoperability between systems and components made by different vendors. Additionally, open systems can be independently reviewed and evaluated, which facilitates identification of bugs and vulnerabilities and rapid development of solutions and updates.

A *closed system* uses proprietary hardware and/or software that may not be compatible with other systems or components. Source code for software in a closed system is not normally available.

Protection rings

The concept of *protection rings* implements multiple domains with increasing levels of trust near the center. The most privileged ring is identified as Ring 0 and normally includes the operating system's security kernel. Additional system components are placed in the appropriate concentric ring based on the principle of least privilege. (For more on this, read Chapter 9.) The MIT MULTICS operating system implements the concept of protection rings in a security architecture.

Security modes

Several *security modes of operation*, based on the classification level of information being processed on a system and the clearance level of authorized users, have been defined. These designations are typically used for US military and government systems and include

- ✔ **Dedicated:** All authorized users must have a clearance level equal to or higher than the highest level of information processed on the system and a valid need-to-know.

- ✔ **System High:** All authorized users must have a clearance level equal to or higher than the highest level of information processed on the system but a valid need-to-know isn't necessarily required.

- ✔ **Multi-level:** Information at different classification levels is stored or processed on a *trusted computer system* (employs all necessary hardware and software assurance measures and meets the specified requirements for reliability and security). Authorized users must have an appropriate clearance level, and access restrictions are enforced by the system accordingly.

- ✔ **Limited access:** Authorized users aren't required to have a security clearance, but the highest level of information on the system is Sensitive But Unclassified (SBU).

Recovery procedures

A hardware or software failure can potentially compromise a system's security mechanisms. Security designs that protect a system during a hardware or software failure include

- ✔ **Fault-tolerant systems:** These systems continue to operate following failure of a computer or network component. The system must be capable of detecting and correcting or circumventing a fault.

- ✔ **Fail-safe systems:** When a hardware or software failure is detected, program execution is terminated, and the system is protected from compromise.

- ✔ **Fail-soft (resilient) systems:** When a hardware or software failure is detected, certain non-critical processing is terminated, and the computer or network continues to function in a degraded mode.

- ✔ **Failover systems:** When a hardware or software failure is detected, the system automatically transfers processing to a hot back-up component, such as a clustered server.

Access Control Models

Models are used to express access control requirements in a theoretical or mathematical framework that precisely describes or quantifies its function. Common access control models include Bell-LaPadula, Access Matrix, Take-Grant, Biba, Clark-Wilson, Information Flow, and Non-interference.

Bell-LaPadula

Published in 1973, the *Bell-LaPadula model* was the first formal confidentiality model of a mandatory access control system. (I discuss mandatory and discretionary access controls in Chapter 3.) It was developed for the US Department of Defense (DoD) to formalize the DoD multilevel security policy. As I discuss in Chapter 5, the DoD classifies information based on sensitivity at three basic levels: Confidential, Secret, and Top Secret. In order to access classified information (and systems), an individual must have *access* (clearance level equal to or exceeding the classification of the information or system) and *need-to-know* (necessary to perform a required job function). The Bell-LaPadula model implements the *access* component of this security policy.

Bell-LaPadula is a *state machine model* that addresses only the confidentiality of information. (A *secure state* is defined and maintained during transitions between secure states.) The basic premise of Bell-LaPadula is that information can't flow downward. Bell-LaPadula defines the following two properties:

- ✓ **Simple security property (ss property):** A subject can't read information from an object with a higher sensitivity label (no read up, or *NRU*).

- ✓ ***-property (star property):** A subject can't write information to an object with a lower sensitivity label (no write down, or *NWD*).

Bell-LaPadula also defines two additional properties that give it the flexibility of a discretionary access control model:

- ✓ **Discretionary security property:** Determines access based on an access matrix

- ✓ **Trusted subject:** An entity that can violate the *-property but not its intent

Access Matrix

An *Access Matrix model*, in general, provides object access rights (Read/Write/Execute, or *R/W/X*) to subjects in a discretionary access control (DAC) system. An Access Matrix consists of access control lists (columns) and capability lists (rows). See Table 8-1 for an example.

Table 8-1	Access Matrix Example		
Subject/Object	*Directory: H/R*	*File: Personnel*	*Process: LPD*
Thomas	Read	Read/Write	Execute
Richard	Read	Read	Execute
Harold	None	None	None

Take-Grant

Take-Grant systems specify the rights that a subject can transfer to or from another subject or object. These rights are defined through four basic operations: create, revoke, take, and grant.

Bell-LaPadula, Access Matrix, and Take-Grant models address confidentiality.

Biba

Published in 1977, the *Biba integrity model* (sometimes referred to as *Bell-LaPadula upside down*) was the first formal integrity model. *Biba* is a lattice-based model that addresses the first goal of integrity: ensuring that modifications to data aren't made by unauthorized users or processes. (See Chapter 5 for a complete discussion of the three goals of integrity.) Biba defines the following two properties:

- **simple integrity property:** A subject can't read information from an object with a lower integrity level (no read down).

- ***-integrity property (star integrity property):** A subject can't write information to an object with a higher integrity level (no write up).

Clark-Wilson

Published in 1987, the *Clark-Wilson integrity model* establishes a security framework for use in commercial activities, such as the banking industry. Clark-Wilson addresses all three goals of integrity and identifies special requirements for inputting data based on the following items and procedures. (See Chapter 5 for more on the three goals of integrity.)

- **Unconstrained data item (UDI):** Data outside the control area, such as input data.

- **Constrained data item (CDI):** Data inside the control area. (Integrity must be preserved.)

- **Integrity verification procedures (IVP):** Checks validity of CDIs.

- **Transformation procedures (TP):** Maintains integrity of CDIs.

The Clark-Wilson integrity model is based upon the concept of a *well-formed transaction*, in which a transaction is sufficiently ordered and controlled in order to maintain internal and external consistency.

Biba and Clark-Wilson address integrity.

Information Flow

An *Information Flow model* is a type of access control model based on information flow rather than access controls. Objects are assigned a security class and value, and their direction of flow is controlled by a security policy. This model type is useful for analyzing covert channels.

Non-interference

A *Non-interference model* ensures that the actions of different objects and subjects aren't seen by and don't interfere with other objects and subjects on the same system.

Evaluation Criteria

Evaluation criteria provide a standard for quantifying the security of a computer system or network. These include the Trusted Computer System Evaluation Criteria (TCSEC), Trusted Network Interpretation (TNI), European Information Technology Security Evaluation Criteria (ITSEC), and the Common Criteria.

Trusted Computer System Evaluation Criteria (TCSEC)

The Trusted Computer System Evaluation Criteria (TCSEC), commonly known as the *Orange Book*, is part of the *Rainbow Series* developed for the US DoD by the National Computer Security Center (NCSC) in 1983. (The current issue was published in 1985.) It is the formal implementation of the Bell-LaPadula model. The evaluation criteria were developed to achieve the following objectives:

- ✔ **Measurement:** Provides a metric for assessing comparative levels of trust between different computer systems.

- ✔ **Guidance:** Identifies standard security requirements that vendors must build into systems to achieve a given trust level.

- ✔ **Acquisition:** Provides customers a standard for specifying acquisition requirements and identifying systems that meet those requirements.

The four basic control requirements identified in the Orange Book are

- ✔ **Security policy:** The rules and procedures by which a trusted system operates. Specific TCSEC requirements include

    - • **Discretionary access control (DAC):** Read more about this in Chapter 3.

    - • **Mandatory access control (MAC):** Read more about this in Chapter 3.

- **Object reuse:** This protects confidentiality of objects that are reassigned after initial use. For example, a deleted file still exists on storage media; only the file allocation table (FAT) and first character of the file have been modified. Thus, residual data may be restored. This describes the problem of *data remanence*. Object reuse requirements define procedures for actually erasing the data.

- **Labels:** Sensitivity labels are required in MAC-based systems. (Read more about this in Chapter 3.) Specific TCSEC labeling requirements include integrity, export, and subject/object labels.

✔ **Assurance:** This guarantees that a security policy is correctly implemented. Specific TCSEC requirements are classified as *operational assurance requirements* (system architecture, system integrity, covert channel analysis, trusted facility management, and trusted recovery) and *life-cycle assurance requirements* (security testing, design specification and verification, configuration management, and trusted distribution).

- **System architecture:** System design features and principles that implement specific security features.

- **System integrity:** Hardware and firmware operate properly and are tested to verify proper operation.

- **Covert channel analysis:** An unintended communication path not protected by a system's normal security mechanisms. A *covert storage channel* conveys information by altering stored system data. A *covert timing channel* conveys information by altering a system resource's performance or timing.

- **Trusted facility management:** The assignment of a specific individual to administer the security-related functions of a system. Closely related to the concepts of *least privilege*, *separation of duties*, and *need-to-know*, which I discuss in Chapters 3 and 9.

- **Trusted recovery:** Ensures that security isn't compromised in the event of a system crash or failure. This involves two primary activities: failure preparation and system recovery, which I discuss in Chapter 9.

- **Security testing:** Specifies required testing by the developer and NCSC.

- **Design specification and verification:** Requires a mathematical and automated proof that the design description is consistent with the security policy.

- **Configuration management:** Identifying, controlling, accounting for, and auditing all changes made to the TCB during the design, development, and maintenance phases of a system life cycle.

- **Trusted distribution:** Protects a system during transport from a vendor (protection) to a customer (site validation).

✔ **Accountability:** The ability to associate users and processes with their actions. Specific TCSEC requirements include

- **Identification and Authentication (I&A):** I discuss this in Chapter 3.

- **Trusted Path:** A direct communications path between the user and the TCB that doesn't require interaction with untrusted applications or operating system layers.

- **Audit:** Recording, examination, analysis, and review of security-related activities in a trusted system, which I discuss in Chapters 3, 9, and 11.

✔ **Documentation:** Specific TCSEC requirements include

- **Security Features User's Guide (SFUG):** User's manual.

- **Trusted Facility Manual (TFM):** System administrator's and/or security administrator's manual.

- **Test documentation:** According to the TSCES manual, must "show how the security mechanisms were tested, and results of the security mechanisms' functional testing."

- **Design documentation:** Defines system boundaries and internal components, such as the TCB.

The Orange Book defines four major hierarchical classes of security protection and numbered sub-classes, as follows. Higher numbers indicate higher security.

✔ **D:** Minimal protection

✔ **C:** Discretionary protection (C1 and C2)

✔ **B:** Mandatory protection (B1, B2, and B3)

✔ **A:** Verified protection (A1)

These classes are further defined in Table 8-2.

Table 8-2		TCSEC Classes
Class	*Name*	*Sample Requirements*
D	Minimal security	Reserved for systems that fail evaluation.
C1	Discretionary protection (DAC)	System doesn't need to distinguish between individual users and types of access.
C2	Controlled access protection (DAC)	System must distinguish between individual users and types of access; object reuse security features required.

Class	Name	Sample Requirements
B1	Labeled security protection (MAC)	Sensitivity labels required for all subjects and storage objects.
B2	Structured protection (MAC)	Sensitivity labels required for all subjects and objects; trusted path requirements.
B3	Security domains (MAC)	ACLs are specifically required; system must protect against covert channels.
A1	Verified design (MAC)	Formal Top-Level Specification (FTLS) required; configuration management procedures must be enforced throughout entire system life cycle.

You don't need to know specific requirements of each TCSEC level for the CISSP exam, but you should know at what levels DAC and MAC are implemented and the relative trust levels of the classes, including numbered sub-classes.

Major limitations of the Orange Book include that it

- ✔ Only addresses confidentiality issues; it doesn't include integrity and availability
- ✔ Isn't applicable to most commercial systems
- ✔ Emphasizes protection from unauthorized access, despite statistical evidence that most security violations involve insiders
- ✔ Doesn't address networking issues

Trusted Network Interpretation (TNI)

Also part of the Rainbow Series, Trusted Network Interpretation (TNI) addresses confidentiality and integrity in trusted computer/communications network systems. Within the Rainbow Series, it's known as the *Red Book*.

European Information Technology Security Evaluation Criteria (ITSEC)

The European Information Technology Security Evaluation Criteria (ITSEC) was developed during the late 1980s, and the current issue was published in 1991. Unlike TCSEC, ITSEC addresses confidentiality, integrity, and availability, and evaluates an entire system, defined as a *Target of Evaluation* (TOE), rather than a single computing platform. ITSEC evaluates *functionality* (security objectives, or *why*; security enforcing functions, or *what*; and security mechanisms, or *how*); and *assurance* (effectiveness and correctness) separately. The ten functionality (F) classes and seven evaluation (E) (assurance) levels are as follows in Table 8-3.

Table 8-3		ITSEC Functionality (F) Classes and Evaluation (E) Levels
(F) Class	*(E) Level*	*Description*
NA	E0	Equivalent to TCSEC level D
F-C1	E1	Equivalent to TCSEC level C1
F-C2	E2	Equivalent to TCSEC level C2
F-B1	E3	Equivalent to TCSEC level B1
F-B2	E4	Equivalent to TCSEC level B2
F-B3	E5	Equivalent to TCSEC level B3
F-B3	E6	Equivalent to TCSEC level A1
F-IN	NA	TOEs with high integrity requirements
F-AV	NA	TOEs with high availability requirements
F-DI	NA	TOEs with high integrity requirements during data communication
F-DC	NA	TOEs with high confidentiality requirements during data communication
F-DX	NA	Networks with high confidentiality and integrity requirements

You don't need to know specific requirements of each ITSEC level for the CISSP exam, but you should know how the basic functionality levels (F– C1 through F–B3) and evaluation levels (E0–E6) correlate to TCSEC levels.

Common Criteria

The Common Criteria for Information Technology Security Evaluation (*Common Criteria*) is an international effort to standardize and improve existing European and North American evaluation criteria. The final draft was published in 1997 and has been adopted as an international standard in ISO15408. The Common Criteria defines eight assurance (EAL) levels as follows in Table 8-4.

Table 8-4		The Common Criteria	
Level	*TCSEC Equivalent*	*ITSEC Equivalent*	*Description*
EAL0	NA	NA	Inadequate assurance
EAL1	NA	NA	Functionally tested
EAL2	C1	E1	Structurally tested
EAL3	C2	E2	Methodically tested and checked
EAL4	B1	E3	Methodically designed, tested, and reviewed
EAL5	B2	E4	Semi-formally designed and tested
EAL6	B3	E5	Semi-formally verified design and tested
EAL7	A1	E6	Formally verified design and tested

You don't need to know specific requirements of each Common Criteria level for the CISSP exam, but you should understand the basic evaluation hierarchy (EAL0–7, in order of increasing levels of trust).

Certification and Accreditation

Certification is a formal methodology for comprehensive testing and documentation of information system security safeguards, both technical and non-technical, in a given environment using established evaluation criteria (TCSEC).

Accreditation is an official, written approval for the operation of a specific system in a specific environment as documented in the certification report. Accreditation is normally granted by a senior executive or *Designated Approving Authority* (DAA). The term *DAA* is used in the US military and government and is normally a senior official, such as a Commanding Officer.

System certification and accreditation must be updated when any changes are made to the system or environment and must also be periodically re-validated, which typically happens every three years.

The certification and accreditation process has been formally implemented in US military and government organizations as the Defense Information Technology Security Certification and Accreditation Process (DITSCAP) and National Information Assurance Certification and Accreditation Process (NIACAP), respectively.

DITSCAP

The Defense Information Technology Security Certification and Accreditation Process (DITSCAP) formalizes the certification and accreditation process for US DoD information systems through four distinct phases:

1. **Definition.** Determines security requirements by defining the organization and system's mission, environment, and architecture

2. **Verification.** Ensures that a system undergoing development or modification remains compliant with the System Security Authorization Agreement (SSAA), which is a baseline security configuration document

3. **Validation.** Confirms compliance with the SSAA

4. **Post-accreditation.** Ongoing activities required to maintain compliance and address new and evolving threats throughout a system's life cycle

NIACAP

The National Information Assurance Certification and Accreditation Process (NIACAP) formalizes the certification and accreditation process for US government national security information systems. NIACAP consists of four phases (Definition, Verification, Validation, and Post-accreditation) that generally correspond to the DITSCAP phases. Additionally, NIACAP defines three types of accreditation:

- **Site accreditation:** Evaluates all applications and systems at a specific location
- **Type accreditation:** Evaluates a specific application or system for multiple locations
- **System accreditation:** Evaluates a specific application or system at a specific location

Additional References

Krutz, Ronald L. and Vines, Russell Dean. *The CISSP Prep Guide: Mastering the Ten Domains of Computer Security,* Chapter 5. John Wiley & Sons, Inc.

Gilster, Ron. *A+ Certification For Dummies*, Chapters 6–9. Hungry Minds, Inc.

Anderson, Ross. *Security Engineering: A Guide to Building Dependable Distributed Systems*, Chapters 7 and 23. John Wiley & Sons, Inc.

Russell, Deborah and Gangemi Sr, G.T. *Computer Security Basics*, Chapter 6. O'Reilly and Associates.

Parker, Donn B. *Fighting Computer Crime: A New Framework for Protecting Information,* pages 256–260. John Wiley & Sons, Inc.

Prep Test

1 The four CPU operating states include all the following except

A ○ Operating
B ○ Problem
C ○ Wait
D ○ Virtual

2 *A computer system that alternates execution of multiple subprograms on a single processor* describes what type of system?

A ○ Multiprogramming
B ○ Multitasking
C ○ Multiuser
D ○ Multiprocessing

3 An address used as the origin for calculating other addresses describes

A ○ Base addressing
B ○ Indexed addressing
C ○ Indirect addressing
D ○ Direct addressing

4 The four main functions of the operating system include all the following except

A ○ Process management
B ○ BIOS management
C ○ I/O device management
D ○ File management

5 *The total combination of protection mechanisms within a computer system, including hardware, firmware, and software, which is responsible for enforcing a security policy* defines

A ○ Reference monitor
B ○ Security kernel
C ○ Trusted Computing Base
D ○ Protection domain

6 *A system that continues to operate following failure of a network component describes which type of system?*

A ○ Fault-tolerant
B ○ Fail-safe
C ○ Fail-soft
D ○ Failover

7 Which of the following access control models addresses availability issues?

A ○ Bell-LaPadula
B ○ Biba
C ○ Clark-Wilson
D ○ None of the above

8 The four basic control requirements identified in the Orange Book include all the following except

A ○ Role-based access control
B ○ Discretionary access control
C ○ Mandatory access control
D ○ Object reuse

9 All the following Orange Book classes require mandatory access control protection except

A ○ B2
B ○ B3
C ○ A1
D ○ A2

10 Which of the following ITSEC classification levels is equivalent to TCSEC level B3?

A ○ E3
B ○ E4
C ○ E5
D ○ E6

Answers

1 **D.** Virtual. The four CPU operating states are operating (or run), problem (or application, supervisory, and wait. *Review "CPU."*

2 **B.** Multitasking. A multiprogramming computer alternates execution of multiple programs on a single processor. A multiuser computer supports several users. A multiprocessing computer executes multiple programs on multiple processors. *Review "CPU."*

3 **A.** Base addressing. Indexed addressing specifies an address relative to an index register. Indirect addressing specifies the address of the desired location. Direct addressing specifies the desired location. *Review "Memory."*

4 **B.** BIOS management. The four main functions of an OS are process management, I/O device management, memory management, and file management. The system BIOS operates independently of the OS. *Review "Software."*

5 **C.** Trusted Computing Base. A reference monitor enforces access controls on an object. A security kernel implements the reference monitor concept. A protection ring is a security concept that implements the principle of least privilege. *Review "Trusted Computing Base (TCB)."*

6 **A.** Fault-tolerant. A fail-safe system terminates program execution. A fail-soft system continues functioning in a degraded mode. A failover system automatically switches to a hot backup. *Review "Recovery procedures."*

7 **D.** None of the above. Bell-LaPadula addresses confidentiality issues. Biba and Clark-Wilson address integrity issues. *Review "Access Control Models."*

8 **A.** Role-based access control. The four basic control requirements identified in the Orange Book are discretionary access control, mandatory access control, object reuse, and labels. *Review "Trusted Computer System Evaluation Criteria (TCSEC)."*

9 **D.** A2. Orange Book levels B1, B2, B3, and A1 all require mandatory access control protection. A2 is a non-existent level. *Review "Trusted Computer System Evaluation Criteria (TCSEC)."*

10 **C.** E5. E3 is equivalent to TCSEC level B1, E4 to B2, and E6 to A1. *Review "European Information Technology Security Evaluation Criteria (ITSEC)."*

Chapter 9

Operations Security

. . . .

In This Chapter

▶ Security operations concepts

▶ Threats and countermeasures

▶ Security operations management

▶ Controls

▶ Auditing

▶ Audit trails

▶ Monitoring

. . . .

*T*he Operations Security domain introduces several key concepts, and it also overlaps other domains, particularly access control — and, to a lesser extent, business continuity planning.

From the Certified Information Security Specialist Professional (CISSP) study guide: "The candidate will be expected to know the resources that must be protected, the privileges that must be restricted, the control mechanisms available, the potential for abuse of access, the appropriate controls, and the principles of good practice."

This chapter discusses everything that an operations group would need to know about security: security operations concepts and management, security threats and countermeasures, security auditing, audit trails, and security monitoring.

Security Operations Concepts

Security operations cover a wide variety of concepts, which I describe in this section. The common theme to these concepts is the mission of protecting the integrity and confidentiality of information assets. Information is protected through the reduction of threats and vulnerabilities.

Anti-virus management

When it comes to viruses — and also worms and Trojan horses — the Internet is a real cesspool of diseases forever seeking fresh victims. Viruses are constantly on the loose, and any organization lacking a strong, multilayer, anti-virus defense will be constantly bombarded. Thus, the desktop and server support teams will spend a lot of time rebuilding systems. Downtime and productivity suffer as well.

To counter the threat of viruses and other malicious code, an organization must develop an effective anti-virus program consisting of enterprise-wide mechanisms to automatically push new signature files (the data containing "signatures" of all known viruses) to all desktop systems and Windows-based servers. Each organization should also seriously consider implementing anti-virus mechanisms on its file, e-mail, and Web proxy servers.

Viruses, worms, and Trojan horses are all examples of malicious code.

Backups of critical information

Things can and do go wrong, ranging from innocent mistakes, bugs in software, hardware failures, and full-blown disasters such as floods and hurricanes. More often than you think, users will make requests to have files restored. These users range from desktop users to computer operations and database administrators.

Management must be absolutely sure that all critical data is backed up as frequently as due care prescribes. Data that changes frequently may need to be backed up more than once per day — if not mirrored or replicated on other online storage systems. Data that doesn't change so frequently can be backed up somewhat less often . . . say, weekly or even monthly.

Performing backups is a form of *due care;* every IT organization should be performing them. See Chapter 11, in which I discuss due care and due diligence. How often must be assessed case by case.

Need-to-know

One of the classic concepts of information security is *need-to-know*. This principle states that only people with a need to know should have access to certain information.

The most difficult challenge with managing need-to-know is the use of controls that enforce need-to-know. Also, information owners need to be able to distinguish *need-to-know* from *want-to-know* and *I'm-just-curious*.

Least privilege

Least privilege is similar to need-to-know, but least privilege applies more to *functionality* and not so much with *access* to data. The principle of least privilege states that persons should have the ability to perform only the tasks that they require to perform their primary job and no more.

To give an individual more privileges than he requires is an invitation for trouble. Offering the temptation to be able to perform more than one requires may sooner or later result in an abuse of privilege.

An example of least privilege is the computer operator who manages a system's print queues. In the UNIX world, for administrative functions such as printing, the user must attain superuser privileges that give the person using it absolute power and control on a system. In UNIX, the root account is generally used to control the print queue. Although most organizations just give the root password to people who manage limited tasks such as managing printing and print queues, a much better approach is to give the root account to the user who manages the print queues.

The principle of least privilege states that persons should have the fewest privileges necessary for them to perform their tasks.

Privileged functions

When I mention *privileged functions*, I sometimes refer to superuser or administrative userids that have the ability to perform all available functions on a system. In this regard, access to privileged functions must be reserved to only those persons whose responsibilities include the management of those systems. Developers, users, and others shouldn't have access to privileged functions.

Privacy

Talk about a hot topic. Privacy has become the buzzword of the new millennium.

Organizations must use caution when collecting and storing personal or private information from employees or customers. Each item of personal or private information should only be collected when a true business need to do so exists. Further, although a justifiable reason may exist to collect and use this information, an organization must also justify *keeping* the information as well as every possible subsequent use of the information after it's stored.

The primary consideration when handling private information is the scourge of identity theft cases. In the United States alone, well over 100,000 cases of identity theft are reported each year.

One of the primary concerns of privacy is the increase in the incidents of identity theft.

Legal requirements

An organization may be bound by national, state, or local ordinances to perform certain functions, possibly even using particular methods. This may include how information is collected and used.

Illegal activities

Most organizations need to have a fraud detection capability to ensure that its employees and customers aren't trying to cheat the organization out of goods, services, or cash. A *fraud detection system* analyzes transactions and provides a list of possibly fraudulent transactions that someone can take a look at.

Organizations also need to examine their business processes and the roles and responsibilities of key personnel as they execute those processes. Among other things, business processes should make it difficult for employees to defraud the organization through *collusion* — it should be as difficult as possible for employees to work together for their illicit personal gain.

Record retention

Organizations are bound by law to collect and store certain pieces of information, as well as to keep it for specified periods of time. An organization must be aware of legal requirements and ensure that it's in compliance with all applicable regulatory bodies.

Handling sensitive information

Sensitive information such as financial records or employee or customer information must be handled according to these guidelines:

✔ **Marking:** This refers to the words that must appear on documents containing sensitive information. An example marking might read `Company confidential, handle according to instructions`.

✔ **Handling:** The organization should have established procedures for the handling of marked documents. These procedures would detail how such documents may be transported, faxed, e-mailed, and sent over networks.

✔ **Storage:** Similar to the handling guideline, the organization must have procedures and requirements specifying how marked information must be stored.

✔ **Destruction:** Sooner or later a document with sensitive information must be destroyed. The organization must have procedures detailing how to destroy sensitive information, whether hard or soft copy.

Threats and Countermeasures

Plenty of threats exist that, if carried out, could cause damage to the organization. I discuss some of these threats here.

Errors and Omissions

Errors and Omissions (E&O) is an insurance term that describes strategic and tactical errors that an organization can commit whether by commission (performing an action) or omission (failure to perform an action). In addition to general liability coverage, insurance companies also sell Errors and Omissions insurance. Errors and Omissions liability is also known as _Professional Liability_.

An example of Errors and Omissions is an error that prevents a company from delivering goods or services on a contract.

Some Errors and Omissions can be prevented through product reviews and quality processes that help to prevent calculation errors or the mishandling of information, for example.

Fraud

Fraud is defined as any deceptive or misrepresented activity that results in a customer knowingly getting products or services from a company for free or for a reduced price. Some examples of fraud include

✔ Writing bad checks

✔ Lying about one's information in order to receive a product or service for which the person is not entitled

Fraud is best countered with controls and processes to ensure that people aren't misrepresenting themselves or the information that they assert. Generally the controls used are those that attempt to confirm information.

Theft

Theft is the taking of property from its owner without the owner's consent. A wide variety of controls can deter and prevent theft, including locks, alarm systems, cameras, audit trails (in the case of information theft), and identifying marks on equipment.

Employee sabotage

Sabotage is the deliberate destruction of property, which could include physical or information assets. This is best deterred and detected with highly visible audit trails and prevented with strict access controls.

Industrial espionage

Industrial espionage is the act of obtaining proprietary or confidential information in order to pass it to a competitor. This is one of the most difficult things to prevent, but you can deter such activity with visible audit trails and access controls.

Loss of physical and infrastructure support

Loss of physical and infrastructure support is a broad category that represents the kinds of actions that result in a data processing operation losing its physical facilities and/or supporting infrastructure. This includes, but isn't limited to, interruptions in public utilities or events that result in the closure or evacuation of a building.

Hackers and crackers

Hackers are computer enthusiasts who enjoy learning the intricacies of computers and programming languages and can often be considered experts. In recent years, however, the term *hacker* has been associated more with individuals who break into computer systems and networks in order to cause disruption or steal information. Hackers insist that those malicious individuals are known as *crackers*.

Malicious code

Malicious code includes viruses, worms, and Trojan horses. Programs containing malicious code generally originate outside the organization and make their way in via e-mail, Web sites, or downloaded files. Malicious code also includes time bombs and logic bombs. These are sections of code in applications that, at a specific time or when certain conditions are met, perform some destructive act such as erasing or corrupting important software or data files.

Inappropriate worker activities

Company workers are capable of all sorts of inappropriate things, such as

- **Fraud:** Workers with detailed knowledge of business processes and/or insider access to information are in a particularly good position to be able to defraud their employer.

- **Collusion:** *Collusion* is the cooperation between two or more persons for some illegal or deceitful purpose.

- **Pornography:** 'Nuf said.

- **Sexual Harassment:** Ditto.

- **Wastefulness:** This covers everything from computer resources to office supplies, time, and money.

- **Theft:** This can include equipment or information.

- **Abuse:** This is a wide-ranging term covering this misuse of company resources for personal gain.

- **Espionage:** Wow. Yes, every employee has a price, and some will stoop to the level of selling information to other organizations.

Criminologists generally describe the criminal as having *means*, *motive*, and *opportunity* to commit a crime. Generally speaking, workers have more means and opportunities to commit damaging acts than do outsiders. They're already entrusted with access (read-only or read-write) to information and equipment. They only need a good opportunity. Outsider-hackers, on the other hand, may have the motivation to damage a company's information assets; but through security measures, they generally lack the means and the opportunity.

Security Operations Management

In this section, I describe some conceptual best practices for protecting the integrity of the business and of the information that makes it go. These best practices all have to do with how people — not technology — work to support the business.

Job requirements and specifications

Before an employer hires a new security-related person, the hiring manager should document the job requirements and specifications. This ensures that the hiring manager knows exactly what skills this position requires.

Background checking

Any organization should get background checks on all employees and contractors. This will help to expose any undesirable candidates based upon their pasts.

Background checks are necessary in order to obtain a detailed assessment of a potential worker.

Background checks can include verification of any of the following:

- Criminal record
- Citizenship
- Credit check
- Employment history
- Education
- Certifications
- Union and association membership

Separation of duties

Separation of duties (sometimes called *segregation of duties*) is the term used to describe the process of assigning parts of tasks to different people. This makes it more difficult for a lone individual to defraud or steal from the organization.

A great example of separation of duties is the way in which banks control safe combinations. Typically a safe has a six-number combination. The bank assigns the first three numbers to one employee and the second three numbers to another employee. A single employee isn't permitted to have all six numbers, so a lone employee is unable to enter the safe and steal its contents.

Job rotation

Job rotation refers to the practice of moving people from job function to job function, with or without notice. Job rotation accomplishes two things:

1. People hesitate to set up the means for periodically or routinely stealing corporate information because they know that they could be moved to another shift at almost any time.

2. People don't work with each other long enough to form collusive relationships that could damage the company.

Job rotation can also include changing workers' workstations and work locations, which are other means for keeping would-be saboteurs off-balance.

Mandatory vacations

Requiring employees to take one or more weeks of their vacation in a single block of time gives the organization an opportunity play Elliot Ness and see whether the employee is regularly committing any forbidden acts.

A week is usually plenty of time for the Information Security department to do a pretty extensive audit of an employee's activities. Knowing this fact deters some employees from performing the kinds of troublesome actions that would appear in such an audit.

Security violations

All known security violations should be documented, and a root-cause analysis should be performed in order to determine whether any changes in processes or technology are needed.

Termination

Employees who violate security policy are subject to termination. Usually this is a last-resort solution, but termination is necessary if the employee has a history of security problems.

Security Controls

Controls are steps in processes that are used to enforce compliance with business or security rules. The enforcement of the control can be based on technology, or it may be a manual step or procedure that an individual performs.

The three major types of controls are

- **Preventive controls:** Used to prevent errors and unauthorized actions.
- **Detective controls:** Used to detect errors and unauthorized activities.
- **Corrective controls:** Used to reverse or minimize the impact of errors and unauthorized events. These are also known as *recovery controls*.

All the controls in this section fall into one or more of these categories.

Operations controls are the processes and procedures that are used to protect business operations and information. The major operations controls are

- Resource protection
- Privileged entity controls
- Change controls
- Media controls
- Administrative controls
- Trusted recovery

Resource protection

Resource protection is the broad category of controls that protect information assets and information infrastructure. The resources that require protection include

- **Communications hardware and software:** This includes routers, switches, firewalls, multiplexers, fax machines, virtual private network (VPN) servers, and so on, as well as the software that these devices use.
- **Computers and their storage systems:** This includes all corporate servers, Redundant Array of Independent Disks (RAID) systems, storage area networks (SANs), network attached storage (NAS), and back-up devices.
- **Business data:** This includes all stored information such as financial data, sales and marketing information, personnel and payroll data, customer and supplier data, and so on.

- ✔ **System data:** This includes operating systems, utilities, userid and password files, audit trails, configuration files, and so forth.
- ✔ **Back-up media:** This includes tapes, removable disks, and so on.
- ✔ **Software:** This includes application source code, programs, tools, libraries, vendor software, and other proprietary software

Privileged entity controls

Privileged entity controls are the mechanisms, generally built into computer operating systems, which give privileged access to hardware, software, and data. In UNIX and Windows NT/2000, the controls that permit privileged functions reside in the operating system.

Change controls

Change controls are the people-operated processes that are used to govern architectural and configuration changes in a production environment. Rather than just make changes to systems and the way that they relate to each other, change control is a formal process of proposal, design, review, approval, and implementation.

The two prevalent forms of change controls are change management and configuration management.

- ✔ **Change management** is the approval-based process that ensures that only approved changes are implemented.
- ✔ **Configuration management** is the control that records all the soft configuration (settings and parameters in the operating system) and software changes that are performed with approval from the change management process.

Media controls

Media controls refer to a broad category of controls that are used to manage information classification and physical media. *Information classification* refers to the tasks of marking information according to its sensitivity, as well as the subsequent handling, storage, and disposal procedures that accompany each classification level. Physical media is similarly marked; likewise, controls specify handling, storage, and disposal procedures.

Administrative controls

Administrative controls refer to the family of controls that includes least privilege, separation of duties, and rotation of duties. These controls form the basis of many processes as well as access control and function control methodologies.

Trusted recovery

Trusted recovery is concerned with the processes and procedures that support the hardware or software recovery of a system. Specifically, the confidentiality and integrity of the information stored on and the functions served by a system being recovered must be preserved at all times.

The primary issue with system recovery is that a system may be operated briefly in maintenance or single-user mode in which all the software controls protecting the operating system and business data may not be functioning.

An organization that's concerned with the integrity and confidentiality of its data will have well-defined processes and procedures for system recovery.

Security Auditing

Auditing is the process of having a third-party examine systems and/or business processes to ensure that they've been properly designed and are being properly used.

Audits are frequently performed to ensure that the business is in compliance with business or security policies/requirements that the business may be subject to. These policies and requirements can include government laws and regulations, legal contracts, and industry or trade group best practices.

Audits are frequently performed by third parties, which gives the audit customers the confidence that the audit results are accurate and not biased because of organizational politics, and so on.

Business critical systems need to be subject to regular audits on a timetable to be dictated by regulatory, contractual, or trade group requirements.

Due care requires that an organization operate using good business practices — usually a set of standards formally or informally stated by industry trade groups. An organization can be held liable for failing to operate with due care.

Audit Trails

Audit trails are the auxiliary records that are created that record transactions and other auditable events. Of the many reasons for having audit trails, here are a few:

- ✔ **Enforcement of accountability:** Employees who know that audit trails capture the details of their actions tend to be more accountable for their actions.

- ✔ **Investigation:** Investigators who need to trace the actions of an individual's activities can rely upon audit trails to see what that person did.

- ✔ **Event reconstruction:** Analysts may need to understand and be able to reconstruct a complex event. Without audit trails, this could be an effort in futility . . . and humility.

- ✔ **Problem identification:** Audit trails can help an analyst or engineer get to the root cause of some sort of a problem.

Anatomy of an audit record

The basic components of an audit record are

- ✔ **Date and time** of the event
- ✔ **Who** performed the event
- ✔ **Where** the event was performed (for instance, which terminal was associated with the event)
- ✔ **Details** about the event (such as old and new values)

Audit or audit trail?

Audit is an activity and the output of the activity — the verification of accuracy of an application or system.

An *audit trail* is a record of events, without regards to correctness or accuracy. It's just a reporting of an event.

Audit trails — the justification for time synchronization

System and network administrators have long recognized the value in synchronizing the time-of-day clocks in their systems with the US National Bureau of Standards (NBS) atomic clock. Although this may be cool to do, the justification for doing so lies in the need for systems to have their time-of-day clocks synchronized to within fractions of a second.

Imagine a situation in which you're trying to piece together a complex set of events that took place on several computers. The order of events that take place on several systems is highly significant. But what if the time-of-day clocks on these systems are several seconds or minutes apart? If the systems' clocks aren't synchronized, it can be difficult to determine the order in which events occurred when several systems are involved.

Types of audit trails

Audit trails (also known as *audit logs*, or just *logs*) come in several shapes and sizes. They include the cryptic `sendmail` logs and `syslog` entries, login logs, network trace logs, and also transaction logs from applications.

Audit trails lack one important feature: consistency of format. It's as though everyone who ever wrote a program that generates an audit log crawled into a cave and invented his own audit log file format. Audit log formats have as much compatibility as taillight lenses share for Fords, Chevys, Toyotas, and Hondas.

This lack of consistency presents a great opportunity to become super-rich by writing the next killer app: audit log consolidation and correlation applications. Imagine ordinary citizens practically bowing down to you when they learn that you've written an audit log correlation utility — that, or they're just getting out of the way of your Humvee.

Finding trouble in them thar logs

After your audit logs are set up and the operating system tools, utilities, and applications are writing to them, how do you differentiate between normal humdrum events and events indicating big trouble?

This is really two problems in one.

First, how do you determine whether an audit log entry is a routine event or an event indicating a problem? You'll have to just work hard to figure these out. You have to RTFM (Read The . . . 'er, Remember This For Mañana) and learn from experience.

Second, do you really believe that someone is actually watching all your organization's audit logs? Not a chance. Nobody eats the parsley garnish on his plate, and nobody reads audit logs. So how do you find out whether something serious is going south? Perform *sampling* and look at the logs now and then.

This is a hard problem. Most modern operating systems lack the tools to *parse* (not to be confused with *parsle-y*) audit logs and send panic messages to your pager, SMS (Short Message Service — as in your cell phone that is also a pager) device, or e-mail inbox. You'll need to shop around for public domain (free, poor documentation, no support) or commercial (expensive, poor documentation, no support) software packages that collect, parse, and wake you up at midnight when something *really bad* is happening.

Problem management and audit trails

In this most fascinating topic of information security, I can practically hear readers asking in unison, "What do we do when we see trouble brewing in the audit log?"

You do two things. First, determine whether the audit trail entry indicates genuine trouble or whether the entry is a false-positive. Ask your more experienced colleagues for help. If real trouble exists, then presumably you have a sound-the-alarm escalation process, whereby you let the cat out of the bag and tell someone that the payroll application is on fire. (Accounts payable, of course, would have a much lower priority.)

Next, audit trails are used to troubleshoot and reconstruct events. Thus, a *root cause analysis* can be developed, which should lead to resolution of the problem — and eventually, the ability to avoid the problem in the future.

Without the audit trail, you're groping in the dark (a bad thing in the security business) — clueless as to what happened, and clueless as to how to avoid it. Time for a career change.

Retaining audit logs

The gigabytes of audit log material produced every day by a firewall or an intrusion detection system (IDS) is one thing that many administrators simply forget to consider, but they find out soon enough when their system runs out of disk space.

I can't tell you how long you should keep your audit logs, but it would be irresponsible for you to just chuck 'em without finding out from someone authoritative how long they should be kept. Audit log retention ultimately becomes a legal issue (complying with federal, state, and local laws) in many cases, especially with applications. Find out how long audit logs are supposed to be kept, and then figure out how to keep them.

Chances are that you'll back up audit logs to tape because having years' worth of audit logs on most systems is infeasible. This introduces a new problem: You need to pick a medium (tape or CD, for example) that will last for the required time period. No, tapes and even CDs aren't forever — they have finite lifetimes that are frequently less than the number of years that a lot of this stuff needs to be kept. Call in an expert if needed; it beats being out of compliance with the law, and you don't want Morley Safer knocking on your door someday asking you questions that you really cannot recall the answers to.

Part of the *Will my media last for* n *years?* problem is just that. Not only do you have to determine just how long the bits will stay on the tape, but you also have to worry about media obsolescence. In other words, if you back up your long-term storage audit log info to SuperDLT tape, you have to ask whether SuperDLT will even *exist* in 15 years. Will the local computer museum even have a working SuperDLT drive? Probably not. This is the quandary of long-term data storage: picking a medium that will be around in a decade for which you can still get hardware support and software drivers in the unlikely event that you will have to actually recover and read this data. Now you know the *real* reason why IT professionals change jobs every few years. Good luck.

Protection of audit logs

I'm really *not* talking down to you when I say that the protection of audit logs is an important issue. The integrity of audit logs is an absolute necessity, but this is another one of those difficult situations that may keep you up at night.

Audit logs must be protected against sabotage and other attacks that would prevent audit logs from properly recording events.

Here's the problem: Audit logs are just data files on a computer. A determined person who wants to either cause trouble or erase his tracks is going to look around for the audit logs and try to alter them. Do you really think you can absolutely prevent this? No way, but you can come close.

With some creativity and an expert on this topic, you can learn about techniques that the really important audit logs can use, such as writing them directly to a sequential access device (tape drive), a CD-ROM, or sneaking them off the subject system over the network to another system.

None of these techniques are foolproof, but these exotic methods can make it more difficult for determined intruders (or insiders) to cause the kind of trouble that they have in mind. But like using The Club on your car's steering wheel to deter theft, perhaps the no-good-doers will notice your nifty audit logging mechanism and move on.

Audit logging can be the object of a Denial of Service (DOS) attack, believe it or not. Here's what can happen. An intruder/insider who wishes to perform some illicit, usually audited transaction(s), is naturally worried about the audit log recording his dirty deed. However, he can launch a DOS attack on the audit log: Either he can perform thousands/millions of transactions or he can consume disk space in some other way to cause the audit trail mechanism to run out of available disk space. After the audit logging mechanism is gagged, the intruder can transact away, and the now-deaf audit log won't hear a thing.

I circle back to the idea that protecting audit logs is vitally important. If they're disk-based, some mechanism (usually tape/CD backup) needs to quickly grab them off the system in case an intruder is going to try to destroy them.

If your intruder is truly nasty and wants to burn down the data center after performing his secret transactions, this should cause you to consider that on-site storage of audit logs is really insufficient. Even without intruders, accidental fires, earthquakes, floods, and other events can ruin both your servers and the audit logs on CDs or tapes in the same room. Off-site storage isn't just an option but a necessity.

Because audit trails are among the most fascinating topics in Information Technology, I wouldn't blame you if you read this section again. But don't read *this* paragraph again or you'll never get to the next section, Monitoring.

Monitoring

Monitoring covers much wider ground than just periodic or constant inspection of audit logs. Monitoring includes the following activities:

- Penetration testing
- Intrusion detection
- Violation processing
- Keystroke monitoring
- Traffic and trend analysis
- Facilities monitoring

The remainder of this section is dedicated to the discussion of these activities.

Packet sniffing isn't all bad

Packet sniffing isn't just a tool used by hackers to pick up userids and passwords from the LAN. Packet sniffing has legitimate uses as well. Primarily, it's used as a diagnostic tool to troubleshoot a problem, such as a firewall (to see whether the desired packets are getting through), routers, switches, and VLANs.

The obvious danger of the packet sniffer falling into the wrong hands is the capability to capture userids and passwords. Equally perilous is the fact that packet sniffers are next to impossible to detect on a network.

Penetration testing

Penetration testing is the general term describing the use of tools that are designed to discover and identify security vulnerabilities.

Penetration testing techniques include

- **Port scanning:** This is a tool that communicates over the network with one or more target systems on various Transmission Control Protocol/Internet Procotol (TCP/IP) ports. A port scan will discover the presence of ports that should probably be deactivated (because they serve no useful or necessary purpose on a particular system) or upgraded/patched (because of a software vulnerability that could lead to a break-in). Some example port scanning tools include SATAN, ISS, and NMAP.

- **Packet sniffing:** A *packet sniffer* is a tool that captures all TCP/IP packets on a network, not just those being sent to the system or device doing the sniffing. Recall that an Ethernet is a shared-media network, which means that all packets on the local area network (LAN) can theoretically be viewed by any or all devices on the LAN. But switched-media Ethernets are becoming more prevalent today for performance reasons; sniffers on switched-media LANs generally pick up only packets intended for the device running the sniffer. I digress; sorry.

  One other term that you need to be familiar with is *promiscuous mode*. This is the altered state in which the network adaptor accepts all packets and sends them to the operating system, not just the packets destined for the system. The reason *promiscuous mode* was chosen to describe this network adaptor setting is an exercise left to the reader.

- **War dialing:** War dialing is one of the oldest hacking techniques. Hackers use *war dialing* to sequentially dial all phone numbers in a range to discover all the modems that are available. The hacker then uses the list of discovered modems to see whether any of them are easily penetrated and are connected to systems or networks worth the trouble to connect to.

✔ **War driving:** *War driving* is the 21st century version of war dialing, wherein someone uses a laptop computer equipped with a wireless LAN card and literally drives around a densely populated area in order to discover unprotected (or poorly protected) wireless LANs. (But is it still called *war driving* if the perpetrator is riding the bus?)

✔ **Radiation monitoring:** *Radio frequency (RF) emanations* describe the electromagnetic radiation emitted by computers and network devices. *Radiation monitoring* is similar to packet sniffing and war driving in that someone uses sophisticated equipment to try to determine what data is being displayed on monitors, transmitted on LANs, or processed in computers.

✔ **Dumpster diving:** *Dumpster diving* is low-tech penetration testing at its best, but still it's sometimes a fruitful way to obtain information about an organization. Organizations in highly competitive environments also need to be concerned about where recycled paper goes and decide whether it should be shredded onsite first.

✔ **Eavesdropping:** *Eavesdropping* is as low-tech as dumpster diving but a little more dignified. Basically an eavesdropper takes advantage of one or more persons who are talking or using a computer — and paying little attention to the fact that someone else may be listening to their conversations or watching them work over their shoulder. The technical term for the latter is *shoulder surfing*.

✔ **Social engineering:** If eavesdropping is passive, then *social engineering* is the active way of getting information from workers. The classic tale of social engineering is the clever individual who makes a number of phone calls, each time pretending to be someone different, in order to piece together the information needed to remotely access a corporate LAN. From one person, the intruder gets the remote access phone number; from others, he gets needed facts about the corporate network; and finally, he poses as a new employee or an employee traveling, calling the help desk to request a password reset. The information that he puts together gives him all he needs to (ahem) legitimately log on to the corporate network. What he does next is up to your imagination.

Intrusion detection

Intrusion detection is the emerging and now popular technique used to detect unauthorized activity on a network. An intrusion detection system is frequently called an *IDS*. The two types of IDSes used today are

↙ *Network-based* **intrusion detection:** This consists of a separate device attached to a LAN that listens to all network traffic by using various methods (which I describe later in this section) to detect anomalous activity.

↙ *Host-based* **intrusion detection:** This is really a subset of network-based IDS, in which only the network traffic destined for a particular host is monitored.

Both network and host-based IDSes use a number of methods:

↙ **Signature-based:** *Signature-based* IDSes compare network traffic that is observed with a list of patterns in a signature file. A signature-based IDS is able to detect any of a known set of attacks, but if an intruder is able to change the patterns that he uses in his attack, then his attack may be able to slip by the IDS without being detected. The other downside of signature-based IDS is that the signature file must be periodically updated.

↙ **Anomaly-based:** *Anomaly-based* IDSes monitor all the traffic over the network and build traffic profiles. Over time, the IDS will report deviations from the profiles that it has built. The upside of anomaly-based IDSes is that there are no signature files to periodically upgrade. The downside is that you may have a high volume of false-positives.

I am obligated to tell you that intrusion detection doesn't stop intruders, but intrusion prevention does stop them . . . or at least it slows them down. *Intrusion prevention* is the collection of security mechanisms that are designed to keep the bad people out and let the good people in. These mechanisms, which I discuss in other chapters in this book, are

↙ **Authentication systems:** Userids and passwords, and possibly also smart cards, tokens, or biometrics (such as fingerprint readers, retina scanners, face scanners, and palm print readers). For more, read through Chapter 3.

↙ **Authorization:** Tools used to enforce users' least privilege settings, preventing them from viewing/changing data and executing functions that they don't require. For more on least privilege, see the earlier section "Least privilege." Find further discussion of privileges in Chapter 3.

↙ **Firewalls:** The systems that filter network traffic and let in (or out) only the network traffic necessary to support the business. Read about the role of the firewall administrator in Chapters 3 and 6.

↙ **VPN:** The modern-day remote access and branch office to headquarters mechanisms that both authenticate and encrypt network traffic. Find more about VPNs in Chapter 4.

Intrusion detection is used to detect known attacks and/or anomalous behavior on a network or host.

Violation analysis

Violation analysis is the science of examining activity and audit logs to discover inappropriate activities. Violation analysis uses *clipping levels*, which are the thresholds that differentiate violations from non-events.

Here's an example. Users on a particular system sometimes type in their passwords incorrectly, so a few errors are allowed. But wisely, you set a clipping level of four failed login attempts per hour. Whenever a user has fewer than four failed attempts, everything's cool. But when the clipping level is exceeded, then a violation has occurred. In this particular example, the violation may indicate that someone is trying to break in to the system by guessing passwords.

Keystroke monitoring

Keystroke monitoring is used to record all input activities on a terminal or workstation. Keystroke monitoring is potentially resource intensive, it can be difficult to hide, and issues exist regarding the privacy rights of the person(s) whose activities are being monitored at this level of scrutiny.

Keystroke monitoring must be used with care — perhaps only as an aid for an active investigation. Only if you want to see yourself on TV should you consider routinely installing keystroke-monitoring software on workstations.

Traffic and trend analysis

Traffic and *trend analysis* are the techniques used to make inferences about the activities of an individual or an organization based upon the type and volume of traffic on a network. For instance, a dramatic rise in network traffic at 2 a.m. might be an indication of backups or batch processing.

Traffic and trend analysis aren't limited to technology. One can observe the comings and going of people at an office location, or perhaps note the number and type of delivery trucks and services. For instance, you can figure that if office furniture and supply trucks are frequenting a building, then that organization is hiring or remodeling. Stretch limos are an indicator of VIPs or foreign dignitaries that may indicate big business details ahead; ambulances may indicate hazardous conditions; pizza deliveries at all hours could mean that they're working hard on something hot; and police cars might mean that the people inside aren't getting along so well.

Facilities monitoring

No monitoring plan is complete without some physical monitoring capabilities. A few methods are

- ✔ Watching the logs of buildings with card-key access control to see whether doors are being propped open or if people are attempting to enter restricted areas
- ✔ Monitoring unmanned entrances and other locations with closed-circuit television (CCTV) monitoring systems
- ✔ Staffing key locations with security guards
- ✔ Installing and monitoring security alarm sensors on doors, windows, and motion sensors in areas not normally manned

Responding to events

Okay, so through your foresight and leadership (and the excellent book that you're reading right now), your organization has full security monitoring capabilities. What do you do when one of the monitoring systems indicates that a security event is unfolding? How will you recognize and respond?

The process of detecting, responding, and fixing a problem is known as *problem management*.

Like business continuity planning and disaster recovery planning (read more about this in Chapter 10), security event recognition requires advance planning:

- ✔ **Monitoring personnel:** Who is monitoring which events, audit logs, and other facilities?
- ✔ **Initial response:** What are the first steps to be performed when a suspicious event is seen? Written procedures would be a good idea here.

✔ **Confirmation:** Who will perform this task, and how will they do it? Someone needs to determine whether the event is a false alarm or not.

✔ **Notification:** How will the appropriate persons or the community affected be notified? Who bears this responsibility? Presuming that the system generating the alarm is being used by someone, key personnel and/or the user community may need to be notified in the event that the event will continue to unfold and interrupt service.

✔ **Escalation:** Who defines which senior managers need to be notified and when? If the event crosses predetermined thresholds, higher levels of management may need to be notified.

✔ **Resolution:** What are the plans for resolution? Most of the time, someone will need to *do* something to manage the event. This could be a server shutdown and reboot, locking a user account, suspending a service, or any number of other actions.

✔ **Event reporting:** Will there be standard reporting formats, and by what means will reports be delivered? How various events will be reported needs to be worked out in advance, too.

✔ **Event review:** How will the event be reviewed in terms of action and prevention? At the conclusion of the event, stakeholders need to discuss the event to determine whether the response was appropriate and whether the event (or ones like it) can be avoided in the future.

Additional References

Krutz, Ronald L. and Vines, Russell Dean. *The CISSP Prep Guide: Mastering the Ten Domains of Computer Security*, Chapter 6. John Wiley & Sons, Inc.

Tipton, Harold F., and Krause, Micki. *Information Security Management Handbook,* 4th Edition, Chapters 22 and 23. Auerbach Publications.

McCrie, Robert D. *Security Operations Management*. Butterworth-Heinemann.

Northcutt, Stephen. *Network Intrusion Detection: An Analysts' Handbook*. New Riders.

Gallegos, Frederick, et al. *Information Technology Control and Audit*. CDC Press.

Prep Test

1 The two types of intrusion detection are

   A ○ Attack-based systems and response-based systems

   B ○ Signature-based systems and anomaly-based systems

   C ○ Knowledge-based systems and scripture-based systems

   D ○ Passive monitoring systems and active monitoring systems

2 Recording data traveling on a network is known as

   A ○ Promiscuous mode

   B ○ Packet sniffing

   C ○ Packet snoring

   D ○ Packing sneaking

3 Which of the following is NOT an example of penetration testing?

   A ○ Radiation monitoring

   B ○ War driving

   C ○ Port scanning

   D ○ War diving

4 Trusted recovery is concerned with

   A ○ The ability of a system to be rebuilt

   B ○ The vulnerability of a system while it's being rebuilt

   C ○ The ability of a system to rebuild itself

   D ○ The willingness of a system to rebuild itself

5 The third-party inspection of a system is known as a(n)

   A ○ Confidence check

   B ○ Integrity trail

   C ○ Audit trail

   D ○ Audit

6 One of the primary concerns with long-term audit log retention is

   A ○ Whether anyone will be around who can find them

   B ○ Whether any violations of privacy laws have occurred

   C ○ Whether anyone will be around who understands them

   D ○ Whether any tape/disk drives will be available to read them

7 The required operating state of a network interface on a system running a sniffer is

A ○ Open mode

B ○ Promiscuous mode

C ○ Licentious mode

D ○ Pretentious mode

8 Filling a system's hard drive so that it can no longer record audit records is known as a(n)

A ○ Audit lock-out

B ○ Audit exception

C ○ Denial of Facilities attack

D ○ Denial of Service attack

9 An investigator who needs to have access to detailed employee event information may need to use

A ○ Keystroke monitoring

B ○ Intrusion detection

C ○ Keystroke analysis

D ○ Trend analysis

10 Which of the following is NOT true about a signature-based IDS?

A ○ It reports a low number of false-positives.

B ○ It requires periodic updating of its signature files.

C ○ It reports a high number of false-positives.

D ○ It can't detect anomalies based on trends.

Answers

1 **B.** Signature-based systems and anomaly-based systems. The two types of IDS systems are signature-based and anomaly-based. *Review "Intrusion detection."*

2 **B.** Packet sniffing. Packet sniffing is the technique used to record network traffic. *Review "Penetration testing."*

3 **D.** War diving. War diving isn't a testing technique, but radiation monitoring, war driving, and port scanning are. *Review "Penetration testing."*

4 **B.** The vulnerability of a system while it's being rebuilt. Most operating systems in single-user mode lack the security controls present in a system that's fully operational. *Review "Security Controls."*

5 **D.** Audit. An *audit* is an inspection of a system or process. *Review "Security Auditing."*

6 **D.** Whether any tape/disk drives will be available to read them. The challenge with audit log retention is choosing a medium that will be readable many years in the future. *Review "Retaining audit logs."*

7 **B.** Promiscuous mode. This is the term that describes the state of a system that is accepting all packets on the network, not just those packets destined for the system. *Review "Penetration testing."*

8 **D.** Denial of Service attack. Filling a system's hard disk is one way to launch a Denial of Service attack on an audit log mechanism. This will prevent the mechanism from being able to write additional entries to the log. *Review "Protection of audit logs."*

9 **A.** Keystroke monitoring. Keystroke monitoring records every key press and mouse movement. *Review "Keystroke monitoring."*

10 **C.** It reports a high number of false-positives. Signature-based IDSes generally have a low number of false-positives. *Review "Intrusion detection."*

Chapter 10

Business Continuity Planning and Disaster Recovery Planning

● ●

In This Chapter

▶ Defining events

▶ Discovering the difference between BCP and DRP

▶ Understanding the Business Continuity Project

▶ Defining Business Impact Assessment

▶ Defining BCP Recovery Plan Development

▶ Developing and implementing the Business Continuity Plan

▶ Planning for disaster recovery

▶ Testing your disaster recovery plan

● ●

*B*usiness Continuity Planning (BCP) and Disaster Recovery Planning (DRP) together provide the organization with the means to continue and recover business operations when a disaster strikes. BCP and DRP are both intensive and highly detailed planning initiatives that result in important-looking three-ring binders full of business continuation and recovery procedures for every participant's bookshelf.

Business Continuity Planning and Disaster Recovery Planning exist for one reason: Bad things happen. Organizations with a desire to survive a disastrous incident need to make formal and extensive plans — contingency plans to keep the business running, and recovery plans to return operations to normal.

Defining Disastrous Events

An amazing variety of disasters can beset an organization's business operations. They fall into two main categories: natural and man-made.

After reading this section, you should no longer be skeptical about the need for Business Continuity Planning and Disaster Recovery Planning.

Natural disasters

In many cases, formal methodologies are used to predict the likelihood of a particular disaster. For example, *50-year flood plain* is a term that you've probably heard that's used to describe the maximum physical limits of a river flood that's likely to occur in a 50-year period. The likelihood of each of these disasters depends greatly upon local and regional geography:

- Fires and explosions
- Hazardous materials spills
- Earthquakes
- Storms (snow, ice, hail, prolonged rain, wind)
- Floods
- Hurricanes, typhoons, and cyclones
- Volcanoes and lava flows
- Tornadoes
- Landslides
- Avalanches
- Tsunamis

Many of these occurrences may have secondary effects, and often it's these secondary effects that disrupt business operations. Some of these ramifications are

- **Utility outages:** Electric power, natural gas, water, and so on
- **Communications outages:** Telephone, cable, wireless, TV, and radio
- **Transportation outages:** Road, airport, train, and port closures
- **Evacuations/unavailability of personnel:** From both home and work locations

Man-made disasters

If natural disasters weren't enough, several other things can disrupt business operations, all as a result of deliberate acts.

- Bombings, sabotage, and other destructive acts
- Strikes, sick-outs, and other protest-related absences of large numbers of employees

Disaster recovery planning and 9-11-2001

The terrorist attacks in New York, Washington DC, and Pennsylvania — and the subsequent collapse of the World Trade Center buildings — had Disaster Recovery Planning and Business Continuity Planning officials all over the world scrambling to update their plans.

The attacks redefined the limits of extreme, deliberate acts of destruction. Previously, the most heinous attacks imaginable were more on the scale of large-scale bombings such as the 1993 attack on the World Trade Center or the 1995 bombing of the Alfred P. Murrah Federal Building in Oklahoma City.

The collapse of the World Trade Center resulted in the loss of life of 40 percent of the employees of the Sandler O'Neill & Partners investment bank. Bond broker Cantor Fitzgerald lost 658 employees in the attack. The sudden loss of a large number of employees had never been figured into BCP and DRP plans before. The previously unheard-of scenario, "What do we do if significant numbers of employees are suddenly lost?" had to be figured into contingency and recovery plans.

In traditional BCP and DRP plans, there were nearly always plenty of insiders around to keep the business rolling. 9-11 changed all that forever.

The Differences between BCP and DRP

Business Continuity Planning and Disaster Recovery Planning are two sides of the same coin. Each springs into action when a disaster strikes. The difference between Business Continuity Planning and DRP can be expressed in the following two statements:

- **BCP:** Business Continuity Planning is concerned with keeping business operations running — perhaps in another location or by using different tools and processes — after a disaster has struck.
- **DRP:** Disaster Recovery Planning is concerned with restoring normal business operations after the disaster takes place.

While the Business Continuity team is busy keeping business operations running via one of possibly several contingency plans, the Disaster Recovery team members are busy restoring the original facilities and equipment so that they can resume normal operations.

BCP and DRP projects have these common elements:

- Identification of **critical business functions** via the Business Impact Assessment and Vulnerability Assessment
- Identification of **possible disaster scenarios**
- **Experts** who understand the organization's critical business processes

---

BCP and DRP: An analogy

Here's the scenario: The business in question is a delivery service with one delivery truck that delivers goods around the city.

Business Continuity Planning is concerned with keeping the delivery service running in case something happens to the truck, presumably with a back-up truck, substitute drivers, maps to get around traffic jams, and other contingencies that can keep the delivery function running.

Disaster Recovery Planning, on the other hand, is concerned with fixing the original delivery truck. This might involve making repairs or even buying/leasing a new truck.

This is where the similarities end. The BCP project diverges on *continuing* business operations whereas the DRP is *recovering* the original business functions.

Understanding BCP Project Elements

Before a BCP project can begin, some basic definitions and assumptions have to be made and understood by everyone on the project team. They are

- ✓ **Project team membership:** Which persons will be chosen to be on the BCP project team? All relevant functions and business units must be represented.

- ✓ **Senior management support:** The development of a Business Continuity Plan is time-consuming, with no immediate or tangible return on investment (ROI). For a BCP project to be successful, it needs the support of senior management, including adequate budget, manpower, and visible statements backing the project. Senior management needs to make explicit statements identifying the responsible parties, as well as on the importance of the BCP project, priorities, urgency, and timing.

- ✓ **Senior management involvement:** Senior management can't just bless the BCP project. Because senior managers and directors may be implicitly and explicitly responsible for the organization's ability to recover from a disaster, senior management needs to have a degree of direct involvement in the BCP planning effort. The careers that these people save may be their own.

- ✓ **Who brings the donuts:** Because it's critical that BCP meetings are well attended, this is an essential success component.

A BCP project typically has four components: scope determination, the Business Impact Assessment, the Business Continuity Plan, and implementation. I discuss each of these components here.

Determining BCP Scope

The success and effectiveness of a Business Continuity Plan depends greatly upon whether its scope is properly defined. Business processes and technology can muddy the waters and make this task difficult. For instance, distributed systems and genuine dependence on at least some desktop systems for vital business functions expands the scope beyond core functions. Geographically dispersed companies — often the result of mergers — complicate matters as well.

Also, large companies are understandably more complex. The boundaries between where a function begins and ends are oftentimes fuzzy and sometimes poorly defined.

Political pressures can influence the scope as well. A department that *thinks* that it's vital but which is outside the BCP scope may lobby to be included therein, appropriately or otherwise. Everybody wants to be important, and some just want to *appear* to be important.

Scope *creep* can become scope *leap* if the BCP project team is weak or inexperienced. For the success of the project, strong leaders must make rational decisions about the scope of the project. Remember that the scope of BCP projects can be changed in later iterations of the project.

Defining the Business Impact Assessment

The *Business Impact Assessment* (BIA) describes the impact that a disaster has on business operations. The impact includes quantitative and qualitative elements. The *quantitative impact* is generally financial, such as loss of revenue. The *qualitative impact* has more to do with the delivery of goods and/or services and things such as the following.

Vulnerability Assessment

Often a BIA includes a *Vulnerability Assessment* that's used to get a handle on obvious and not-so-obvious weaknesses in business critical systems. Like a Risk Assessment, a Vulnerability Assessment has quantitative (financial) and qualitative (operational) sections.

The purpose of a Vulnerability Assessment is to determine the impact — both quantitative and qualitative — of the loss of a critical business function.

Quantitative losses include

- ✔ Loss of revenue
- ✔ Loss of operating capital
- ✔ Loss because of personal liabilities
- ✔ Increase in expenses
- ✔ Penalties because of violations of business contracts
- ✔ Violations of laws and regulations

Qualitative losses include loss of

- ✔ Competitive advantages
- ✔ Market share
- ✔ Prestige and reputation

The Vulnerability Assessment identifies *critical support areas*, which are business functions that, if lost, would cause irreparable harm to the business by jeopardizing critical business processes or the lives and safety of personnel. Critical support areas should be studied carefully in the Vulnerability Assessment to identify the resources that they require to continue functioning.

Quantitative losses include an increase in operating expenses attributable to any higher costs associated with executing the contingency plan.

Criticality Assessment

The BCP team should inventory all high-level business functions (for example, customer support, order processing, returns, accounts receivable, and so forth) and rank them in order of criticality, and also describe the impact of a disruption of each function on overall business operations.

Essential to the Criticality Assessment is an analysis of the impact of a disruption based upon its duration. You can see the vast difference in business impact of a disruption lasting one minute compared with one hour, one day, one week, or longer. Generally, the criticality of a business function depends upon the degree of impact that its impairment has on the business.

Identifying key players

Although you can consider a variety of angles when evaluating vulnerability and criticality, commonly you start with a high-level organization chart (hip people call this the *org chart*). In most companies, the major functions pretty much follow the structure of the organization.

Following an org chart helps the BCP project team to consider all the steps in a critical process. A walk through the org chart, stopping at each manager's or director's position and asking, "What does he do?" and "What does she do?" will help to jog your memory and to better see all the parts of the big picture.

One important thing that you can easily overlook is the inclusion of outsourced functions when cruising an org chart. For instance, if Accounts Payable (A/P) is outsourced, you might miss it if you don't see it on an org chart. Okay, maybe this is a bad example because the absence of *all* of A/P would probably be noticed. But if *part* of A/P — say, a group that detects and investigates A/P fraud (looking for payment patterns that would suggest the presence of phony payment requests) — were outsourced, *that* vital function would probably not be on the org chart.

Setting Maximum Tolerable Downtime

An extension of the Criticality Assessment is a statement of Maximum Tolerable Downtime (MTD) for each critical business function. *Maximum Tolerable Downtime* is the maximum period of time that a critical business function can be inoperative before the company fails to be viable.

If you're having trouble understanding this, imagine your favorite online merchant — a bookseller, an auction house, or an online trading company — being down for an hour or a day or a week. At some point, you have to figure that a prolonged disruption will literally sink the ship and that the business won't survive. This is what MTD is all about.

The Maximum Tolerable Downtime assessment should be a major factor that determines the criticality — and priority — of business functions. A function that can only withstand two hours of downtime obviously has a higher priority than another function that can withstand several days of downtime.

Maximum Tolerable Downtime is a measure of the longest period of time that a critical business function can be disrupted without threatening the survivability of the organization.

Defining the Resource Requirements

The *Resource Requirements* portion of the BIA is a listing of the resources that are required to continue operating each critical business function. In an organization with finite resources (which is pretty much everyone), the most critical functions are going to get first pick, with the lower priority functions getting the leftovers.

BCP Recovery Plan Development

A complete Business Recovery Plan consists of several components that handle not only the continuation of critical business functions but also all the functions and resources that support those critical functions.

Emergency response

Emergency response teams must be identified for every possible type of disaster. These response teams need written procedures to keep critical business functions operating.

Written procedures are vital for two reasons. First, the people who perform critical functions may not be familiar with them: They may not be the same persons who perform them under usual circumstances (during a disaster, the people who ordinarily perform the function may be unavailable). Second, the procedures and processes for performing the critical functions during a disaster will probably be different than under normal conditions.

Personnel notification

The Continuity Plan must have some provisions for notifying all affected personnel that a disaster has occurred. Multiple methods for notifying key business continuity personnel are needed in cases in which public communications infrastructures are interrupted.

Throughout a disaster and its recovery, management must be given regular status reports as well as tactical issues so that management can align resources to support critical business operations that function on a contingency basis. For instance, a manager of a corporate facilities department can loan equipment that critical departments need to keep functioning.

Backups and off-site storage

The information stored on each computer system that supports critical business processes must be regularly backed up. The back-up media must also be stored off-site in the event that the facility housing those systems is damaged. Having back-up tapes in the data center is of little value if they're destroyed along with their respective systems.

For systems with large amounts of data, that data must be understood in order to determine what kinds of backups need to be performed (full, differential, incremental) and how frequently. The factors that need to be considered are the time that it takes to perform backups, the effort required to restore data, and procedures for restoring data from backups compared with other methods for re-creating the data. For example, is restoring application software from back-up tapes faster than just installing them from release media?

Off-site storage of back-up media and other materials (documentation, and so on) must be chosen carefully. Factors to consider include survivability of the off-site storage facility as well as the distance from the off-site facility to the data center, airports, and alternate processing sites.

Some organizations have one or more databases that are so large that they literally *can* not (or, at any rate, *do* not) back them up to tape. Instead, they keep one or more replicated copies of the database on other computers in other cities. BCP planners need to consider this possibility when developing continuity plans.

The purpose of off-site media storage is to make up-to-date data available in the event that the primary data center is damaged.

Software escrow agreements

Your organization should consider software escrow agreements with the software vendors whose applications support critical business functions. In the event that a disaster (this could include bankruptcy) strikes the software vendor and it is thus unable to recover from it, your organization must be able to consider all options for the continued maintenance for those critical applications, including in-house support.

External communications

The Corporate Communications, External Affairs, and (if applicable) Investor Relations departments should all have plans in place for communicating the facts about a disaster to the press and public. Contingency plans for these functions are critical if the organization is to continue communicating to the outside world. Open communication during a disaster is vital so that customers, suppliers, and investors don't panic because they don't know the true extent of the disaster.

Who says External Affairs is non-essential?

Here's a hypothetical example. Suppose the headquarters building for a large company burns to the ground. (This is very unlikely in modern buildings, but stay with me.) All personnel escaped unharmed. In fact, the organization is very well off because all the information in the building was duplicated and stored in an off-site facility. However, the External Affairs department, which was housed in that building, lost everything. It took two days to recover the capability of communicating to the outside world. However, because of this time lag, the company had lost half of its customers, who feared the worst. This is especially unfortunate and ironic because the company was actually in pretty good shape.

Utilities

Data-processing facilities supporting critical business functions must keep running in the event of a power failure. Although every situation is different, the principle is not: The BCP team must determine for what period of time the data-processing facility must be able to continue operating without utility power. A power engineer can find out the length of power outages in your area and the mean time between outages. By using that information, as well as having an inventory of the data center's equipment and environmental equipment, you can determine whether an uninterrupted power supply (UPS) alone, or a UPS *and* an electric generator, is needed.

Uninterruptible power supplies (UPS) and emergency electric generators are used to provide electric power during prolonged power outages.

Logistics and supplies

The BCP team needs to study every aspect of critical functions that can be made to continue despite a disaster. Every resource that's needed to sustain the critical operation must be identified and then considered against every possible disaster scenario to determine whether any special plans must be made. For instance, if a business operation relies upon a just-in-time shipment of materials for its operation and an earthquake has closed the region's only highway (or airport or sea/lake port), then alternative means for acquiring those materials must be determined in advance. Or, perhaps an emergency ration of those materials needs to be stockpiled so that the business function can continue uninterrupted.

Fire protection

Many natural disasters disrupt public utilities, including water supplies or delivery. In the event that a disaster has interrupted water delivery, will your affected facility be allowed to operate without the means for fighting a fire should one occur?

Documentation

Any critical business function must be able to continue operating after a disaster strikes. An essential item for sustained operations includes all relevant documentation for every piece of equipment as well as every critical process and procedure that's performed in a given location.

Don't be lulled into taking for granted the emerging trend of hardware and software products not coming with any documentation. After all, many vendors deliver their documentation *only* over the Internet, or they charge extra for hard copy. But many types of disasters may disrupt Internet communications, thereby leaving an operation high and dry with no instructions on how to use or manage tools or applications.

At least one set of hard copy documentation should be stored at the same offsite storage facility that stores the organization's back-up tapes.

Continuity and recovery documentation must exist in hard copy in the event that it's unavailable via technical means such as laptop computers.

Data processing continuity planning

Data processing facilities are so vital to business today that a lot of emphasis is placed on them. Generally this comes down to these variables: where and how the business will continue to sustain its data processing functions.

Because data centers are so expensive and time-consuming to build, better business sense dictates having an alternate processing site available. The most common are

- **Cold site:** A *cold site* is basically an empty computer room with environmental facilities (UPS; heating, ventilation, and air conditioning [HVAC]; and so on) but no equipment. This is the least costly option, but more time is required to be able to assume a workload because computers need to be brought in from somewhere and set up, and data and applications need to be loaded. Connectivity to other locations also needs to be installed.

✔ **Warm site:** A *warm site* is basically a cold site but with computers and communications links. In order to take over production operations, the computers must be loaded with application software and business data.

✔ **Hot site:** Indisputably the most expensive option, a *hot site* is equipped with the same computers as the production system, with application changes, operating system changes, and even patches kept in sync with the live production system counterparts. Even business data is kept up-to-date at the hot site with mirroring or transaction replication. Because they are trained on operating the organization's business applications (and they have documentation), the staff there knows what to do to take over data processing operations at a moment's notice.

✔ **Multiple data centers:** Larger organizations can consider the option of running daily operations out of two or more regional data centers that are hundreds of miles (or more) apart. The advantage of this arrangement is that the organization doesn't have to make arrangements with outside vendors for hot/warm/cold sites, and the organization's staff is already onsite and familiar with business and computer operations.

A hot site provides the most rapid recovery ability, but it's also the most expensive because of the effort that it takes to maintain its readiness.

Table 10-1 compares these options side by side.

Table 10-1　Data Processing Continuity Planning Site Comparison

Feature	Hot Site	Warm Site	Cold Site	Multiple Data Centers
Cost	Highest	Medium	Low	No additional
Computer-equipped	Yes	Yes	No	Yes
Connectivity-equipped	Yes	Yes	No	Yes
Data-equipped	Yes	No	No	Yes
Staffed	Yes	No	No	Yes
Typical lead time to readiness	Minutes to hours	Hours to days	Days to weeks	Minutes to hours

Development of the BCP Plan

By now you've defined the scope of the BCP project and developed the Business Impact Assessment. What you know so far is

✔ What portion of the organization is included in the plan.

✔ Of this portion of the organization, which business functions are so critical that the business would fail were these functions to be interrupted for long (or even short) periods of time.

✔ You have some quantitative and qualitative data that give you an idea of the degree of impact on the business when one of the critical functions fails.

The hard part of the Business Continuity Project begins now: This is where you develop the strategy for continuing each critical business function when disasters occur. This is known as the *Continuity Strategy*.

Developing a Continuity Strategy is the time for looking at the excruciating details of critical business functions. This is the time for strong coffee, pizzas, and buckets of Rolaids.

Identifying success factors

The critical success factors for this important and time-consuming phase of the project include

✔ **Call a spade a spade:** No biases. No angles. No politics. No favorites. No favors. This isn't the time for screwing around — you're trying to save the business before the disaster strikes.

✔ **Build smaller teams of experts:** Each critical business function should have teams dedicated to just that function. That team's job is to analyze just one critical business function and figure out how it can be made to continue despite a disaster of some sort. Pick the right people for each team — people who *really* understand the details of the business process being examined.

✔ **Have teams share results with each other:** Teams working on individual continuity strategies can learn from each other. Each team can share highlights of its work over the past week or two. Some of the things that they say will spark ideas on other teams. The entire effort will be better off for it.

✔ **No competition between teams:** Don't pit the teams against each other. This is not a zero-sum game: Everyone needs to do an excellent job.

✔ **Retain a BCP mentor/expert:** If your organization doesn't have experienced business continuity planners on staff, you need to bring in a consultant — someone who has helped to develop plans for other organizations. Even more important than that — someone who has been there when disaster struck and who saw the business continuity plan in action.

Simplifying large or complex critical functions

Some critical business functions may be too large and complex to examine in one big chunk. Complex functions can be broken down into smaller components, perhaps like this:

- ✔ **People:** The team can identify the critical people — or more appropriately, the critical functions — required to keep the function running.

- ✔ **Facilities:** In the event that the function's primary facilities are unavailable, where will the function be performed?

- ✔ **Technology:** What hardware, software, and other computing/network components support the critical function? If parts or all these components are unavailable, what other equipment will support the critical business functions? Will the functions be performed any differently?

- ✔ **Miscellaneous:** What supplies, other equipment, and services are required to support the critical business function?

If a team analyzing a large complex business function breaks into groups such as these listed here, these groups need to get together frequently to ensure that their respective strategies eventually become a cohesive whole. Eventually, these four (or whatever number) groups need to come back together and integrate their separate materials into one complete plan.

Documenting the strategy

Now for the part that everyone loves: documentation. The details of the continuity plans for each critical function must be described in minute detail, step by step by step.

Why? The people who develop the strategy may very well *not* be the people who execute it. The people who develop the strategy may change roles in the company or change jobs altogether. Or, the scope of an actual disaster may be wide enough that the critical personnel just aren't available. Any skeptics should consider 9-11 and the impact that this disaster had on a number of companies that lost virtually everyone.

Best practices for documenting Business Continuity Plans exist. Here is another reason to have that expert around. For $300/hour, he can spend a couple of weeks developing templates. But watch out — he might just download them from a BCP Web site, tweak them a little bit, and spend the rest of his time playing DOOM.

Why hire an expert?

Most of us don't do Business Continuity Planning for a living. Although we may be the experts on our business processes, we're not necessarily the right people for knowing all the angles of contingency planning.

Turn this question around for a minute: What would you think if an IT shop developed a security strategy without having a security expert's help? Do you think that this would result in a sound, viable strategy?

The same argument fits equally well with BCP.

For the remaining skeptics, do yourself a favor: Hire a BCP expert for just a short time to help validate your framework and plan. If he says that your plan is great, then you can consider it money well spent to confirm your suspicions. If he says that your plan needs help, have him show you where and how. Then you decide whether to rework and improve your plan.

Implementing the Business Continuity Plan

It is an accomplishment indeed when the BCP documentation has been written, reviewed, edited, and placed into three-ring binders. However, the job isn't yet done. The Business Continuity Plan needs senior management buy in, the plan must be announced and socialized throughout the organization, and one or more persons must be dedicated to keeping the plan up-to-date.

Securing senior management approval

After the entire plan has been documented and reviewed by all stakeholders, it's time for senior management to examine it and approve it. Not only must senior management approve the plan, but senior management must also *publicly* approve it.

Senior management approval is needed so that all affected and involved employees in the organization understand the importance of emergency planning.

Promoting organizational awareness

Everyone in the organization needs to be made aware of the existence of the plan and of his or her role in it. This may mean training for potentially large numbers of people who are expected to *be there* when a disaster strikes.

All employees in the organization must be made aware of the existence of the Business Continuity Plan.

Maintaining the plan

No, the plan isn't finished. It has just begun! Now the BCP *person* (the project team members by this time have collected their denim shirts and their pen-and-pencil sets) needs to periodically chase The Powers That Be to make sure that they know about all significant changes to the environment. In fact, if the BCP person has any leadership left in him, he needs to start attending the Change Control Board (or whatever his company calls it) meetings and to jot down notes that may mean that some detail in a BCP document may need some changes.

The Business Continuity Plan is easier to modify than it is to create out of thin air. Once or twice each year, someone knowledgeable ought to examine the detailed strategy and procedure documents in the BCP to make sure that they'll still work.

Disaster Recovery Planning

As I describe in the earlier section "The Difference between BCP and DRP," the planning for both Disaster Recovery and Business Continuity have common roots. Both need to assemble similar project teams; both need executive sponsorship and support; and both must identify critical business processes.

Here the similarity ends. In the remainder of this chapter, I discuss the development and implementation of the Disaster Recovery Plan.

Developing a Disaster Recovery Plan

While the BCP folks develop a plan to keep business operations rolling, the DRP people develop a plan to restore the damaged facility so that the critical business functions can operate there again.

Preparing for emergency response

Emergency response teams must be prepared for every possible scenario. Members of these teams need a variety of specialized training to deal with such things as water and smoke damage, structural damage, flooding, and hazardous materials.

All the types of response must be documented so that the response teams know what to do. The emergency response documentation consists of two major parts: how to respond to each type of incident, and up-to-date facts about the facilities and equipment that the organization uses. In other words, you want your teams to know how to deal with water damage, smoke damage, structural damage, hazardous materials, and many other things. Your teams also need to know everything about every company facility: where things such as utility entrances, electrical equipment, HVAC, fire control, elevators, communications, data closets, and so on are located, which vendors maintain and service them, and so forth.

Responding to an emergency branches into two activities: salvage and recovery. Tangential to this is preparing financially for the costs associated with salvage and recovery.

Salvage

The salvage team is concerned with restoring full functionality to the damaged facility. This includes several activities:

- **Damage assessment:** The facility must be thoroughly examined to identify the full extent and nature of damage. Frequently this is performed by outside experts such as structural engineers and the like.

- **Salvage assets:** Computer equipment, records, furniture, inventory, and so on need to be removed from the facility.

- **Cleaning:** The facility needs to be thoroughly cleaned to eliminate smoke damage, water damage, debris, and so forth. This is frequently performed by outside companies that specialize in these services.

- **Restoring facility to operational readiness:** The final step to full recovery is the completion of repairs and re-stocking/re-equipping the facility to return it to pre-disaster readiness. At this point, the facility is ready for business functions to resume there.

The salvage team is primarily concerned with the restoration of a facility to return it to operational readiness.

Recovery

Recovery comprises equipping the BCP team with any logistics, supplies, or coordination in order to get alternate functional sites up and running. This activity should be heavily scripted, with lots of procedures and checklists in order to ensure that every detail is handled.

Financial readiness

The salvage and recovery operations can be very expensive. The organization must be prepared for potentially large expenses (at least several times the total monthly operating cost) to restore operations to the original facility.

Not only response, but also prevention

On the surface, it appears that Disaster Recovery Planning is all about cleaning up and restoring business operations after a hurricane, tornado, or flood. However the DRP project can add considerable value to the organization if it also points out things that are putting the business at risk in the first place. For instance, the DRP planning team may discover a design flaw in a building that makes it more vulnerable to damage during a flood. The planning team can make a recommendation to make the necessary repairs in order to reduce the likelihood of flood damage.

Notifying personnel

The disaster recovery team needs to have communication plans prepared in advance of any disaster. The DRP team must have a way of notifying employees about facilities that are closed, and note that one or more traditional means of communications may also have been adversely affected by the same event that damaged business facilities. For example, if a building has been damaged, the voice-mail system that you would expect people to call into for checking messages and getting workplace status might not be working.

Facilitating external communications

The corporate departments that communicate with customers, investors, government, and the media are equipped with pretty much the same information as for Business Continuity Planning. There are really no differences and no need for any significant differences in planning for external communications between DRP and BCP.

Maintaining physical security

Looting and vandalism may occur after significant events. The organization must be prepared to deploy additional guards as well as temporary fencing and other physical barriers in order to protect its physical assets until facilities are secured and law and order are restored.

Testing the Disaster Recovery Plan

By the time that an organization has completed a DRP, it will probably have spent hundreds of man-hours and possibly tens or hundreds of thousands of dollars on consulting fees. You would think that after making this large of an investment, any organization would want to test its DRP to make sure that it works when a real emergency strikes.

Five methods available for testing the Disaster Recovery Plan are

- ✔ **Checklist:** This amounts to a review or read-through of the disaster recovery plan documentation. By itself, this is an insufficient, but logical starting place. One of the following tests should be performed afterwards.

- ✔ **Structured walkthrough:** The step-by-step review of the DRP is performed by a team of experts (in a fancy mountain retreat).

- ✔ **Simulation:** In a *simulation*, all the designated disaster recovery personnel practice going through the motions associated with a real recovery. In a simulation, the team doesn't actually perform any recovery or alternate processing.

- ✔ **Parallel:** A *parallel test* involves performing all the steps of a real recovery except that the real, live production computers are kept running. They run in parallel with the disaster recovery computers. This is a very time-consuming test, but it does test the accuracy of the applications because analysts compare data on the test recovery systems with production data.

- ✔ **Interruption:** An *interruption test* is similar to a parallel test except that in an interruption test, the function's computer systems are actually shut off or disconnected. An interruption test is the ultimate test of a disaster recovery plan because one or more of the business' critical functions actually depends upon the availability, integrity, and accuracy of the recovery systems.

The parallel test includes the loading of data onto recovery systems without taking production systems down.

Additional References

Myers, Kenneth N. *Manager's Guide to Contingency Planning for Disasters: Protecting Vital Facilities and Critical Operations.* John Wiley & Sons, Inc.

Fulmer, Kenneth L. *Business Continuity Planning, 2000 Edition: A Step-By-Step Guide With Planning Forms on CD-ROM.* Rothstein Associates.

Barnes, James C. and Rothstein, Philip Jan. *A Guide to Business Continuity Planning.* John Wiley & Sons, Inc.

Tipton, Harold F. and Krause, Micki. *Information Security Management Handbook,* 4th Edition, Chapter 24. Auerbach Publications.

Prep Test

1 The longest period of time that a business can survive without a critical function is called

   A ○ Downtime Tolerability Period

   B ○ Greatest Tolerable Downtime

   C ○ Maximum Survivable Downtime

   D ○ Maximum Tolerable Downtime

2 Which of the following is NOT a natural disaster?

   A ○ Avalanche

   B ○ Stock market crash

   C ○ Fire

   D ○ Storage drought

3 The impact of a disaster on business operations is contained in

   A ○ Local newspapers

   B ○ Business Impact Assessment

   C ○ Operations Impact Assessment

   D ○ Vulnerability Assessment

4 The decision whether to purchase an emergency generator is based upon

   A ○ Wholesale electric rates

   B ○ Retail electric rates

   C ○ The duration of a typical outage

   D ○ The income rate of affected systems

5 The purpose of a UPS is

   A ○ To provide instantaneous power cutover when utility power fails

   B ○ A lower cost for overnight shipping

   C ○ The need to steer the vehicle after it's moving again

   D ○ To restore electric power within 24 hours

6 The Business Impact Assessment

   A ○ Describes the impact of disaster recovery planning on the budget

   B ○ Describes the impact of a disaster on business operations

   C ○ Is a prerequisite to the Vulnerability Assessment

   D ○ Is the first official statement produced after a disaster

7 **To maximize the safety of back-up media, it should be stored**

A ○ At a specialized off-site media storage facility

B ○ At the residences of various senior managers

C ○ In the operations center in a locking file cabinet

D ○ Between 50° F–60° F

8 **An alternate information processing facility with all systems, patches, and data mirrored from live production systems is known as a**

A ○ Warm site

B ○ Hot site

C ○ Recovery site

D ○ Mutual Aid Center

9 **The greatest advantage of a cold site is**

A ○ It can be build nearly everywhere

B ○ Its high responsiveness

C ○ Its low cost

D ○ Its close proximity to airports

10 **The most extensive Disaster Recovery Plan**

A ○ Has dual failover

B ○ Is a waste of paper

C ○ Is known as a parallel test

D ○ Is known as an interruption test

Answers

1 **D.** Maximum Tolerable Downtime. This is the term that describes the maximum period of time that a business function can suspend operations and the company can still survive. *Review "Defining the Business Impact Assessment."*

2 **B.** Stock market crash. A stock market crash is a man-made (non-natural) disaster. *Review "Defining Disastrous Events."*

3 **B.** Business Impact Assessment. The BIA describes the impact that a disaster will have on business operations. *Review "Defining the Business Impact Assessment."*

4 **C.** The duration of a typical outage. The average and worst-case duration of electrical power outages help to determine whether an emergency generator should be purchased. *Review "BCP Recovery Plan Development."*

5 **A.** To provide instantaneous power cutover when utility power fails. A UPS provides continuous electric power to all equipment connected to it. *Review "BCP Recovery Plan Development."*

6 **B.** Describes the impact of a disaster on business operations. A Business Impact Assessment (BIA) contains quantitative and qualitative estimates of the impact of a disaster. *Review "Defining the Business Impact Assessment."*

7 **A.** At a specialized off-site media storage facility. Such a specialized facility is designed to withstand most disastrous events. *Review "BCP Recovery Plan Development."*

8 **B.** Hot site. Although a hot site is the most expensive to build and maintain, it provides the greatest possible performance. *Review "BCP Recovery Plan Development."*

9 **C.** Its low cost. Cold sites are inexpensive but are also the slowest to set up and get running. *Review "BCP Recovery Plan Development."*

10 **D.** Is known as an interruption test. The interruption test performs an actual failover of applications to the servers. *Review "Testing the Disaster Recovery Plan."*

Chapter 11

Law, Investigations, and Ethics

● ●

In This Chapter

▶ Major categories and types of laws

▶ Major categories of computer crime

▶ Types of laws relevant to computer crimes

▶ Investigations, evidence, and incident response

▶ Standards of ethical conduct

● ●

Security professionals are said to be cut from one of two cloths: those with a legal background and some technical expertise or, more commonly, those with a technical background and some legal expertise. Either way, knowledge of the legal aspects of computer crimes and investigations is essential for the security professional. Knowledge of and adherence to ethical standards are required for the Certified Informational Systems Security Professional (CISSP) and security professionals in general. Those CISSP candidates from the first cloth described above may want to study the ethics section a little harder. (Ouch! Okay, I apologize — that was a cheap shot at lawyers. I promise no more than one or two lawyer jokes in this chapter!)

In this chapter, I cover the ninth domain of the Systems Security Certifications Consortium [(ISC)^2] Common Body of Knowledge (CBK) — Law, Investigations, and Ethics.

Major Categories and Types of Laws

My discussion of the major categories and types of laws consists of US and international law. The focus here, as with the CISSP exam, is primarily on the US common law system.

The (ISC)^2 CISSP Study Guide states "the current CBK has been updated to remove specific reference to laws and policy of the United States government and include reference to international standards." However, as of this writing, the CISSP exam still focuses primarily on US law, although this is subject to change in the near future.

US common law

Under the common law system of the United States, three major categories of laws are defined at the federal and state levels: *criminal*, *civil* (or *tort*), and *administrative* (or *regulatory*) laws.

Criminal law

Criminal law defines those crimes committed against society, even when the actual victim is a business or individual(s). Criminal laws are enacted to protect the general public. As such, in the eyes of the court, the victim is incidental to the greater cause.

Criminal penalties

Penalties under criminal law have two main purposes:

- ✔ **Punishment:** Penalties may include jail/prison sentences, probation, fines, and/or financial restitution to the victim.

- ✔ **Deterrence:** Penalties must be severe enough to dissuade any further criminal activity by the offender or anyone else considering a similar crime.

Burden of proof under criminal law

To be convicted under criminal law, a jury must believe *beyond a reasonable doubt* that the defendant is guilty. Therefore, the burden of proof in a criminal case rests firmly with the prosecution.

Classifications of criminal law

These are the two main classifications of criminal law depending upon severity, such as type of crime/attack or total loss in dollars:

- ✔ **Felony:** More serious crimes, normally resulting in jail/prison terms of more than one year. Convicted felons also lose their right to vote forever.

- ✔ **Misdemeanor:** Less serious crimes, normally resulting in fines or jail/prison terms of less than one year.

Civil law

Civil (tort) law addresses wrongful acts committed against an individual or business, either willfully or negligently, resulting in damage, loss, injury, or death.

Civil penalties

Unlike criminal penalties, civil penalties don't include jail or prison terms. Instead, civil penalties provide financial restitution to the victim as follows:

- ✓ **Compensatory damages:** Actual damages to the victim including attorney/legal fees, lost profits, investigative costs, and so forth.
- ✓ **Punitive damages.** Determined by a jury and intended to punish the offender.
- ✓ **Statutory damages:** Mandatory damages determined by law and assessed for violating the law.

Burden of proof under civil law

Convictions under civil law are easier to obtain than under criminal law because the burden of proof is much less. To be convicted under civil law, a jury must believe *based upon the preponderance of the evidence* that the defendant is guilty. This simply means that the weight of the evidence leads the jury to a conclusion of guilt.

Liability and due care

The concepts of liability and due care are germane to civil law cases but are also applicable under administrative law, which I discuss in the next section.

The standard criteria for assessing the legal requirements for implementing recommended safeguards is to evaluate the cost of the safeguard and the estimated loss from the corresponding threat, if realized. If the cost is less than the estimated loss and the organization doesn't implement a safeguard, then a legal liability may exist. This is based on the principle of *proximate causation,* in which an action taken or not taken was part of a sequence of events that resulted in negative consequences.

Under the Federal Sentencing Guidelines, senior corporate officers may be personally liable if their organization fails to comply with applicable laws. Such individuals must follow the *prudent man rule,* which requires them to perform their duties:

- ✓ In good faith
- ✓ In the best interests of the enterprise, and
- ✓ With the care and diligence that ordinary, prudent persons in a like position would exercise under similar circumstances

The concepts of *due care* and *due diligence* are related but distinctly different:

- ✓ **Due care:** The steps that an organization takes to implement security best practices.
- ✓ **Due diligence:** The prudent management and execution of due care.

Lawyer-speak

Although the information in this sidebar is not tested on the CISSP examination, the Law, Investigations, and Ethics domain does require some knowledge of the US common law system and specific computer crime laws. When attempting to learn the various laws, you'll find it helpful to know the correct parlance (fancy-speak for *jargon*) used. For example:

> 18 U.S.C. § 1030 (1986) (the Computer Fraud and Abuse Act of 1986) refers to Section 1030 in Title 18 of the 1986 edition of the United States Code, not 18 University of Southern California squiggly-thingy 1030 (1986).

Federal statutes and administrative laws are usually cited in the following format:

- ✔ **The title number** (titles are grouped by subject matter)

- ✔ **The abbreviation for the code:** for example, *U.S.C.* is United States Code; *C.F.R.* is Code of Federal Regulations

- ✔ **The section number** (*§* means "*The Word Formerly Known As Section*")

- ✔ **The year of publication**

Other important abbreviations to understand include:

- ✔ **Fed. Reg.:** Federal Register

- ✔ **Fed. R. Evid.:** Federal Rules of Evidence

- ✔ **PL:** Public Law

- ✔ **§§:** Sections; for example, 18 U.S.C. §§ 2701–11

- ✔ **v.:** versus; such as, United States v. Moore. *Note:* The rest of the civilized world understands *vs.* to mean *versus* and *v.* to mean *version* or *volume*, but remember two important points here: Lawyers are not part of the civilized world, and they apparently charge by the letter!

Another important aspect of due care is the principle of *culpable negligence*. If an organization fails to follow a standard of due care in the protection of its assets, the organization may be held culpably negligent. In such cases, jury awards may be adjusted accordingly, and the organization's insurance company may be required to pay only a portion of any loss.

Administrative law

Administrative (regulatory) laws define standards of performance and conduct for major industries (including banking, energy, and health care), organizations, and officials. These laws are typically enforced by various government agencies, and violations may result in financial penalties and/or imprisonment.

International law

Given the global nature of the Internet, it's often necessary for many countries to cooperate in order to bring a computer criminal to justice. Unfortunately, because practically every country in the world has its own unique legal system, such cooperation is always difficult and often impossible. As a starting point, many countries disagree on exactly what justice is. Other problems include:

- **Lack of universal cooperation:** I can't answer the question, "Why can't we all just get along?" but I can tell you that it's highly unlikely that a 14-year-old hacker in some remote corner of the world will commit some dastardly crime that unites us all in our efforts to take him down, bringing about a lasting world peace!

- **Different interpretations of laws:** What's illegal in one country is not necessarily illegal in another.

- **Different rules of evidence:** This can include different rules for obtaining and collecting evidence and different rules for admissibility of evidence.

- **Low priority:** Different nations have different views regarding the seriousness of computer crimes; and in the realm of international relations, computer crimes are normally of minimal concern.

- **Outdated laws and technology:** Technology varies greatly throughout the world, and many countries (not only third-world countries) lag far behind others. For this reason and many others, computer crime laws are often a low priority and aren't kept current. This problem is further exacerbated by the different technical capabilities of the various law enforcement agencies that may be involved in an international case.

- **Extradition:** Many countries don't have extradition treaties and won't extradite suspects to a country with different or controversial practices, such as capital punishment. Although capital punishment for a computer crime may sound extreme, recent events and the threat of cyberterrorism make this a very real possibility.

Major Categories of Computer Crime

Webster's defines a *crime* as an act or the commission of an act that's forbidden by law. Webster's defines a *computer crime* as . . . well, Webster's doesn't define computer crime. Perhaps this is because of real-world difficulties in defining computer crimes. Several reasons why computer crimes are hard to define include:

- **Lack of understanding:** In general, legislators, judges, attorneys, law enforcement officials, and jurors don't understand the many different technologies and issues involved in a computer crime.

- **Inadequate laws:** Laws are slow to change, and fail to keep pace with rapidly evolving, new technology.

- **Multiple roles of computers in crime:** These include crimes committed *against* a computer (such as hacking into a system and stealing information) and crimes committed by *using* a computer (such as using a system to launch a distributed denial of service attack).

Computer crimes are often difficult to prosecute for the reasons that I just listed and also because of the following issues:

- **Lack of tangible assets:** Traditional rules of property often don't apply in a computer crime case. However, property rules have been extended in many countries to include electronic information. Computing resources, bandwidth, and data (in the form of magnetic particles) are often the only assets at issue. These can be very difficult to quantify and assign a value to. The asset valuation process, which I discuss in Chapter 5, can provide key information in such a case.

- **Rules of evidence:** Often, original documents aren't available in a computer crime case. Most evidence in such a case is considered hearsay evidence (which I discuss later in the upcoming section "Hearsay rule") and must meet certain requirements to be admissible in court.

- **Definition of loss:** A loss of confidentiality or integrity of data goes far beyond the normal definition of loss in a criminal or civil case.

- **Criminal profiles:** Computer criminals typically aren't hardened criminals and may include the following:
  - **Juveniles:** Juvenile laws in many countries aren't taken seriously and are inadequate to deter crime. A busy prosecutor is unlikely to pursue a low-profile crime committed by a juvenile that results in a three-year probation sentence for the offender.
  - **Trusted individuals:** Many computer criminals are individuals that hold a position of trust within a company and have no prior criminal record. Such an individual will likely be able to afford a Dream Team for legal defense, and a judge may be inclined to levy a more lenient sentence for the first-time offender.

The CISSP CBK identifies six major categories of computer crimes, as follows:

- **Terrorist attacks**
- **Military and intelligence attacks**
- **Financial attacks**
- **Business attacks**
- **Grudge attacks**
- **"Fun" attacks**

Terrorist attacks

Terrorism exists at many levels on the Internet. In April of 2001, during a period of tense relations between China and the US (resulting from the crash landing of a US Navy reconnaissance plane on Hainan Island), Chinese hackers (cyberterrorists) launched a major effort to disrupt critical US infrastructure, which included US government and military systems.

Following the terrorist attacks against the US on September 11, 2001, the general public became painfully aware of the extent of terrorism on the Internet. Terrorist organizations and cells are using online capabilities to coordinate attacks, transfer funds, harm international commerce, disrupt critical systems, disseminate propaganda, and gain useful information about developing techniques and instruments of terror, including nuclear, biological, and chemical weapons.

Military and intelligence attacks

Military and intelligence attacks are perpetrated by criminals, traitors, or foreign intelligence agents seeking classified law enforcement or military information. Such attacks may also be carried out by governments during times of war and conflict. For example, during Operation Desert Shield/ Desert Storm, the US government disrupted the Iraqi communications infrastructure as part of its war strategy.

Financial attacks

Banks, large corporations, and e-commerce sites are the targets of financial attacks, all of which are motivated by greed. Financial attacks may seek to steal or embezzle funds, gain access to online financial information, extort individuals or businesses, or obtain personal credit card numbers.

Business attacks

Businesses are becoming the target of more and more computer and Internet attacks. These attacks include competitive intelligence gathering, denial of service, and other computer-related attacks. Businesses are often targeted for several reasons including

✔ **Lack of expertise:** Despite heightened security awareness, a shortage of qualified security professionals still exists, particularly in private enterprise.

✔ **Lack of resources:** Businesses often lack the resources to prevent, or even detect, attacks against their systems.

✔ **Lack of reporting or prosecution:** Because of public relations concerns and the inability to prosecute computer criminals due to either a lack of evidence or a lack of properly handled evidence, the majority of business attacks still go unreported.

The cost to businesses can be significant, including loss of trade secrets or proprietary information, loss of revenue, and loss of reputation.

Grudge attacks

Grudge attacks are targeted at individuals or businesses and are motivated by revenge or the desire to "get back" at someone or something. A disgruntled employee, for example, may steal trade secrets, delete valuable data, or plant a logic bomb in a critical system or application.

Fortunately, these attacks (at least in the case of a disgruntled employee) can be easier to prevent or prosecute than many other types of attacks because: the attacker is often known to the victim; the attack has a visible impact that produces a viable evidence trail; most businesses (already sensitive to the possibility of wrongful termination suits) have well-established termination procedures; and specific laws (such as the US Economic Espionage Act of 1996, which I discuss later in this chapter) provide very severe penalties for such crimes.

"Fun" attacks

These attacks are perpetrated by thrill seekers and script kiddies who are motivated by curiosity or excitement. Although these attackers may not intend to do any harm or use any of the information that they access, they're still dangerous and their activities are still illegal.

These attacks can also be relatively easy to detect and prosecute. Because the perpetrators are often script kiddies or otherwise inexperienced hackers, they may not know how to cover their tracks effectively.

Also, because no real harm is normally done nor intended against the system, it may be tempting (although ill-advised) for a business to prosecute the individual and put a positive public relations spin on the incident. You've seen the film at 11: "We quickly detected the attack, prevented any harm to our network, and prosecuted the responsible individual; our security is *unbreakable!*" Such action, however, will likely motivate others to launch a more serious and concerted grudge attack against the business.

Many computer criminals in this category only seek notoriety. Although it's one thing to brag to a small circle of friends about defacing a public Web site, the wily hacker who appears on CNN reaches the next level of hacker celebrity-dom. These twisted individuals want to be caught to revel in their 15 minutes of fame.

Types of Laws Relevant to Computer Crimes

Given the difficulties in defining and prosecuting computer crimes that I discuss in the earlier sections of this chapter, many prosecutors seek to convict computer criminals on more traditional criminal statutes, such as theft, fraud, extortion, and embezzlement. Intellectual property rights and privacy laws, in addition to specific computer crime laws, also exist to protect the general public and assist prosecutors.

The CISSP candidate should understand that because of the difficulty in prosecuting computer crimes, prosecutors often use more traditional criminal statutes, intellectual property rights, and privacy laws to convict criminals. In addition, you should also realize that specific computer crime laws do exist.

Intellectual property

Intellectual property is protected by US law under one of four classifications as follows:

- ✔ Patents
- ✔ Trademarks
- ✔ Copyrights
- ✔ Trade secrets

Intellectual property rights worldwide are agreed, defined, and enforced by various organizations and treaties, including the World Intellectual Property Organization (WIPO), World Customs Organization (WCO), World Trade Organization (WTO), United Nations Commission on International Trade Law (UNCITRAL), European Union (EU), and Trade-Related Aspects of Intellectual Property Rights (TRIPs).

Licensing violations are one of the more prevalent examples of intellectual property rights infringement. Other examples include plagiarism, software piracy, and corporate espionage.

Patents

A *patent*, as defined by the US Patent and Trademark Office (PTO) is "the grant of a property right to the inventor." A patent grant confers upon the owner "the right to exclude others from making, using, offering for sale, selling or importing the invention." Computer hardware or a physical device in firmware are examples of computer-related objects that may be protected by patents.

A patent is granted by the PTO for an invention that has been sufficiently documented by the applicant and that has been verified as original by the PTO. A patent is generally valid for 20 years from the date of application and is effective only within the US, including territories and possessions. The owner of the patent may then grant a license to others for use of the invention or its design, often for a fee.

US patent (and trademark) laws and rules are covered in 35 U.S.C. and 37 C.F.R., respectively. The Patent Cooperation Treaty (PCT) provides some international protection for patents. As of December 2001, 115 countries worldwide have adopted the PCT.

Patents grants were previously valid for only 17 years but have recently been changed, for newly granted patents, to 20 years.

Trademark

A *trademark*, as defined by the PTO, is "any word, name, symbol, or device, or any combination, used, or intended to be used, in commerce to identify and distinguish the goods of one manufacturer or seller from goods manufactured or sold by others." A corporate brand or an operating system logo are examples of computer-related objects that may be protected by trademarks.

US Public Law 105–330, the Trademark Law Treaty Implementation Act, provides some international protection for US registered trademarks.

Copyright

A *copyright* is a form of protection granted to the authors of "original works of authorship," both published and unpublished. A copyright protects a tangible form of expression rather than the idea or subject matter itself. Under the original Copyright Act of 1909, publication was generally the key to obtaining a federal copyright. However, the Copyright Act of 1976 changed this requirement, and copyright protection now applies to any original work of authorship immediately from the time that it's created in a tangible form. Object code or documentation are examples of computer-related objects that may be protected by copyrights.

Copyrights can be registered through the Copyright Office of the Library of Congress, but a work doesn't need to be registered to be protected by copyright. Copyright protection generally lasts for the lifetime of the author plus 70 years.

Trade secret

A *trade secret* is proprietary or business-related information that a company or individual uses and has exclusive rights to. To be considered a trade secret, the information must meet the following requirements:

- ✔ **Must be genuine and not obvious.**
- ✔ **Must provide the owner a competitive or economic advantage and therefore have value to the owner.**
- ✔ **Must be reasonably protected from disclosure.** This doesn't mean that it must be kept absolutely and exclusively secret, but the owner must exercise due care in its protection.

Software source code or firmware code are examples of computer-related objects that may be protected by trade secrets.

Privacy laws

Privacy laws are enacted to protect information collected and maintained on individuals from unauthorized disclosure or misuse. Privacy laws are one area in which the United States lags behind other countries, particularly the EU, which has defined more restrictive privacy regulations that prohibit the transfer of personal information to countries (including the United States) that don't equally protect such information. The EU privacy rules include the following requirements about personal data and records:

- ✔ **Must be collected fairly and lawfully.**
- ✔ **Must only be used for the purposes for which it was collected and only for a reasonable period of time.**
- ✔ **Must be accurate and kept up-to-date.**
- ✔ **Must be accessible to individuals who request a report on personal information held about themselves.**
- ✔ **Individuals have the right to have any errors in their personal data corrected.**
- ✔ **Personal data cannot be disclosed to other organizations or individuals unless authorized by law or consent of the individual.**
- ✔ **Transmission of personal data to locations where equivalent privacy protection cannot be assured is prohibited.**

Two important pieces of privacy legislation in the United States are the US Federal Privacy Act of 1974 and the US Health Insurance Portability and Accountability Act of 1996.

US Federal Privacy Act of 1974, 5 U.S.C. § 552A

The Federal Privacy Act of 1974 protects records and information maintained by US government agencies about US citizens and lawful permanent residents. Except under certain specific conditions, no agency may disclose any record about an individual "except pursuant to a written request by, or with the prior written consent of, the individual to whom the record pertains." The Privacy Act also has provisions for access and amendment of individual records by the individual, except in cases of "information compiled in reasonable antici-pation of a civil action or proceeding." The Privacy Act provides individual penalties for violation including a misdemeanor charge and fines up to $5,000.

US Health Insurance Portability and Accountability Act (HIPAA) of 1996, PL 104-191

HIPAA was signed into law effective August 1996. The HIPAA legislation pro-vided Congress three years from this date to pass comprehensive health pri-vacy legislation. If Congress failed to pass legislation by this deadline, the Department of Health and Human Services (HHS) was given the authority to develop the privacy and security regulations for HIPAA. In October 1999, HHS released proposed HIPAA privacy and security regulations entitled "Privacy Standards for Individually Identifiable Health Information." The general dead-lines for compliance (with some exceptions) are

- ✔ **October 2002: Transactions and Code Sets**
- ✔ **April 2003: Privacy**

Organizations that must comply with HIPAA regulations are referred to as *cov-ered entities* and include

- ✔ **Payers (or health plan):** An individual or group health plan that pro-vides, or pays the cost of, medical care; for example, insurers
- ✔ **Health care clearinghouses:** A public or private entity that processes or facilitates the processing of nonstandard data elements of health infor-mation into standard data elements, such as data warehouses
- ✔ **Health providers:** A provider of medical or other health services, such as hospitals, HMOs, doctors, specialists, dentists, and counselors

HIPAA is composed of five titles. Title II, Subsection F, "Administrative Simplification," pertains to information privacy and security. The HIPAA secu-rity standard addresses four key areas:

✔ **Administrative procedures:** Formally documented security management practices, including policies and procedures, business continuity and disaster recovery plans, internal audits, incident handling procedures, and security awareness training.

✔ **Physical safeguards:** Various protections for computer systems and related buildings from environmental hazards and intrusion, including physical access controls and media controls.

✔ **Technical security services:** Processes that protect information and control access, including access controls, auditing, and authentication, authorization, and accounting (AAA) services.

✔ **Technical security mechanisms:** Protection of data during transit including message authentication, integrity controls, and encryption.

Civil Penalties for HIPAA violations include fines of $100 per incident, up to $25,000 per provision, per calendar year. Criminal penalties include fines up to $250,000 and potential imprisonment of corporate officers for up to 10 years. Additional state penalties may also apply.

Computer crime laws

Important computer crime laws in the United States that the CISSP candidate should be familiar with include

✔ **Computer Fraud and Abuse Act of 1986** (as amended)

✔ **Electronic Communications Privacy Act of 1986**

✔ **Computer Security Act of 1987**

✔ **Federal Sentencing Guidelines of 1991** (not necessarily specific to computer crime, but certainly relevant)

✔ **Economic Espionage Act of 1996**

✔ **Child Pornography Prevention Act of 1996**

✔ **USA Patriot Act of 2001**

US Computer Fraud and Abuse Act of 1986, 18 U.S.C. § 1030 (as amended)

In 1984, the first US federal computer crime law, the US Computer Fraud and Abuse Act, was passed. This intermediate act was narrowly defined and somewhat ambiguous. The law covered

✔ Classified national defense or foreign relations information

✔ Records of financial institutions or credit reporting agencies

✔ Government computers

The US Computer Fraud and Abuse Act of 1986 enhanced and strengthened the 1984 law, clarifying definitions of criminal fraud and abuse for federal computer crimes and removing obstacles to prosecution.

The act established two new felony offenses for the unauthorized access of *Federal interest* computers and a misdemeanor for unauthorized trafficking in computer passwords.

Major provisions of the act established three new crimes (two felonies and one misdemeanor) as follows:

- **Felony:** Unauthorized access, or access that exceeds authorization, of a Federal interest computer to further an intended fraud, shall be punishable as a felony [Subsection (a)(4)].

- **Felony:** Altering, damaging, or destroying information in a Federal interest computer or preventing authorized use of the computer or information, that causes an aggregate loss of $1,000 or more during a one-year period or potentially impairs medical treatment, shall be punishable as a felony [Subsection (a)(5)]. This provision was stricken in its entirety and replaced with a more general provision, which I discuss later in this section, in the 1994 amendment.

- **Misdemeanor:** Trafficking in computer passwords or similar information if it affects interstate or foreign commerce or permits unauthorized access to computers used by or for the US government [Subsection (a)(6)].

A *Federal interest computer* (actually the term was changed to *protected computer* in the 1996 amendments to the act) is defined in the act as a computer:

- "exclusively for the use of a financial institution or the United States Government, or, in the case of a computer not exclusively for such use, used by or for a financial institution or the United States Government and the conduct constituting the offense affect that use by or for the financial institution or the Government;"

    or

- "which is used in interstate or foreign commerce or communication."

Several minor amendments to the US Computer Fraud and Abuse Act were made in 1988, 1989, and 1990, and more significant amendments were made in 1994, 1996 (by the Economic Espionage Act of 1996), and 2001 (by the USA Patriot Act of 2001). The act, in its present form, establishes seven specific computer crimes. In addition to the three that I discuss above, these include the following five provisions [Subsection (a)(5) is re-introduced here in its current form]:

✔ Unauthorized access, or access that exceeds authorization, to a computer that results in *disclosure of U.S. national defense or foreign relations information* [Subsection (a)(1)].

✔ Unauthorized access, or access that exceeds authorization, to a protected computer to *obtain any information on that computer* [Subsection (a)(2)].

✔ Unauthorized access to a protected computer, or access that exceeds authorization, to a protected computer that *affects the use* of that computer by or for the U.S. Government [Subsection (a)(3)].

✔ Unauthorized access to a protected computer causing damage or reckless damage, or *intentionally transmitting malicious code* which causes damage to a protected computer [Subsection (a)(5), as amended].

✔ Transmission of interstate or foreign commerce communication *threatening to cause damage* to a protected computer for the purpose of extortion [Subsection (a)(7)].

I discuss major amendments to the US Computer Fraud and Abuse Act of 1986 (as amended) introduced in 2001 in the upcoming "USA Patriot Act of 2001" section.

The US Computer Fraud and Abuse Act of 1986 is *the* major computer crime law currently in effect. The CISSP exam will likely test your knowledge of the act in its original 1986 form, but you should also be prepared for revisions to the exam that may cover the more recent amendments to the act.

US Electronic Communications Privacy Act (ECPA) of 1986

The ECPA complements the US Computer Fraud and Abuse Act of 1986 and prohibits eavesdropping, interception, or unauthorized monitoring of wire, oral, and electronic communications. However, the ECPA does provide specific statutory exceptions allowing network providers to monitor their networks for legitimate business purposes when the network users are notified of the monitoring process.

The ECPA was amended extensively by the USA Patriot Act of 2001. These changes are discussed in the upcoming "USA Patriot Act of 2001" section.

The US Electronic Communications Privacy Act (ECPA) provides the legal basis for network monitoring.

US Computer Security Act of 1987

The US Computer Security Act of 1987 requires federal agencies to take extra security measures to prevent unauthorized access to computers holding sensitive information. In addition to identifying and developing security plans for sensitive systems, the act requires those agencies to provide security-related awareness training for their employees. The act also assigns formal government responsibility for computer security to the National Institute of Standards and Technology (NIST) for information security standards in general and to the National Security Agency (NSA) for cryptography in classified government/ military systems and applications.

US Federal Sentencing Guidelines of 1991

In November 1991, the United States Sentencing Commission published Chapter 8, Federal Sentencing Guidelines for Organizations, of the US Federal Sentencing Guidelines. These guidelines establish written standards of conduct for organizations, provide relief in sentencing for organizations that have demonstrated due diligence, and place responsibility for due care on senior management officials with penalties for negligence including fines of up to $290 million.

US Economic Espionage Act of 1996

The US Electronic Espionage Act (EEA) of 1996 was enacted to curtail industrial espionage, particularly when such activity benefits a foreign entity. The EEA makes it a criminal offense to take, download, receive, or possess trade secret information that has been obtained without the owner's authorization. Penalties include fines of up to $10 million, up to 15 years in prison, and forfeiture of any property used to commit the crime. The EEA also enacted the 1996 amendments to the US Computer Fraud and Abuse Act, which I discuss earlier in the section "US Computer Fraud and Abuse Act of 1986, 18 U.S.C. § 1030 (as amended)."

US Child Pornography Prevention Act of 1996

The US Child Pornography Prevention Act (CPPA) of 1996 was enacted to combat the use of computer technology to produce and distribute pornography involving children, including adults portraying children.

The USA Patriot Act of 2001, which I cover in the next section, changes many of the provisions in the computer crime laws, particularly the US Computer Fraud and Abuse Act of 1986 (as amended) and the Electronic Communications Privacy Act of 1986, which I detail in the earlier section "US Electronic Communications Privacy Act (ECPA) of 1986." As security professionals, we must keep abreast of current laws and affairs to perform our jobs effectively. Current exam questions in this domain are likely to be based on the laws discussed above in their original form. However, questions that reflect recent changes in the USA Patriot Act could begin appearing on the CISSP examination in the near future.

USA Patriot Act of 2001

Following the terrorist attacks against the United States on September 11, 2001, the USA Patriot Act of 2001 was enacted in October 2001. This act takes great strides to strengthen and amend existing computer crime laws, including the US Computer Fraud and Abuse Act and the US Electronic Communications

Privacy Act (ECPA), as well as to empower US law enforcement agencies, if only temporarily. Most of the provisions in the act have a sunset provision expiring December 31, 2005. Also, because of the emergency conditions and necessary haste in drafting the act, it is sure to be contested and certain parts or provisions may be struck down by the courts. The relevant sections of the act are

- ✔ **Section 202 – Authority to Intercept Voice Communications in Computer Hacking Investigations:** Under previous law, investigators couldn't obtain a wiretap order for violations of the Computer Fraud and Abuse Act. This amendment authorizes such action for felony violations of the Computer Fraud and Abuse Act.

- ✔ **Section 209 – Obtaining Voice-mail and Other Stored Voice Communications:** Under previous law, investigators could obtain access to e-mail under the ECPA but not voice-mail, which was covered by the more restrictive wiretap statute. This amendment authorizes access to voice mail with a search warrant rather than a wiretap order.

- ✔ **Section 210 – Scope of Subpoenas for Electronic Evidence:** Under previous law, subpoenas of electronic records were restricted to very limited information. This amendment expands the list of records that can be obtained and updates technology-specific terminology.

- ✔ **Section 211 – Clarifying the Scope of the Cable Act:** This amendment governs privacy protection and disclosure to law enforcement of cable, telephone, and Internet service records that were extremely restrictive under previous law.

- ✔ **Section 212 – Emergency Disclosures by Communication Providers:** Prior to this amendment, no special provisions existed that allowed a communications provider to disclose customer information to law enforcement officials in emergency situations, such as an imminent crime or terrorist attack, without exposing the provider to civil liability suits from the customer.

- ✔ **Section 216 – Pen Register and Trap and Trace Statute:** This amendment clarifies law enforcement authority to trace communications on the Internet and other computer networks and authorizes the use of a pen/trap device nationwide rather than limiting it to the jurisdiction of the court. This particular statute is not subject to the sunset provision.

- ✔ **Section 217 – Intercepting the Communications of Computer Trespassers:** Under previous law, it was permissible for organizations to monitor activity on their own networks but not necessarily for law enforcement to assist these organizations in monitoring, even when such help was specifically requested. This amendment allows organizations to authorize persons "acting under color of law" to monitor trespassers on their computer systems.

- ✔ **Section 220 – Nationwide Search Warrants for E-mail:** This removes jurisdictional issues in obtaining search warrants for e-mail. For an excellent example of this problem, read *The Cuckoo's Egg* by Clifford Stoll (Doubleday).

✔ **Section 814 – Deterrence and Prevention of Cyberterrorism:** This amendment greatly strengthens the US Computer Fraud and Abuse Act, including raising the maximum prison sentence from 10 years to 20 years.

✔ **Section 815 – Additional Defense to Civil Actions Relating to Preserving Records in Response to Government Requests:** This amendment clarifies the "statutory authorization" defense for violations of the ECPA.

✔ **Section 816 – Development and Support of Cybersecurity Forensic Capabilities:** This statute requires the Attorney General to establish regional computer forensic laboratories, maintain existing laboratories, and provide forensic and training capabilities.

See a timeline of major US computer crime laws in Figure 11-1.

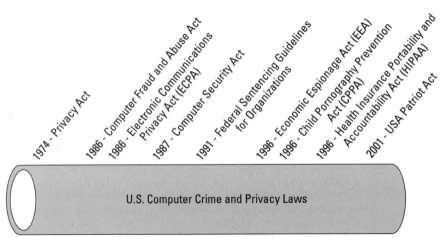

Figure 11-1:
Timeline of major US computer crime laws.

Investigations

Computer forensics is the science of conducting a computer crime investigation to determine what has happened and who is responsible, and to collect legally admissible evidence for use in a computer crime case.

Closely related to, but distinctly different from investigations, is incident handling (or response). The purpose of an investigation is to determine what happened, who is responsible, and collect evidence. Incident handling is done to determine what happened, contain and assess damage, and restore normal operations.

Investigations and incident handling must often be conducted simultaneously in a well-coordinated and controlled manner to ensure that the initial actions of either activity don't destroy evidence or cause further damage to the organization's assets. For this reason, it's important that Computer Incident (or Emergency) Response Teams (CIRT or CERT, respectively) be properly trained and qualified to secure a crime scene or incident while preserving evidence. Ideally, the CIRT includes individuals who will actually be conducting the investigation.

An analogy to this would be an example of a police patrolman who discovers a murder victim. It's important that the patrolman quickly assesses the safety of the situation and secures the crime scene; but at the same time, he must be careful not to destroy any evidence. The homicide detective's job is to gather and analyze the evidence. Ideally, the homicide detective would be the individual who discovers the murder victim, allowing her to assess the safety of the situation, secure the crime scene, and begin collecting evidence.

Evidence

Evidence is information presented in a court of law to confirm or dispel a fact that's under contention. A case can't be brought to trial without sufficient evidence to support the case. Thus, properly gathering evidence is one of the most important and most difficult tasks of the investigator.

The types of evidence, rules of evidence, admissibility of evidence, chain of custody, and evidence life cycle comprise the main elements to be tested in the Investigations portion of this domain.

Types of evidence

Sources of legal evidence that can be presented in a court of law generally fall into one of four major categories:

- **Direct evidence:** Oral testimony or a written statement based on information gathered through the witness's five senses (an eyewitness account) that proves or disproves a specific fact or issue.

- **Real (or physical) evidence:** Tangible objects from the actual crime, such as the tools or weapons used and any stolen or damaged property. May also include visual or audio surveillance tapes generated during or after the event. Physical evidence from a computer crime is rarely available.

✔ **Documentary evidence:** Includes originals and copies of business records, computer-generated and computer-stored records, manuals, policies, standards, procedures, and log files. Most evidence presented in a computer crime case is documentary evidence. The *hearsay rule*, which I discuss in an upcoming section, is an extremely important test of documentary evidence that must be understood and applied to this type of evidence.

✔ **Demonstrative evidence:** Used to aid the court's understanding of a case. Opinions are considered demonstrative evidence and may be either *expert* (based on personal expertise and facts) or *non-expert* (based on facts only). Other examples include models, simulations, charts, and illustrations.

Other types of evidence that may fall into one or more of the above major categories include

✔ **Best evidence:** Original, unaltered evidence, which is preferred by the court over secondary evidence. Read more about this in its upcoming section "Best evidence rule."

✔ **Secondary evidence:** A duplicate or copy of evidence, such as a tape backup, screen capture, or photograph.

✔ **Corroborative evidence:** Supports or substantiates other evidence presented in a case.

✔ **Conclusive evidence:** Incontrovertible and irrefutable: you know, the smoking gun.

✔ **Circumstantial evidence:** Relevant facts that can't be directly or conclusively connected to other events but about which a reasonable inference can be made.

Rules of evidence

Important rules of evidence for computer crime cases include the best evidence rule and hearsay evidence rule. The CISSP candidate must understand both of these rules and their applicability to evidence in computer crime cases.

Best evidence rule

The best evidence rule, defined in the Federal Rules of Evidence, states that "to prove the content of a writing, recording, or photograph, the original writing, recording, or photograph is [ordinarily] required."

However, an exception to this rule is also defined in the Federal Rules of Evidence, as follows:

> "[i]f data are stored in a computer or similar device, any printout or other output readable by sight, shown to reflect the data accurately, is an "original".

This means that data extracted from a computer — that is a fair and accurate representation of the original data — satisfies the best evidence rule and may normally be introduced into court proceedings as such.

Hearsay rule

Hearsay evidence is that evidence that is not based on personal, first-hand knowledge of the witness but rather was obtained through other sources. Under the Federal Rules of Evidence, hearsay evidence is normally not admissible in court. This rule exists to prevent unreliable statements by witnesses from improperly influencing the outcome of a trial.

Business records, including computer records, have traditionally, and perhaps mistakenly, been considered hearsay evidence by most courts because these records cannot be proven accurate and reliable. One of the most significant obstacles for a prosecutor to overcome in a computer crime case is seeking the admission of computer records as evidence.

A prosecutor may be able to introduce computer records as best evidence rather than hearsay evidence as I discuss in the preceding section.

Several courts have acknowledged that the hearsay rules are applicable to *computer-stored* records containing human statements but are not applicable to *computer-generated* records untouched by human hands.

Perhaps the most successful and commonly applied test of admissibility for computer records in general, has been the *business records exception*, established in the Federal Rules of Evidence, for records of regularly conducted activity, meeting the following criteria:

1. **Made at or near the time of occurrence of the act**

2. **Made by a person with knowledge or from information transmitted by a person with knowledge**

3. **Made and relied upon during the regular conduct of business, as verified by the custodian or other witness familiar with their use**

4. **Kept for motives that tend to assure their accuracy**

5. **In the custody of the witness on a regular basis (as required by the chain of evidence)**

Admissibility of evidence

Because computer-generated evidence can often be easily manipulated, altered, or tampered with, and because it's not easily and commonly understood, this type of evidence is usually considered suspect in a court of law. In order to be admissible, evidence must be

✓ **Relevant:** It must tend to prove or disprove facts that are relevant and material to the case.

✓ **Reliable:** It must be reasonably proven that what is presented as evidence is what was originally collected and that the evidence itself is reliable. This is accomplished, in part, through proper evidence handling and the chain of custody. (I discuss this in the upcoming section "Chain of custody and the evidence life cycle.")

✓ **Legally permissible:** It must be obtained through legal means. Evidence that's not legally permissible may include evidence obtained through the following means:

- **Illegal search and seizure:** Law enforcement personnel must obtain a prior court order; however, non-law enforcement personnel, such as a supervisor or system administrator, may be able to conduct an authorized search under some circumstances.

- **Illegal wiretaps or phone taps:** Anyone conducting wiretaps or phone taps must obtain a prior court order.

- **Entrapment or enticement:** *Entrapment* encourages someone to commit a crime that the individual may have had no intention of committing. Conversely, *enticement* lures someone toward certain evidence (a honey pot, if you will) after that individual has already committed a crime. Enticement is not necessarily illegal but does raise certain ethical arguments and may not be admissible in court.

- **Coercion:** Coerced testimony or confessions are not legally permissible.

- **Unauthorized or improper monitoring:** Active monitoring must be properly authorized and conducted in a standard manner; users must be notified that they may be subject to monitoring.

Chain of custody and the evidence life cycle

The *chain of custody* (or evidence) provides accountability and protection for evidence throughout its entire life cycle and includes the following information, which is normally kept in an evidence log:

✓ **Persons involved (*Who*):** Identify any and all individual(s) who discovered, collected, seized, analyzed, stored, preserved, transported, or otherwise controlled the evidence. Also identify any witnesses or other individuals present during any of the above actions.

✓ **Description of evidence (*What*):** Ensure that all evidence is completely and uniquely described.

✓ **Location of evidence (*Where*):** Provide specific information about the evidence's location when it is discovered, analyzed, stored, or transported.

✔ **Date/Time (*When*):** Record the date and time that evidence is discovered, collected, seized, analyzed, stored, or transported. Also, record date and time information for any evidence log entries associated with the evidence.

✔ **Methods used (*How*):** Provide specific information about how evidence is discovered, collected, stored, preserved, or transported.

Any time that evidence changes possession or is transferred to a different media type, it must be properly recorded in the evidence log to maintain the chain of custody.

Law enforcement officials must strictly adhere to chain of custody requirements, and this adherence is highly recommended for anyone else involved in collecting or seizing evidence. Security professionals and incident response teams must fully understand and follow the chain of custody, no matter how minor or insignificant a security incident may initially appear.

Even properly trained law enforcement officials sometimes make crucial mistakes in evidence handling. Most attorneys won't understand the technical aspects of the evidence that you may present in a case, but they will definitely know evidence-handling rules and will most certainly scrutinize and attack your actions in this area. Improperly handled evidence, no matter how conclusive or damaging, will likely be inadmissible in a court of law.

The *evidence life cycle* describes the various phases of evidence from its initial discovery to its final disposition.

The evidence life cycle has the following five stages:

✔ **Collection and identification**

✔ **Analysis**

✔ **Storage, preservation, and transportation**

✔ **Presentation in court**

✔ **Return to victim (owner)**

Collection and identification

Collecting evidence involves taking that evidence into custody. Unfortunately, evidence can't always be collected and must instead be seized. Many legal issues are involved in seizing computers and other electronic evidence. The publication *Searching and Seizing Computers and Obtaining Evidence in Criminal Investigations (January 2001)*, published by the US Department of Justice (DOJ) Computer Crime and Intellectual Property Section (CCIPS) provides comprehensive guidance on this subject. Find this publication available for download at www.cybercrime.gov.

In general, law enforcement officials can search and/or seize computers and other electronic evidence under any of four circumstances:

- **Voluntary** or **consensual:** The owner of the computer or electronic evidence can freely surrender the evidence.

- **Subpoena:** A court issues a subpoena to an individual ordering that individual to deliver the evidence to the court.

- **Search warrant** or **Writ of Possession:** A *search warrant* is issued to a law enforcement official by the court, allowing that official to search and seize specific evidence. A *Writ of Possession* is a similar order issued in civil cases.

- **Exigent circumstances:** If probable cause exists and the destruction of evidence is imminent, that evidence may be searched or seized without a warrant.

When evidence is collected, it must be properly marked and identified. This ensures that it can later be properly presented in court as actual evidence gathered from the scene or incident. The collected evidence must be recorded in an evidence log with the following information:

- A **description** of the particular piece of evidence including any specific information, such as make, model, serial number, physical appearance, material condition, and pre-existing damage

- The **name(s)** of the person(s) who discovered and collected the evidence

- The exact **date and time, specific location,** and **circumstances** of the discovery/collection

Additionally, the evidence must be marked, using the following guidelines:

- **Mark the evidence:** If possible without damaging the evidence, mark the actual piece of evidence with the collecting individual's initials, the date, and the case number (if known). Seal the evidence in an appropriate container and again mark the container with the same information.

- **Or use an evidence tag:** If the actual evidence cannot be marked, attach an evidence tag with the same information as above, seal the evidence and tag in an appropriate container, and again mark the container with the same information.

- **Seal evidence:** Seal the container with evidence tape and mark the tape in a manner that will clearly indicate any tampering.

- **Protect evidence:** Use extreme caution when collecting and marking evidence to ensure that it's not damaged. If you're using plastic bags for evidence containers, be sure that they're static-free.

Always collect and mark evidence in a consistent manner so that you can easily identify evidence and describe your collection and identification techniques to an opposing attorney in court, if necessary.

Analysis

Analysis involves examining the evidence for information pertinent to the case. Analysis should be conducted with extreme caution, by properly trained and experienced personnel only, to ensure the evidence is not altered, damaged, or destroyed.

Storage, preservation, and transportation

All evidence must be properly stored in a secure facility and preserved to prevent damage or contamination from various hazards, including intense heat or cold, extreme humidity, water, magnetic fields, and vibration. Evidence that's not properly protected may be inadmissible in court, and the party responsible for collection and storage may be liable. Care must also be exercised during transportation to ensure that evidence is not lost, damaged, or destroyed.

Presentation in court

Evidence to be presented in court must continue to follow the chain of custody and be handled with the same care as at all other times in the evidence life cycle. This process continues throughout the trial until all testimony related to the evidence is completed and the trial is over.

Return to victim (owner)

After the conclusion of the trial or other disposition, evidence is normally returned to its proper owner. However, under some circumstances, certain evidence may be ordered destroyed, such as contraband, drugs, or paraphernalia. Any evidence obtained through a search warrant is legally under the control of the court, possibly requiring the original owner to petition the court for its return.

Conducting investigations

A computer crime investigation should begin immediately upon report of an alleged computer crime or incident. Any incident should be handled, at least initially, as a computer crime investigation until a preliminary investigation determines otherwise.

The CISSP candidate should be familiar with the general steps of the investigative process, which include the following steps:

✔ **Detection and containment:** Early detection is critical to a successful investigation. Unfortunately, passive or reactive detection techniques (such as the review of audit trails and accidental discovery) are usually the norm in computer crimes, which often leaves a cold evidence trail. Containment is essential to minimize further loss or damage. Enter the CIRT, which I discuss in the next section.

✔ **Notification of management:** Management must be notified of any investigations as soon as possible. Knowledge of the investigations should be limited to as few people as possible, on a need-to-know basis. Out-of-band communications methods (reporting in person) should be used to ensure an intruder does not intercept sensitive communications about the investigation.

✔ **Preliminary investigation:** This is necessary to determine whether a crime has actually occurred. Most incidents are actually honest mistakes rather than criminal conduct. This step includes reviewing the complaint or report, inspecting damage, interviewing witnesses, examining logs, and identifying further investigation requirements.

✔ **Disclosure determination:** The first and most important determination is whether disclosure of the crime or incident is required by law. Next, determine whether disclosure is desired. This should be coordinated with a public relations or public affairs official of the organization.

✔ **Conduct the investigation:**

- **Identify potential suspects.** This includes insiders and outsiders to the organization. One standard discriminator to help determine or eliminate potential suspects is the MOM test: Did the suspect have the Motive, Opportunity, and Means to commit the crime?

- **Identify potential witnesses.** Determine who will be interviewed and who will conduct the interviews. Be careful not to alert any potential suspects to the investigation; focus on obtaining facts, not opinions, in witness statements.

- **Prepare for search and seizure.** This includes identifying the types of systems and evidence to be searched or seized, designating and training the search and seizure team members (CIRT), obtaining and serving proper search warrants (if required), and determining potential risk to the system during a search and seizure effort.

✔ **Report findings:** The results of the investigation, including evidence, should be reported to management and turned over to proper law enforcement officials or prosecutors, as appropriate.

MOM: Motive, Opportunity, and Means.

Incident handling (Or response)

Incident response begins before an incident has actually occurred. Preparation is the key to a quick and successful response. A well-documented and regularly practiced incident response plan ensures effective preparation. The plan should include:

- ✔ **Response procedures:** Detailed procedures that address different contingencies and situations should be included.

- ✔ **Response authority:** Roles, responsibilities, and levels of authority for all members of the CIRT must be clearly defined.

- ✔ **Available resources:** People, tools, and external resources (consultants and law enforcement agents) that are available to the CIRT should be identified. Training should include use of these resources, when possible.

- ✔ **Legal review:** The incident response plan should be evaluated by appropriate legal counsel to determine compliance with applicable laws and to determine whether they're enforceable and defensible.

Additional steps in incident response include:

- ✔ **Determination:** This is similar to the detection and containment step in the investigative process, and includes defining what constitutes a security incident for your organization. Upon determination that an incident has occurred, it's important to immediately begin detailed documentation of every action taken throughout the incident response process.

- ✔ **Notification:** This step and specific procedures are identical to the notification of management step in the investigative process but also includes the disclosure determination step from the investigative process. All contact information should be documented before an incident, and all notifications and contacts during an incident should be documented in the incident log.

- ✔ **Containment:** Again similar to the detection and containment step in the investigative process, the purpose of this step is to minimize further loss or damage. This may include eradicating a virus, denying access, and disabling services.

- ✔ **Assessment:** This includes determining the scope and cause of damage, as well as the responsible (or liable) party.

- ✔ **Recovery:** This may include rebuilding systems, repairing vulnerabilities, improving safeguards, and restoring data and services. This step should be done in accordance with a business continuity plan (BCP) with priorities for recovery properly identified.

- ✔ **Evaluation:** This is the final phase of an incident response plan and includes the lessons learned. *Lessons learned* should include not only what went wrong but also what went right.

Investigations and incident response have similar steps but different purposes: The distinguishing characteristic of an investigation is the gathering of evidence for possible prosecution, whereas incident response focuses on containing the damage and returning to normal operations.

Ethics

Ethics (or moral values) are not easily defined, and a fine line often hovers between ethical and unethical activity. Ethical activity doesn't necessarily equate to illegal activity. And what may be acceptable in some organizations, cultures, or societies may be unacceptable or even illegal in others.

Ethical standards can be based on a common or national interest, individual rights, laws, tradition, culture, or religion. One helpful distinction between laws and ethics is that laws define what we *must* do and ethics define what we *should* do.

Many common fallacies abound about computers and the Internet, which contribute to this gray area:

- **The Computer Game Fallacy:** Any system or network that's not properly protected is fair game.

- **The Law-Abiding Citizen Fallacy:** If no physical theft is involved, it really isn't stealing.

- **The Shatterproof Fallacy:** Any damage done will have a limited effect.

- **The Candy-from-a-Baby Fallacy:** It's so easy, it can't be wrong.

- **The Hacker's Fallacy:** Computers provide a valuable means of learning that will, in turn, benefit society. The problem here lies in the distinction between *hackers* and *crackers*. Although both may have a genuine desire to learn, crackers do it at the expense of others.

- **The Free Information Fallacy:** Any and all information should be free and thus can be obtained through any means.

Most every recognized group of professionals defines a code of conduct or standards of ethical behavior by which its members must abide. For the CISSP, it is the (ISC)² Code of Ethics. The CISSP candidate must be familiar with the (ISC)² Code of Ethics and Request for Comments (RFC) 1087 for professional guidance on ethics (and the exam).

(ISC)² Code of Ethics

As a requirement for (ISC)² certification, all Certified Information Systems Security Professionals (CISSPs) must subscribe to and fully support the (ISC)² Code of Ethics.

The (ISC)² Code of Ethics consists of a mandatory preamble and four mandatory canons. Additional guidance is provided for each of the canons on the (ISC)² Web site at www.isc2.org.

Internet Activities Board (IAB) – "Ethics and the Internet" (RFC 1087)

Published by the Internet Activities Board (IAB) in January 1989, RFC 1087 characterizes as unethical and unacceptable any activity that purposely:

1. *"Seeks to gain unauthorized access to the resources of the Internet."*

2. *"Disrupts the intended use of the Internet."*

3. *"Wastes resources (people, capacity, computer) through such actions."*

4. *"Destroys the integrity of computer-based information."*

5. *"Compromises the privacy of users."*

Other important tenets of RFC 1087 include

"Access to and use of the Internet is a privilege and should be treated as such by all users of [the] system."

"Many of the Internet resources are provided by the U.S. Government. Abuse of the system thus becomes a Federal matter above and beyond simple professional ethics."

"Negligence in the conduct of Internet-wide experiments is both irresponsible and unacceptable."

"In the final analysis, the health and well-being of the Internet is the responsibility of its users who must, uniformly, guard against abuses which disrupt the system and threaten its long-term viability."

Additional References

Krutz, Ronald L. and Vines, Russell Dean. *The CISSP Prep Guide: Mastering the Ten Domains of Computer Security*, Chapter 9. John Wiley & Sons, Inc.

Tipton, Harold F. and Krause, Micki. *Information Security Management Handbook,* 4th Edition, Chapters 28–30. Auerbach Publications.

Parker, Donn B. *Fighting Computer Crime: A New Framework for Protecting Information*, Chapters 4, 6, and 15. John Wiley & Sons, Inc.

Pipkin, Donald L. *Information Security: Protecting the Global Enterprise*, Chapters 21–31. Prentice Hall PTR.

Mandia, Kevin and Prosise, Chris. *Incident Response: Investigating Computer Crime*, Chapters 1–5 and Appendix C. Osborne/McGraw-Hill.

Allen, Julia H. *The CERT Guide to System and Network Security Practices*, Chapters 1 and 7. Addison-Wesley.

Prep Test

1 **Penalties for conviction in a civil case can include**

- **A** ○ Imprisonment
- **B** ○ Probation
- **C** ○ Fines
- **D** ○ Community service

2 **Possible damages in a civil case are classified as all the following except**

- **A** ○ Compensatory
- **B** ○ Punitive
- **C** ○ Statutory
- **D** ○ Financial

3 **Computer attacks motivated by curiosity or excitement describes**

- **A** ○ "Fun" attacks
- **B** ○ Grudge attacks
- **C** ○ Business attacks
- **D** ○ Financial attacks

4 **Intellectual property includes all the following except**

- **A** ○ Patents and trademarks
- **B** ○ Trade secrets
- **C** ○ Copyrights
- **D** ○ Computers

5 **Under the Computer Fraud and Abuse Act of 1986 (as amended), which of the following is not considered a crime?**

- **A** ○ Unauthorized access
- **B** ○ Altering, damaging, or destroying information
- **C** ○ Trafficking child pornography
- **D** ○ Trafficking computer passwords

6 **Which of the following is not considered one of the four major categories of evidence?**

- **A** ○ Circumstantial evidence
- **B** ○ Direct evidence
- **C** ○ Demonstrative evidence
- **D** ○ Real evidence

7 **In order to be admissible in a court of law, evidence must be**

A ○ Conclusive

B ○ Relevant

C ○ Incontrovertible

D ○ Immaterial

8 **What term describes the evidence-gathering technique of luring an individual toward certain evidence after that individual has already committed a crime; is this considered legal or illegal?**

A ○ Enticement/Legal

B ○ Coercion/Illegal

C ○ Entrapment/Illegal

D ○ Enticement/Illegal

9 **In a civil case, the court may issue an order allowing a law enforcement official to seize specific evidence. This order is known as a(n)**

A ○ Subpoena

B ○ Exigent Circumstances Doctrine

C ○ Writ of Possession

D ○ Search warrant

10 **The IAB "Ethics and the Internet" (RFC 1087) characterizes all the following activities as unethical except**

A ○ Seeking to gain unauthorized access to resources

B ○ Wasting resources

C ○ Compromising user privacy

D ○ Downloading pornography

Answers

1 **C.** Fines. Fines are the only penalty a jury can award in a civil case. The purpose of a fine is financial restitution to the victim. *Review "Civil penalties."*

2 **D.** Financial. Although damages in a civil case are of a financial nature, they are classified as compensatory, punitive, and statutory. *Review "Civil penalties."*

3 **A.** "Fun" attacks. Grudge attacks are motivated by revenge. Business attacks may be motivated by a number of factors including competitive intelligence. Financial attacks are motivated by greed. *Review "Major Categories of Computer Crime."*

4 **D.** Computers. Patents and trademarks, trade secrets, and copyrights are all considered intellectual property and are protected by intellectual property rights. Computers are considered physical property. *Review "Intellectual property."*

5 **C.** Trafficking child pornography. The Child Pornography Prevention Act (CPPA) of 1996 addresses child pornography. Review *"US Child Pornography Prevention Act of 1996."*

6 **A.** Circumstantial evidence. Circumstantial evidence is a type of evidence but is not considered one of the four main categories of evidence. In fact, circumstantial evidence may include circumstantial, direct, or demonstrative evidence. *Review "Types of evidence."*

7 **B.** Relevant. The tests for admissibility of evidence include relevance, reliability, and legal permissibility. *Review "Admissibility of evidence."*

8 **A.** Enticement/Legal. Entrapment is the act of encouraging someone to commit a crime that the individual may have had no intention of committing. Coercion involves forcing or intimidating someone to testify or confess. Enticement does raise certain ethical arguments but is not normally illegal. *Review "Admissibility of evidence."*

9 **C.** Writ of Possession. A subpoena requires the owner to deliver evidence to the court. The exigent circumstances doctrine provides an exception to search and seizure rules for law enforcement officials in emergency or dangerous situations. A search warrant is issued in criminal cases. *Review "Collection and identification."*

10 **D.** Downloading pornography. Although certainly unethical and even illegal in many countries, societies, communities, organizations, and situations, pornography is not universally considered unethical. *Review "Internet Activities Board (IAB) – 'Ethics and the Internet' (RFC 1087)."*

Chapter 12

Physical Security

. . . .

In This Chapter

▶ Threats to physical security

▶ Facility requirements planning

▶ Physical access controls

▶ Technical controls

▶ Environmental and life safety controls

▶ Administrative controls

. . . .

*I*f you've already read Chapter 3, you may recall my analogy that castles are normally built in a strategic location with towering walls. But what makes a location strategic, and how high is towering? Exactly where should the battlements and bastions be positioned? Who should guard the entrance, and what are the procedures for raising and lowering the drawbridge? And what should you do after burning and pillaging? This is the realm of the physical security domain.

For the tenth domain (Physical Security) of the Common Body of Knowledge (CBK), the Certified Information Systems Security Professional (CISSP) candidate must fully understand the various threats to physical security, the elements of facility requirements planning and design, and the various physical security controls, including access controls, technical controls, environmental and life safety controls, and administrative controls, as covered in this chapter.

 Many CISSP candidates underestimate the physical security domain. As a result, exam scores are often lowest in this domain. Although much of the information in this domain is redundant and may seem to be common sense, the CISSP exam does ask very specific questions from this domain, and many candidates lack practical experience in fighting fires!

Physical Security Threats

Threats to physical security come in many forms including natural disasters, emergency situations, and man-made threats. All possible threats must be identified in order to perform a complete and thorough risk analysis and to develop an appropriate and effective control strategy. Some of the more common threats to physical security include

✔ **Fire:** Threats from fire can be potentially devastating and lethal. Proper precautions, preparation, and training not only help limit the spread of fire and damage but, more importantly, can save lives. *Saving human lives is the first priority in any life-threatening situation.* Other hazards associated with fires include smoke, explosions, building collapse, release of toxic materials or vapors, and water damage.

Fire requires three elements to burn: heat, oxygen, and fuel. These three elements are sometimes referred to as the *fire triangle.* (See Figure 12-1.) Fire suppression and extinguishing systems fight fires by removing one of these three elements or by temporarily breaking up the chemical reaction between these three elements: that is, separating the fire triangle. Fires are classified according to the fuel type, as listed in Table 12-1.

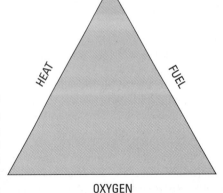

Figure 12-1:
A fire needs these three elements to burn.

Table 12-1　Fire Classes and Suppression/Extinguishing Methods

Class	Description (Fuel)	Extinguishing Method
A	Common combustibles, such as paper, wood, furniture, and clothing	Water or soda acid
B	Burnable fuels, such as gasoline or oil	CO_2, soda acid, or Halon (I discuss this in the later section "Detection systems")

Class	Description (Fuel)	Extinguishing Method
C	Electrical fires, such as computers or electronics	CO_2 or Halon (**Note:** Most important step: Turn off electricity first!)
D	Special fires, such as chemical or grease fires	May require total immersion or other special techniques

Saving human lives is the first priority in any life-threatening situation.

You must be able to describe Class A, B, and C fires and their primary extinguishing methods. Class D is less common and is not relevant to the CISSP exam.

✔ **Water:** Water damage (and damage from liquids in general) can occur from many different sources including pipe breakage, firefighting efforts, leaking roofs, spilled drinks, and flooding. Wet computers and other electrical equipment pose a potentially lethal hazard.

✔ **Vibration and movement:** Causes may include earthquakes, landslides, and explosions. Equipment may also be damaged by sudden or severe vibrations, falling objects, or equipment racks tipping over. More seriously, vibrations or movement may weaken structural integrity, causing a building collapse.

✔ **Severe weather:** This includes hurricanes, tornadoes, high winds, severe thunderstorms and lightning, rain, snow, sleet, and ice. Such forces of nature may cause fires, water damage and flooding, structural damage, loss of communications and utilities, and personnel hazards.

✔ **Electricity:** Sensitive equipment can be damaged or affected by various electrical hazards and anomalies, including

• **Electrostatic discharge (ESD):** The ideal humidity range for computer equipment is 40–60 percent. Higher humidity causes condensation and corrosion. Lower humidity increases the potential for ESD (static electricity). A static charge of as little as 40 volts (V) can damage sensitive circuits, and 2,000V can cause a system shutdown. The minimum discharge that can be felt by humans is 3,000V, and discharges of over 25,000V are possible.

The ideal humidity range for computer equipment is 40–60 percent.

• **Electrical noise:** This includes Electromagnetic Interference (EMI) and Radio Frequency Interference (RFI). EMI is generated by the different charges between the three electrical wires (hot, neutral, and ground) and can be *common-mode noise* (caused by hot and ground) or *traverse mode noise* (caused by hot and neutral). RFI is caused by electrical components, such as fluorescent lighting and electric cables. A *transient* is a momentary line noise disturbance.

- **Electrical anomalies:** These include the following, as listed in Table 12-2.

Table 12-2	Electrical Anomalies
Electrical Event	*Definition*
Blackout	Total loss of power
Fault	Momentary loss of power
Brownout	Prolonged drop in voltage
Sag	Short drop in voltage
Inrush	Initial power rush
Spike	Momentary rush of power
Surge	Prolonged rush of power

You may want to come up with some meaningless mnemonic for the above list such as "Bob Frequently Buys Shoes In Shoe Stores" because you will need to know these terms for the CISSP exam.

- **Lightning strikes:** Approximately 10,000 fires are started every year by lightning strikes in the United States alone, despite the fact that only 20 percent of all lightning ever reaches the ground. Lightning can heat the air in immediate contact with the stroke to 54,000° Fahrenheit (F), which translates to 30,000° Celsius (C), and lightning can discharge 100,000 amperes of electrical current.

- **Magnetic fields:** Monitors and storage media (including floppy diskettes and hard drives) can be permanently damaged or erased by magnetic fields.

✔ **Sabotage/theft/vandalism:** Both internal and external threats must be considered. A heightened security posture is prudent during certain situations, including labor disputes, corporate downsizing, hostile terminations, bad publicity, demonstrations/protests, and civil unrest.

✔ **Equipment failure:** Equipment failures are inevitable. The effects can be mitigated by maintenance and support agreements, ready spare parts, and redundant systems.

✔ **Loss of communications and utilities:** These include voice and data, electricity, and heating, ventilation, and air conditioning (HVAC). Loss of communications and utilities may be due to any of the above factors, as well as human error or mistakes.

✔ **Personnel loss:** This can be due to illness, injury, death, transfer, labor disputes, resignations, and terminations. The effects of a personnel loss can be mitigated through good security practices, such as documented procedures, job rotations, cross training, and redundant functions.

Facility Requirements Planning

Astute organizations will involve security professionals during the design, planning, and construction of new or renovated facilities. Proper facility requirements planning during the early stages of construction helps ensure that a new building or data center is adequate, safe, and secure — all of which can help an organization avoid costly mistakes later.

Choosing a secure location

Location, location, location! Although to a certain degree this bit of conventional business wisdom may be less important to profitability in the age of e-commerce, it's still a critical factor in physical security. Important factors when considering a location include

✔ **Climatology and natural disasters:** Although an organization is unlikely to choose a geographic location based on the likelihood of hurricanes or earthquakes, these factors must be considered when designing a safe and secure facility. Other related factors may include floodplain avoidance, location of evacuation routes, and adequacy of civil and emergency preparedness.

✔ **Local considerations:** Is the location in a high crime area? Are there nearby hazards, such as hazardous materials storage, railway freight lines, or flight paths for the local airport? Is the area heavily industrialized: That is, will air and noise (including vibration) pollution affect your systems?

✔ **Visibility:** Will your employees and facilities be targeted for crime and vandalism? Is the site near another high visibility organization that may attract undesired attention? Keeping a low profile is generally better; avoid external building markings if possible.

✔ **Accessibility:** Consider local traffic patterns, convenience to airports, proximity to emergency services (police, fire, and medical facilities), and availability of adequate housing. For example, will on-call employees have to drive for an hour to respond when needed?

✔ **Utilities:** Where is the facility located in the power grid? Is electrical power stable and clean? Is sufficient fiber optic cable already in place to support telecommunications requirements?

✔ **Joint tenants:** Will you have full access to all necessary environmental controls? Can (and should) boundary protection costs and responsibilities be shared between joint tenants?

Designing a secure facility

Many of the physical and technical controls that I discuss later in this chapter should be considered during the initial design of a secure facility. Doing so will often help reduce the costs and improve the overall effectiveness of these controls. Other building design considerations include

✔ **Exterior walls:** Ideally, exterior walls should be able to withstand high winds (tornadoes and hurricanes/typhoons) and reduce emanations (tempests). If possible, windows should be avoided throughout the building, particularly on lower levels. Metal bars over windows on lower levels may be necessary. Any windows should be fixed (cannot be opened), shatterproof, and sufficiently opaque to conceal inside activities.

✔ **Interior walls:** Interior walls adjacent to secure or restricted areas must extend from the floor to the ceiling (through raised flooring and drop ceilings) and must comply with applicable building and fire codes. Walls adjacent to storage areas (such as closets containing janitorial supplies, paper, media, or other flammable materials) must meet minimum fire ratings, which are typically higher than for other interior walls. Ideally, Kevlar (bulletproof) walls should protect the most sensitive areas.

✔ **Floors:** Flooring (both slab and raised) must be capable of bearing loads in accordance with local building codes (typically 150 pounds per square foot). Additionally, raised flooring must have a nonconductive surface and be properly grounded.

✔ **Ceilings:** Weight bearing and fire ratings must be considered. Drop ceilings may temporarily conceal water leaks; conversely, drop ceilings can reveal leaks while impeding water damage.

✔ **Doors:** Doors must be of sufficient strength and design to resist forcible entry and have a fire rating equivalent to adjacent walls. Emergency exits must remain unlocked from the inside and should also be clearly marked and monitored or alarmed. Electronic lock mechanisms and other access control devices should fail open in the event of an emergency to permit emergency egress. Many doors swing out to facilitate emergency egress; thus, door hinges are located on the outside. These must be properly secured to prevent an intruder from easily lifting hinge pins and removing the door.

✔ **Lighting:** Exterior lighting for all physical spaces and buildings in the security perimeter (including entrances and parking areas) should be sufficient to provide personnel safety as well as to discourage prowlers and casual intruders.

✔ **Wiring:** All wiring, conduits, and cable runs must comply with building and fire codes and be properly protected. Plenum cabling must be used below raised floors and above drop ceilings because PVC cabling releases toxic chemicals when burning.

✔ **Electricity and HVAC:** Electrical load and HVAC requirements must be carefully planned to ensure that sufficient power is available in the right locations and that proper climate ranges (temperature and humidity) are maintained. I discuss additional controls later in the section "Electrical and life safety controls."

✔ **Pipes:** Shutoff valves for water, steam, or gas pipes should be located and appropriately marked. Drains should have positive flow; that is, carry drainage away from the building.

Physical Security Controls

Physical security controls include a combination of physical access controls, technical controls, environmental and life safety controls, fire detection and suppression, and administrative controls.

Physical access controls

Physical access controls consist of the systems and techniques used to restrict access to a security perimeter and provide boundary protection. These include fencing, security guards, dogs, locks, storage areas, security badges, and biometric access controls.

Fencing

Fencing is the primary means for securing an outside perimeter or external boundary and an important element of physical security that the CISSP candidate must know for the exam. Fencing provides physical access control and includes fences, gates, turnstiles, and mantraps. A *mantrap* is a physical access control method consisting of a double set of locked doors or turn-stiles. The mantrap may be guarded or monitored, may require different levels of access to pass through both doors or in a different direction and, in more advanced systems, may have a weight-sensing floor to prevent more than one person from passing through at once. The main disadvantages of fencing are cost and appearance. General fencing height requirements are listed in Table 12-3.

Table 12-3	General Fencing Height Requirements
Height	*General Effect*
3–4 ft (1m)	Deters casual trespassers
6–7 ft (2m)	Too high to climb easily
8 ft (2.4m) + 3-strand barbed wire	Deters more determined intruders

Security guards

Throughout history, guards have been used to provide physical security for many different situations and environments. Although modern surveillance equipment, biometric access controls, and intrusion detection systems (IDS) may seem to diminish the role of security guards, on the contrary, these tools have increased the need for skilled physical security personnel capable of operating advanced technology and applying discerning judgment. The major advantages of security guards include

- ✔ **Discernment:** Guards can apply human judgment to different situations.
- ✔ **Visibility:** Guards provide a visible deterrent, response, and control capability.
- ✔ **Dual functions:** Guards can also perform receptionist and visitor escort functions.

Some disadvantages include

- ✔ **Unpredictability:** Pre-employment screening and bonding doesn't necessarily assure reliability or integrity.
- ✔ **Imperfections:** Along with human judgment comes the element of human error.
- ✔ **Cost:** Maintaining a full-time security force (including training) or outsourcing these functions can be very expensive.

The main advantage of security guards is their ability to use human judgment when responding to different situations.

Dogs

Like human guards, dogs also provide a highly visible deterrent, response, and control capability. Additionally, dogs are typically more loyal and reliable than humans, with more acute sensory abilities (smell and hearing). However, the use of guard dogs is typically restricted to an outside security perimeter. Other considerations include

> ✔ **Limited judgment capability**
>
> ✔ **Cost and maintenance**
>
> ✔ **Potential liability issues**

Locks

Doors, windows, and other access points into secure or sensitive areas need to be protected. One of the simplest ways to accomplish this is with a lock. The two basic types of locks are

> ✔ **Preset:** These are basic mechanical locks that consist of latches, cylinders, and deadbolts; all require a key to open them.
>
> ✔ **Programmable:** These can be mechanical (such as dial combination or five-key pushbutton) or electronic (cipher lock or keypad). *Shoulder surfing*, a social engineering technique commonly used against these types of locks, involves casually observing an authorized individual entering an access code.

Storage areas

Storage areas containing spare equipment and parts, consumables, and deliveries should be locked and controlled to help prevent theft. Additionally, you should be aware of any hazardous materials being stored in such areas and any environmental factors or restrictions that may affect the contents of the storage area.

Security badges

Security badges (or access cards) are used for identification and authentication of authorized personnel entering a secure facility or area.

A *photo identification card* (also referred to as a *dumb card*) is a simple ID card with a facial photograph of the bearer. Typically, no technology is embedded in these cards for authentication purposes, requiring that a security guard determines whether entry is permitted by the bearer.

Smart cards are digitally encoded cards that contain an integrated chip (IC) or magnetic stripe (possibly in addition to a photo). Various types of smart cards include

> ✔ **Magnetic stripe:** The most basic type of smart card. Information is encoded in a magnetic stripe. Common examples include credit cards and automatic teller machine (ATM) cards.
>
> ✔ **Optical-coded:** Similar to, but more reliable than, a magnetic stripe card. Information is encoded in a laser-burned lattice of digital dots. These are becoming more common on US state driver's licenses.

✔ **Electric circuit:** Contains a printed IC on the card surface. These are true smart cards, commonly used for logical access control to computer systems.

✔ **Proximity card:** Doesn't require the bearer to physically insert the card into the reader. Instead, the reader senses the card in the general area and takes the appropriate action. The three common types of system-sensing proximity cards are

- **Passive:** These devices contain no battery or power on the card. They use the electromagnetic field transmitted by the reader to transmit access information (identification) at different frequency levels.

- **Field-powered:** These devices contain active electronics, an RF transmitter, and power supply on the card.

- **Transponders:** Both the card and reader contain a transceiver, control logic, and battery. The reader transmits an interrogating signal (challenge) causing the card to transmit an access code (response).

Although more common in logical access controls, smart cards can also provide two-factor authentication in physical access control systems by requiring the user to enter a personal identification number (PIN) or password, or by incorporating an authentication token or other challenge-response mechanism.

Smart cards, and their associated access control systems, can be programmed to permit multilevel access, restrict access to certain periods (day and time), and log access information.

In the Physical Security domain, *smart card* is used as a general term to describe any security badge or access card with built-in identification and authentication features, such as embedded technology. This may be as simple as a magnetic stripe on an ID card that's swiped through a card reader. However, in the Access Control domain, a *smart card* refers to a very specific, highly specialized type of access card: A magnetic stripe doesn't qualify.

Biometric access controls

Biometrics provides the only absolute method for positively identifying an individual based on some unique physiological or behavioral characteristic of that individual (something you are). I discuss biometrics extensively in Chapter 3. Although biometrics in the Physical Security domain refers to *physical* access control devices (rather than *logical* access control devices, as in the Access Control Systems and Methodology domain), the underlying concepts and technologies are the same. To review, the major biometric systems in use today include

✔ **Finger scan systems**

✔ **Hand geometry systems**

- ✓ **Retina pattern**
- ✓ **Iris pattern**
- ✓ **Voice recognition**
- ✓ **Signature dynamics**

The accuracy of a biometric system is normally stated as a percentage, in the following terms:

- ✓ **False Reject Rate (FRR) or Type I error:** Authorized users who are incorrectly denied access, stated as a percentage.
- ✓ **False Accept Rate (FAR) or Type II error:** Unauthorized users who are incorrectly granted access, stated as a percentage.
- ✓ **Crossover Error Rate (CER):** The point at which the FRR equals the FAR, stated as a percentage.

Technical controls

Technical controls include monitoring and surveillance, intrusion detection systems (IDS), and alarms that alert personnel to physical security threats and allow them to respond appropriately.

Surveillance

Visual surveillance systems include photographic and electronic equipment that provide preventive, detective, and deterrent controls. When used to monitor live events, these systems are a preventive control. When used to record live events, they're a detective control. The visible use of these systems also provides a deterrent control.

Electronic systems such as closed-circuit television (CCTV) are used to extend and improve the monitoring and surveillance capability of security guards. Photographic systems, including videocassette recorders, are used to record events for later analysis or as evidence for prosecution.

Intrusion detection

Intrusion detection in the physical security domain refers to systems that detect attempts to gain unauthorized physical access to a building or area. Modern intrusion detection systems (IDS) commonly use the following types of sensors:

- ✓ **Photoelectric sensors:** A grid of visible or infrared light is projected over the protected area. If a beam of light within the grid is disturbed, an alarm is sounded.

- ✔ **Dry contact switches and metallic tape:** These systems are inexpensive and commonly used along a perimeter or boundary on door and window frames. For example, if the circuit switch is opened or the metallic tape broken, an alarm is sounded.

- ✔ **Motion detectors:** Three categories of motion detectors are

  - **Wave pattern:** Generates a low frequency, ultrasonic, or microwave field over a protected area up to 10,000 square feet (3,000 square meters). Any motion changes the frequency of the reflected wave pattern, causing an alarm to be sounded.

  - **Capacitance:** Monitors an electrical field for changes in electrical capacitance caused by motion. This type of motion detector is typically used for spot protection within a few inches of a protected object.

  - **Audio:** Passive system (doesn't generate a wave pattern or electrical field) triggered by any abnormal sound. This type of device generates more false alarms and should only be used in areas with low ambient noise.

Don't confuse intrusion detection systems (IDS) used to detect physical intruders in the Physical Security domain with network-based and host-based intrusion detection systems (IDS) used to detect cyber-intruders.

Alarms

Alarms are activated when a certain condition is detected. Examples of systems employing alarms include fire and smoke detectors, motion sensors and intrusion detection systems (IDS), metal and explosives detectors, access control systems (physical and logical), and climate control monitoring systems.

Alarm systems should have separate circuitry and a back-up power source. *Line supervision,* comprising technology and processes used to detect attempts to tamper with or disable an alarm system, should also be implemented.

The five general types of alarm systems are

- ✔ **Local systems:** An audible alarm is sounded on the local premises. These systems require a local response capability; that is, someone must call the police/fire department and/or respond directly.

- ✔ **Central station systems:** These systems are operated and monitored by private security organizations connected directly to the protected site via leased lines.

- ✔ **Proprietary systems:** These are similar to central station systems but are operated and monitored directly on the premises.

✔ **Auxiliary station systems:** These systems — which require prior authorization — use local municipal police or fire circuits to transmit an alarm to the appropriate police or fire headquarters. These systems are typically used in conjunction with one of the above systems (particularly central station systems) to improve response capabilities.

✔ **Remote station systems:** These systems are similar to auxiliary station systems but don't use police and fire circuits and also don't necessarily send the alarm to a police or fire department. An automatic dial-up fire alarm that dials a local police or fire department and plays a pre-recorded message is an example of a remote station system.

Environmental and life safety controls

These are the controls necessary for maintaining a safe and acceptable operating environment for computers and personnel. These include electrical power, HVAC, and fire detection and suppression.

Electrical power

General considerations for electrical power include having a dedicated feeder(s) from one or more utility substations or power grids and also ensuring that adequate physical access controls are implemented for electrical distribution panels and circuit breakers. An Emergency Power Off (EPO) switch should be installed near major systems and exit doors to shut down power in case of fire or electrical shock. Additionally, a back-up power source should be established, such as a diesel power generator. Back-up power should only be provided for critical facilities and systems including emergency lighting, fire detection and suppression, mainframes and servers (and certain workstations), HVAC, physical access control systems, and telecommunications equipment.

Protective controls for ESD include

✔ **Maintain proper humidity levels (40–60 percent)**

✔ **Ensure proper grounding**

✔ **Use anti-static flooring, anti-static carpeting, and floor mats**

Protective controls for electrical noise include

✔ **Install power line conditioners**

✔ **Ensure proper grounding**

✔ **Use shielded cabling**

Using an Uninterruptible Power Supply (UPS) is perhaps the most important protection against electrical anomalies. A UPS provides clean power to sensitive systems and a temporary power source during electrical outages (blackouts); it's important that this power supply is sufficient to properly shut down the protected systems. ***Note:*** A UPS should not be used as a back-up power source. A UPS — even a building UPS — is designed to provide temporary power, typically for 10–30 minutes, in order to allow a proper shutdown of protected systems.

Surge protectors and surge suppressors provide only minimal protection for sensitive computer systems and are more commonly (and dangerously) used to overload an electrical outlet or as a daisy-chained extension cord. The protective circuitry in most of these units costs no more than one dollar (compare the cost of a low-end surge protector with that of a 6' extension cord), and you get what you pay for — these glorified extension cords provide only minimal spike protection. True, a surge protector does provide more protection than nothing at all, but don't be lured into a false sense of security by these units — check them regularly for proper use and operation and don't accept them as a viable alternative to a UPS.

HVAC

Heating, ventilation, and air conditioning (HVAC) systems maintain the proper environment for computers and personnel. HVAC requirements planning involves complex calculations based on numerous factors including the average BTUs (British Thermal Units) produced by the estimated computers and personnel occupying a given area, the size of the room, insulation characteristics, and ventilation systems.

The ideal temperature range for computer equipment is between 50–80° F (10–26° C). At temperatures as low as 100° F (38° C), magnetic storage media can be damaged.

The ideal temperature range for computer equipment is between 50–80° F (10–26° C).

The ideal humidity range for computer equipment is between 40–60 percent. Higher humidity causes condensation and corrosion. Lower humidity increases the potential for ESD or static electricity.

Doors and side panels on computer equipment racks should be kept closed (and locked, for physical access control) to ensure proper airflow for cooling and ventilation.

Heating and cooling systems should be properly maintained and air filters cleaned regularly to reduce dust contamination and fire hazards.

Most gas discharge systems will automatically shut down HVAC systems prior to discharging, but a separate EPO should be installed near exits to facilitate a manual emergency shutdown.

Ideally, HVAC equipment should be dedicated, controlled, and monitored. If the systems aren't dedicated or independently controlled, proper liaison with the building manager is necessary to ensure that escalation procedures are effective and understood. Monitoring systems should alert the appropriate personnel when operating thresholds are exceeded.

Fire detection and suppression

Fire detection and suppression systems are some of the most essential life safety controls for protecting facilities, equipment, and most importantly, human lives.

Detection systems

The three main types of fire detection systems are

- ✔ **Heat-sensing:** These devices either sense temperatures exceeding a pre-determined level *(fixed-temperature detectors)* or rapidly rising temperatures *(rate-of-rise detectors)*. The former are more common and exhibit a lower false alarm rate.

- ✔ **Flame-sensing:** These devices either sense the flicker (or pulsing) of flames or the infrared energy of a flame. These systems are relatively expensive but provide an extremely rapid response time.

- ✔ **Smoke-sensing:** These devices either sense variations in light intensity *(photoelectric sensors)* or disturbances in the normal ionization current of radioactive materials *(radioactive sensors)*. These systems are typically used as early warning devices in ventilation systems.

The three main types of fire detection systems are heat-sensing, flame-sensing, and smoke-sensing.

Suppression systems

The two primary types of fire suppression systems are

- ✔ **Water sprinkler systems:** Water extinguishes fire by removing the heat element from the fire triangle and is most effective against Class A fires. Water is the primary fire-extinguishing agent for all business environments. Although water can potentially damage equipment, it's one of the most effective, inexpensive, readily available, and least harmful (to humans) extinguishing agents available. The four variations of water sprinkler systems are

  - **Wet pipe (or closed head system):** Most commonly used and considered the most reliable. Pipes are always charged with water and ready for activation. Typically a fusible link in the nozzle melts or ruptures, opening a gate valve that releases the water flow. Disadvantages include flooding because of nozzle or pipe failure and because of frozen pipes in cold weather.

- **Dry pipe:** No standing water in the pipes. Upon activation, a clapper valve opens, air is blown out of the pipe, and water flows. This type of system is less efficient than wet pipe systems but reduces the risk of accidental flooding; the time delay provides an opportunity to shut down computer systems (or remove power), if conditions permit.

- **Deluge:** Operates similar to a dry pipe system but is designed to quickly deliver large volumes of water. Deluge systems are typically not used for computer equipment areas.

- **Preaction:** Combines wet and dry pipe systems. Pipes are initially dry. When a heat-sensor is triggered, the pipes are charged with water, and an alarm is activated. Water isn't actually discharged until a fusible link melts (like in wet pipe systems). This system is recommended for computer equipment areas because it reduces the risk of accidental discharge by permitting manual intervention.

The four main types of water sprinkler systems are wet pipe, dry pipe, deluge, and preaction.

✔ **Gas discharge systems:** Gas discharge systems may be portable (such as a CO_2 extinguisher) or fixed (beneath a raised floor). These systems are typically classified according to the extinguishing agent that's employed. These include

- **Carbon dioxide (CO_2):** CO_2 is a commonly used colorless, odorless gas that extinguishes fire by removing the oxygen element from the fire triangle. (Refer to Figure 12-1.) CO_2 is most effective against Class B and C fires. Because it removes oxygen, its use is potentially lethal and best suited for unmanned areas or with a delay action (with manual override) in manned areas.

  CO_2 is also used in portable fire extinguishers, which should be located near all exits and within 50 feet (15 meters) of any electrical equipment. All portable fire extinguishers (CO_2, water, and soda acid) should be clearly marked (listing the extinguisher type and the fire classes to be used for) and periodically inspected. Additionally, all personnel should receive training on proper fire extinguisher use.

- **Soda acid:** This includes a variety of chemical compounds that extinguish fires by removing the fuel element (suppressing the flammable components of the fuel) of the fire triangle. (Refer to Figure 12-1.) Soda acid is most effective against Class A and B fires. It is not used for Class C fires because of the highly corrosive nature of many of the chemicals used.

- **Halon:** Halon systems suppress fire by separating the elements of the fire triangle (a chemical reaction) and are most effective against Class B and C fires. (Refer to Figure 12-1.) Halon doesn't damage computer equipment, leaves no liquid or solid residue, mixes thoroughly with the air, and spreads extremely fast.

However, Halon in concentrations above 10 percent is harmful if inhaled, and it degrades into toxic chemicals (hydrogen fluoride, hydrogen bromide, and bromine) when used on fires with temperatures above 900° F (482° C).

The two types of Halon used are Halon 1211 (liquid steaming agent used in portable extinguishers) and Halon 1301 (gas agent used in fixed flooding systems). However, because of its ozone-depleting characteristics, the Montreal Protocol of 1987 prohibited the further production and installation of Halon systems beginning in 1994, instead encouraging replacement of existing systems. Acceptable replacements for Halon include FM-200 (most effective), CEA-410 or CEA-308, NAF-S-III, FE-13, Argon or Argonite, and Inergen.

Halon is an ozone-depleting substance. Acceptable replacements include FM-200, CEA-410 or CEA-308, NAF-S-III, FE-13, Argon or Argonite, and Inergen.

Administrative controls

These include the policies and procedures necessary to ensure that physical access, technical controls, and environmental and life safety controls are properly implemented and achieve an overall physical security strategy.

Restricted areas

Areas in which sensitive information is handled or processed should be formally designated as restricted areas with additional security controls implemented. Restricted areas should be clearly marked, and all employees should know the difference between authorized and unauthorized personnel: specifically, how to detect whether someone on premises is authorized or not.

Visitors

Visitor policies and escort requirements should be clearly defined in the organizational security policy. All visitors should be required to present proper identification to a security guard or receptionist, sign a visitor log, complete a non-disclosure agreement (when appropriate), and wear a conspicuous badge that both identifies them as a visitor and clearly indicates whether an escort is required (often done with color-coded badges). If an escort is required, the assigned escort should be identified by name and held responsible for the visitor at all times while on the premises.

Audit trails and access logs

Audit trails and access logs are detective controls that provide a record of events. These records can be analyzed for unauthorized access attempts and patterns of abuse; they can also potentially be used as evidence. I cover audit trails extensively in Chapter 11.

Asset classification and control

Asset classification and control, particularly physical inventories, are an important detective control. The proliferation of desktop PCs, notebooks, personal digital assistants (PDAs), and wireless devices has made theft a very common and difficult physical security threat to counter. An accurate inventory helps identify missing equipment and may potentially be used as evidence.

Emergency procedures

Emergency procedures must be clearly documented, readily accessible (often posted in appropriate areas), periodically updated, and routinely practiced (in training and drills). Additional copies may also be kept at secure off-site facilities. Emergency procedures should include emergency system shutdown procedures, evacuation plans and routes, and business continuity plan/disaster recovery plan (BCP/DRP), which I cover in Chapter 10.

General housekeeping

Good housekeeping practices are an important aspect of physical security controls. Implementing and enforcing a no-smoking policy helps to reduce not only potential fire hazards but also contamination of sensitive systems. Cleaning dust and ventilation systems helps maintain a cleaner computing environment and also reduces static electricity and fire hazards. Keeping work areas clean and trash emptied reduces potential fire hazards (combustibles) and also helps identify and locate sensitive information that may have been improperly or carelessly handled.

Pre-employment and post-employment procedures

These include procedures for background and reference checks, obtaining security clearances, granting access, and termination procedures. These procedures are covered extensively in Chapters 5 and 9.

Additional References

Krutz, Ronald L. and Vines, Russell Dean. *The CISSP Prep Guide: Mastering the Ten Domains of Computer Security*, Chapter 10. John Wiley & Sons, Inc.

Tipton, Harold F. and Krause, Micki. *Information Security Management Handbook,* 4th Edition, Chapter 31. Auerbach Publications.

Russell, Deborah and Gangemi Sr, G.T. *Computer Security Basics*, Chapter 9. O'Reilly and Associates.

Parker, Donn B. *Fighting Computer Crime: A New Framework for Protecting Information*, pages 249–252. John Wiley & Sons, Inc.

Prep Test

1 The three elements of the fire triangle necessary for a fire to burn include all the following except

A ○ Fuel

B ○ Oxygen

C ○ Heat

D ○ Nitrogen

2 Electrical fires are classified as what type of fire and use what extinguishing methods?

A ○ Class B; CO_2 or soda acid

B ○ Class B; CO_2 or Halon

C ○ Class C; CO_2 or Halon

D ○ Class A; Water or soda acid

3 A prolonged drop in voltage describes what electrical anomaly?

A ○ Brownout

B ○ Blackout

C ○ Sag

D ○ Fault

4 What type of cabling should be used below raised floors and above drop ceilings?

A ○ CAT-5

B ○ Plenum

C ○ PVC

D ○ Water-resistant

5 In order to deter casual trespassers, fencing should be a minimum height of

A ○ 1–3 ft

B ○ 3–4 ft

C ○ 6–7 ft

D ○ 8 ft or greater

6 **Three types of intrusion detection systems (IDS) used for physical security include photoelectric sensors, dry contact switches, and which of the following?**

A ○ Motion detectors

B ○ Anomaly-based

C ○ Host-based

D ○ Network-based

7 **A water sprinkler system in which no water is initially present in the pipes and upon activation delivers a large volume of water describes what type of system?**

A ○ Wet pipe

B ○ Dry pipe

C ○ Deluge

D ○ Preaction

8 **Portable CO_2 fire extinguishers are classified as what type of extinguishing system?**

A ○ Gas discharge systems

B ○ Water sprinkler systems

C ○ Deluge systems

D ○ Preaction systems

9 **Which of the following extinguishing agents fights fires by separating the elements of the fire triangle?**

A ○ Water

B ○ Soda acid

C ○ CO_2

D ○ Halon

10 **Production of Halon has been banned for what reason?**

A ○ It is toxic at temperatures above 900° F.

B ○ It is an ozone-depleting substance.

C ○ It is ineffective.

D ○ It is harmful if inhaled.

Answers

1 **D.** Nitrogen. The fire triangle consists of fuel, oxygen, and heat. *Review "Physical Security Threats."*

2 **C.** Class C; CO_2 or Halon. Class B fires consist of burnable fuels and are extinguished using CO_2, soda acid, or Halon. Class A fires consist of common combustible materials. *Review "Physical Security Threats."*

3 **A.** Brownout. A blackout is a total loss of power, a sag is a short drop in voltage, and a fault is a momentary loss of power. *Review "Physical Security Threats."*

4 **B.** Plenum. CAT-5 cabling can be either plenum or PVC-coated. PVC cabling releases toxic vapors when burned. Both PVC and plenum coatings are water resistant. *Review "Designing a secure facility."*

5 **B.** 3–4 ft. Fencing of 1–3 ft might deter a toddler or a duck! 6–7 ft is too high to climb easily. Eight-foot high or greater fencing (with three-strand barbed wire) will deter a more determined intruder. *Review "Fencing."*

6 **A.** Motion detectors. Anomaly-based, host-based, and network-based systems are types of intrusion detection systems (IDS) used for computer systems and networks. *Review "Intrusion detection."*

7 **C.** Deluge. A wet pipe system always has water present in the pipes. A dry pipe system is similar to a deluge system but doesn't deliver a large volume of water. A preaction system combines elements of both wet and dry pipe systems. *Review "Suppression systems."*

8 **A.** Gas discharge systems. Water sprinkler systems are fixed systems that discharge water. Deluge and preaction systems are types of water sprinkler systems. *Review "Suppression systems."*

9 **D.** Halon. Water fights fires by removing the heat element. Soda acid fights fires by suppressing the fuel element. CO_2 fights fires by removing the oxygen element. *Review "Suppression systems."*

10 **B.** It is an ozone-depleting substance. Halon does release toxic chemicals at temperatures above 900° F and is harmful if inhaled in concentrations greater than 10 percent, but these are not the reasons that its production was banned. Halon is one of the most effective fire extinguishing agents currently available. *Review "Suppression systems."*

Part III
The Part of Tens

The 5th Wave   By Rich Tennant

Oh come on—
how fatal
can it be?

FATAL
ERROR

In this part . . .

Ya know 'em, ya love 'em. Short chapters with ten key ideas to make the exam easier and increase your score. Read the chapter title, savor the wisdom on the pages.

Chapter 13

Ten Security Domains

In This Chapter

▶ Listing the ten (ISC)² domains of information security

▶ Defining the ten (ISC)² domains of information security

*I*f you've read everything in this book to this point, you should be painfully aware of the CISSP CBK. But just to recap, the Common Body of Knowledge (CBK), which defines a basic and common knowledge base for all security professionals, is commonly referred to as the *ten domains of information security*. These ten domains are roughly analogous to test objectives defined by (ISC)² for the CISSP exam (www.isc2.org).

Access Control Systems and Methodology

This domain encompasses the set of mechanisms employed to restrict or direct the behavior, use, and content of a system. It defines a user's rights on a system, including what a user can or cannot do and what resources are available to a user.

In Chapter 3, I discuss all sorts of wonderful aspects of access control including concepts, techniques, and models, administration, methodologies, implementation, identification and authentication, accountability, monitoring, and methods of attack.

Telecommunications and Network Security

This domain encompasses the structures, transmission methods, transport formats, and security measures used to provide confidentiality, integrity, availability, and authentication for transmissions over private and public networks.

In Chapter 4, I discuss the Open Systems Interconnection (OSI) model and all the nitty-gritty details of telecommunications and networking.

Security Management Practices

This domain encompasses

- **Security management:** The identification of an organization's information assets and the development, documentation, and implementation of policies, standards, procedures and guidelines that ensure confidentiality, integrity, and availability

- **Risk management:** The identification, measurement, control, and minimization of loss associated with uncertain events or risks, including overall security review, risk analysis, selection and evaluation of safeguards, cost benefit analysis, management decision, safeguard implementation, and effectiveness review

See Chapter 5 for all the details.

Applications and Systems Development Security

This domain encompasses the controls included within systems and applications software and the steps used in their development. In this chapter (Chapter 6), I also delve into database security, system life cycles, and covert channels (no, not the scrambled channels on your cable TV box).

Cryptography

This domain encompasses the principles, means, and methods of disguising information to ensure its confidentiality, integrity, and authenticity. I discuss public and private key algorithms, digital signatures, PKI, and methods of attack. See Chapter 7 for more *"Tales from the Crypt-o!"*

Security Architecture and Models

This domain encompasses the concepts, principles, structures, and standards used to design, implement, monitor, and secure operating systems, equipment, networks, and applications. In Chapter 8, I discuss these topics and more, including Bell-LaPadula, Clark-Wilson, Biba, and others.

Operations Security

This domain encompasses the controls over hardware, media, and operators with access privileges to resources, including monitoring and auditing. This domain provides a good broad brush stroke of many of the individual concepts that I discuss throughout this book. Chapter 9 is kind of a the-sum-is-greater-than-the-parts type of chapter that gives you the big picture of how all these concepts combine to form a good, cohesive security strategy.

Business Continuity Planning (BCP) and Disaster Recovery Planning (DRP)

This domain encompasses the preparation, testing, and updating of specific actions to protect critical business processes from the effect of major system and network failures.

- **BCP:** Ensures that an organization can continue to function (or resume business functions) during an emergency
- **DRP:** Ensures that an organization can quickly recover from an emergency and attempts to minimize the impacts of an emergency

BCP and DRP deserve a little R-E-S-P-E-C-T and are covered extensively in Chapter 10.

Law, Investigations, and Ethics

This domain encompasses computer crime laws and regulations, incident handling, investigative measures and techniques, evidence gathering, ethical issues, and codes of conduct for security professionals.

All other domains in the CISSP CBK are primarily concerned with what you do *before* a security incident or violation has occurred. The Law, Investigations, and Ethics domain (covered extensively in Chapter 11) is largely devoted to what happens *after* a security incident or violation has occurred.

Physical Security

This domain encompasses the threats, vulnerabilities, and countermeasures used to physically protect an enterprise's resources and sensitive information including people, facilities, data, equipment, support systems, media, and supplies. See Chapter 12.

Chapter 14

Ten More Security Certifications

Many professional and technical security certifications are available that can either help a candidate prepare for Certified Information Systems Security Professional (CISSP) certification or complement the CISSP certification. Listed below are several security certifications listed in general order of popularity and relevance.

All costs and fees cited in this chapter are listed in US dollars.

Check Point

www.checkpoint.com/services/education/certification

The Check Point Certified Professional Program provides product-focused certifications based on the most popular firewall product on the market today: Check Point FireWall-1. Certifications exams are available at Prometric and VUE testing centers and include

- ✔ Check Point Certified Security Administrator (CCSA)
- ✔ Check Point Certified Security Expert (CCSE)
- ✔ Check Point Certified Security Expert Plus (CCSE Plus)

Cisco

www.cisco.com

Earning a Cisco Security Specialist 1 certification demonstrates proficiency in designing, installing, and supporting Cisco security products. Cisco Security

Specialist certification requires CCNA (Cisco Certified Network Associate) certification and four additional exams:

- ✔ Managing Cisco Network Security (MCNS)
- ✔ Cisco Secure PIX Firewall Advanced (CSPFA)
- ✔ Cisco Secure Intrusion Detection System (CSIDS)
- ✔ Cisco Secure VPN (CSVPN)

Finally, the mother of all certifications, the crème de la crème . . . the Cisco Certified Internetworking Expert (CCIE) offers a security track requiring satisfactory completion of a 2-hour, 100-question multiple choice qualification exam and a 1-day hands-on lab.

CIW

www.ciwcertified.com

The Certified Internet Webmaster (CIW) is a vendor-neutral certification program. The CIW Security Analyst Specialization requires the candidate to have earned Microsoft Certified Systems Engineer (MCSE), Certified Novell Engineer (CNE), Cisco Certified Network Professional (CCNP) or Cisco Certified Internetworking Expert (CCIE), Linux Professional Institute (LPI) Level II, or Software Architecture Implementation and Realization (SAIR) Linux and GNU Certified Engineer (LCE) Level II certification, and pass the CIW Security Professional Exam. For more on LPI and LCE certification, see the upcoming section "SAIR Linux/GNU."

CompTIA

www.comptia.org

The CompTIA Security+ examination is currently under development and expected to be released late 2002. CompTIA provides industry-supported, vendor-neutral certifications that test a candidate's understanding of basic foundation skills and core competencies in a given subject area. Although deemed entry-level by many, CompTIA certifications nonetheless provide a valuable and trusted certification in any technical career path. Several popular CompTIA certifications, including A+, Network+, and Server+, are accepted for credit toward various vendor-sponsored certifications including Microsoft (MCSE and MCSA) and CIW.

CompTIA exams also have the advantage, at least in the realm of vendor-neutral security certifications, of being readily available (administered by Prometric and VUE testing centers and relatively inexpensive). The Security+ certification will likely provide a very useful benchmark for candidates preparing for CISSP certification. Security topics expected to be covered on the Security+ exam include the following:

- Cryptography
- Firewalls
- Forensics
- Incident reporting
- Intrusion detection
- Malicious code and viruses
- Network auditing/vulnerability analysis
- Network defense and countermeasures
- Operating system security and patch installation
- Public Key Infrastructure (PKI) fundamentals and standards
- Remote access
- Security law
- Security policy
- User authentication, smart cards, biometrics, and digital certificates
- Virtual private networks
- Wireless devices and network security

DRII

www.dr.org

Disaster Recovery Institute International (DRII) provides three levels of certification in business continuity planning and disaster recovery, including

- **Associate Business Continuity Planner (ABCP):** For individuals who don't have two years of industry experience in the Professional Practices, which I describe below.

✔ **Certified Business Continuity Planner (CBCP):** For individuals with a minimum of two years of industry experience in at least three of the Professional Practices subject areas described below (and verified by two references).

✔ **Master Business Continuity Professional (MBCP):** For individuals with a minimum of five years of industry experience. Requires completion of a directed research paper or a 3½ hour case study exam for an additional $250 fee.

The exam is a multiple-choice exam administered at various locations and dates throughout the year. The cost for the exam is $250 (re-takes within 12 months are $50) and an application fee of $50 for ABCP, $250 for CBCP, and $300 for MBCP.

The exam tests the candidate's knowledge in ten subject areas covered in the Professional Practices for Business Continuity Planners document:

✔ Project initiation and management

✔ Risk evaluation and control

✔ Business impact analysis

✔ Developing business continuity strategies

✔ Emergency response and operations

✔ Developing and implementing business continuity plans

✔ Awareness and training programs

✔ Maintaining and exercising business continuity plans

✔ Public relations and crisis coordination

✔ Coordination with public authorities

ISACA

www.isaca.org

The Information Systems Audit and Control Association and Foundation (ISACA) administers the Certified Information Systems Auditor (CISA) certification, which has been earned by more than 27,000 professionals worldwide. In 2002, more than 10,000 individuals registered for the CISA certification exam.

Requirements for CISA certification include successful completion of the CISA examination and a minimum of five years of professional experience in information systems auditing, control, or security.

The CISA exam, offered only once a year, is a 4-hour, 200-question multiple choice exam. Costs range from $295 for ISACA members to $460 for non-members registering late. The exam covers the following areas:

- The IS Audit Process
- Management, Planning, and Organization of IS
- Technical Infrastructure and Operational Practices
- Protection of Information Assets
- Disaster Recovery and Business Continuity
- Business Application System Development, Acquisition, Implementation, and Maintenance
- Business Process Evaluation and Risk Management

(ISC)²

www.isc2.org

In addition to the CISSP certification, International Information Systems Security Certifications Consortium [(ISC)²] offers the Systems Security Certified Practitioner (SSCP) certification. Developed in 1998, the SSCP certifies network and systems administrators who implement security policies, standards, and procedures. The SSCP tests the candidate's knowledge in seven domains that comprise the Information Systems Security Administrator Common Body of Knowledge (CBK):

- Access controls
- Administration
- Audit and monitoring
- Risk, response, and recovery
- Cryptography
- Data communications
- Malicious code/malware

Similar in format to the CISSP exam, the SSCP exam is a paper-based 125-question multiple choice examination. The candidate has three hours to complete the exam. A minimum of one year of related work experience in at least one of the seven domains is also required. The exam cost is $295 if you register more than 21 days in advance.

Microsoft

www.microsoft.com

Although Microsoft doesn't offer a security certification, several security-relevant exams are available in the MCSE electives, including:

- ✔ Designing Security for a Microsoft Windows 2000 Network
- ✔ Implementing and Supporting Microsoft Proxy Server 2.0
- ✔ Installing, Configuring, and Administering Microsoft ISA Server 2000, Enterprise Edition

SAIR Linux/GNU

www.linuxcertification.com

Like Microsoft certifications, SAIR Linux/GNU certifications offer security-relevant exams in the course of certification requirements. The three levels of SAIR certification are

- ✔ Level I: SAIR Linux and GNU Certified Administrator (LCA)
- ✔ Level II: SAIR Linux and GNU Certified Engineer (LCE)
- ✔ Level III: Master SAIR Linux and GNU Certified Engineer (MLCE)

These certifications each require successful completion of four exams in the following system usage areas:

- ✔ Linux Installation
- ✔ Network Connectivity
- ✔ System Administration
- ✔ Security, Ethics, and Privacy

SANS/GIAC

> www.sans.org

> www.giac.org

The Global Information Assurance Certification (GIAC) was founded by the SANS (Systems Administration, Networking, and Security) Institute in 1999. GIAC certification is more technical and hands-on certification than the CISSP certification. Candidates for GIAC certification must first complete a written practical assignment. Passing assignments are posted on the SANS Web site and qualify the individual to take a technical certification to complete GIAC certification. GIAC currently offers ten individual certifications:

- ✔ GIAC Security Essentials Certification (GSEC)
- ✔ GIAC Certified Firewall Analyst (GCFW)
- ✔ GIAC Certified Intrusion Analyst (GCIA)
- ✔ GIAC Certified Incident Handler (GCIH)
- ✔ GIAC Certified Windows Security Administrator (GCWN)
- ✔ GIAC Certified UNIX Security Administrator (GCUX)
- ✔ GIAC Information Security Officer - Basic (GISO-Basic)
- ✔ GIAC Systems and Network Auditor (GSNA)
- ✔ GIAC Certified Forensic Analyst (GCFA)
- ✔ GIAC Security Leadership Certificate (GSLC)

A more advanced certification, the GIAC Security Engineer (GSE), is available for candidates who have completed the GSEC, GCFW, GCIA, GCIH, GCWN, and GCUX certifications and who excel in at least one of the subject area modules.

GIAC examination costs range from $250 if taken with SANS online or conference training to $425 if taken independently. Additionally, CISSP certified individuals qualify for a 40 percent discount on the GIAC Security Essentials Certification (GSEC) training *and* certification!

Chapter 15

Ten Security Web Sites

*L*iterally hundreds (if not thousands) of security Web sites can be found on the Internet. This list is by no means complete. Security Web sites come in many flavors (including black hat and white hat) and certainly some Web sites out there are better than others, with more being developed every day. However, this is a brief list of sites that I've found useful, both in preparing for the CISSP exam and in doing my job as a security professional. Please explore these sites, bookmark them, or add them to your Favorites (if you're so inclined), and continue your never-ending quest for knowledge.

(ISC)²

```
www.isc2.org
```

Your quest for the Certified Information Systems Security Professional (CISSP) certification begins here at the International Information Systems Security Certifications Consortium [(ISC)²] Web site. Read about the certification, request a free copy of the CISSP Study Guide, view the exam schedule, and register for your exam.

Other important and valuable information on this Web site includes review seminar schedules, information about post certification requirements, the (ISC)² Code of Ethics, (ISC)² events, and the Commonly Accepted Security Practices and Recommendations (CASPR) forum.

CISSP Open Study Guide

```
www.cccure.org/studytips.php
```

The CISSP Open Study Guide (OSG) Web site includes many valuable study resources for the CISSP candidate, such as study guides, downloads, study presentations, an online quiz, books, news, and access to numerous study groups.

Cissps.com

```
www.cissps.com
```

This Web portal for the CISSP includes an exam FAQ, study guides, a CISSP directory, information security resources, career opportunities for those with CISSP certifications, an online bookstore, and links to many other security Web sites.

Network Security Library

```
www.secinf.net
```

The Network Security Library is an excellent source of free online books, articles, FAQs, and HOWTOs. Subjects include Windows, Unix, Netware, firewalls, IDs, security policy, the Internet, the National Computer Security Center (NCSC) and DoD Rainbow Series, harmless hacking, and many more.

The SANS Institute

```
www.sans.org
```

The SANS (System Administration, Networking, and Security) Institute sponsors the Global Information Assurance Certification (GIAC) Program, a series of security certifications with a more technical hands-on focus than the CISSP certification. It's an excellent complement to CISSP certification, and SANS offers a 40 percent discount on its GSEC (GIAC Security Essentials Certification) certification for those with CISSP certification.

This Web site also includes SANS conference schedules, an extremely helpful security digest, the SANS online bookstore, various projects, resources, security links, sample security policies, white papers, GIAC student practicals, and security tools.

The site also includes the SANS/FBI Top Twenty Vulnerabilities list. This list, co-sponsored by the FBI National Infrastructure Protection Center (NIPC), helps organizations prioritize security efforts by listing and describing the top 20 Internet security vulnerabilities in 3 categories: General Vulnerabilities, Windows Vulnerabilities, and Unix Vulnerabilities.

The Shmoo Group

www.shmoo.com

The Shmoo Group hosts news mail archives with various subjects including Check Point Firewall-1, firewalls, Bugtraq, and intrusion detection systems. It is also the new home for the SecurityGeeks news site.

www.simovits.com

www.simovits.com/trojans/trojans.html

This site hosts a database of Trojans sorted by ports, Trojan common name, Trojan filename, file size, actions, affected systems, country of origin, and programming language.

Carnegie Mellon SEI CERT Coordination Center

www.cert.org

The Carnegie Mellon Software Engineering Institute (SEI) CERT Coordination Center includes vulnerabilities, incidents and fixes, security practices and evaluations, survivability research and analysis, and training and education resources.

Common Vulnerabilities and Exposures

```
cve.mitre.org
```

The Common Vulnerabilities and Exposures (CVE) is a list (maintained by the MITRE Corporation) of standardized names for vulnerabilities and other information security exposures. You can download the CVE dictionary from this Web site.

HierosGamos Guide to Computers and the Law

```
www.hg.org/compute.html
```

This Web site, sponsored by HierosGamos, includes a comprehensive guide to US and international laws and regulations relevant to the computer industry.

Chapter 16

Ten Test Preparation Tips

In This Chapter

▶ Studying for the CISSP exam

▶ Preparing for exam logistics

So much information, so little time! In this chapter, I recommend several (ten or so) tips for helping you prepare for that special day. (No, not *that* special day; read *Weddings For Dummies* for that one.) I'm talking about the CISSP exam here.

Get a Networking Certification First

The Telecommunications and Network Security domain is the most comprehensive domain tested on the Certified Information Systems Security Professional (CISSP) exam. Although its purpose is to test your security knowledge, you must have a complete understanding of telecommunications and networking basics. For this reason, I highly advise that you earn a networking certification first, such as the CompTIA Network+ or the Cisco Certified Network Associate (CCNA), before attempting the CISSP exam. (For more information on these certifications, see www.comptia.org and www.cisco.com, respectively.) An additional benefit is that you will then have another valuable technical certification in high demand within the computer industry.

If you already have one of these certifications, you should find that most of the information in the Telecommunications and Network Security domain to be very basic. In this case, a quick review focusing on security concepts (particularly methods of attack) should be sufficient for this domain. I dedicate Chapter 4 of this book to the Telecommunications and Network Security domain and Chapter 3 to the Access Control Systems and Methodology domain.

Register NOW!

Go online and register for the CISSP exam at www.isc2.org — NOW!

Committing yourself to a test date is the best cure for procrastination, especially because the test costs $450 (US) . . . and an additional $100 (US) if you must change your exam date! This will help you plan and focus your study efforts.

Also, unlike most certification exams, the CISSP exam isn't conveniently available at Prometric Testing Centers. You need to look at the schedule on the International Information Systems Security Certifications Consortium [(ISC)²] Web site to find a suitable date and location. Some travel may be necessary, which will require advance planning as well.

Finally, expect an additional $100 (US) late registration fee if you register less than 21 days before the exam.

A 60-Day Study Plan

After you register for the CISSP exam, commit yourself to a 60-day study plan. Of course, your daily experiences and professional reading should span a much greater period, but for your final preparations leading up to the CISSP exam, plan on a 60-day period of intense study.

Exactly how intense depends on your own personal experience and learning ability, but plan on a minimum of 2 hours a day for 60 days. If you're a slow learner or reader, or perhaps find yourself weak in many areas, plan on four to six hours a day and more on the weekends. Regardless, try to stick to the 60-day plan. If you feel that you need 360 hours of study, you may be tempted to spread this out over a 6-month period for 2 hours a day. But committing to six months of intense study is much harder (on you, as well as your family and friends) than two months. In the end, you'll find yourself studying only as much as you would have in a 60-day period.

Get Organized and READ!

A wealth of security information is available for the CISSP candidate. However, studying everything is impractical. Instead, get organized, determine your strengths and weaknesses, and then READ!

Begin by requesting an official *CISSP Certification CBK Study Guide* from the (ISC)^2 Web site (www.isc2.org). It's free and will be e-mailed to you as a password-protected Adobe Acrobat PDF document. This provides a good outline of the subjects on which you'll be tested.

Next, read this book, take the practice exam in Appendix A, and review the materials on the accompanying CD-ROM. *CISSP For Dummies* is written to provide the CISSP candidate with an excellent overview of all the broad topics covered on the CISSP exam. If the CISSP Study Guide is the bread in a CISSP sandwich, this is the meat!

Next, focus on weak areas that you identify. Read additional references (I list several great ones at the end of each chapter throughout this book. As a minimum, I highly recommend *The CISSP Prep Guide: Mastering the Ten Domains of Computer Security* by Ronald L. Krutz and Russell Dean Vines (John Wiley & Sons, Inc.) and the *Information Security Management Handbook,* 4th Edition by Harold F. Tipton and Micki Krause (Auerbach Publications). If you really want to know what's in the meat, this is your source.

You should also download and review the Tipton and Rothke presentations and the ten domain guides available at www.cccure.org/studytips.php. This is the lettuce and tomato of your CISSP sandwich.

You can also find several study guides at www.cissps.com, www.cccure.org, and www.cramsession.com. Mayonnaise and mustard.

Finally, in the final week before your exam, you should have been through all your selected study materials at least once. Review or read *CISSP For Dummies* one more time, as well as your own personal study notes, and do as many practice questions as you can.

Join a Study Group

There is strength in numbers. Joining or creating your own study group will help you stay focused and provide a wealth of information from the broad perspectives and experiences of other security professionals. Perhaps the best study group for CISSP candidates and security professionals is the CISSPstudy 1 list at yahoogroups.com. You can subscribe via a link from www.cccure.org/studytips.php.

Take Practice Exams

No practice exams are available that exactly duplicate the CISSP exam — and forget about brain dumps. However, many resources are available for practice questions. You'll find some practice questions too hard, others too easy, and some that are just plain irrelevant. However, the repetition of practice questions will help reinforce important information that you need to know in order to successfully answer questions on the CISSP exam. For this reason, I recommend taking as many practice exams as possible. Use the practice test in Appendix A of this book, use the Flash Cards on the accompanying CD-ROM, try the practice questions on the CISSP Open Study Guide (OSG) Web site (www.cccure.org/studytips.php), and use the Boson CISSP Exams #2 and #3 (www.boson.com).

Take a CISSP Review Seminar

Finally, you can take an official (ISC)² CISSP Review Seminar. Choose from a one-day "Introduction to the CISSP Exam and CBK" or a more extensive five-day "CBK Review Seminar." Like the exam, the review seminars can be quite expensive and may require some travel. Schedules and additional information are available at www.isc2.org.

Develop a Test-Taking Strategy

The CISSP certification exam is a unique exam in many regards. One obvious difference from other certification exams is that it's not computer-based. This requires a different approach, and you should consider things such as how you will complete your answer sheet, writing in the exam booklet, and allotting time for guessing.

One strategy is to go through the entire exam, answering only the questions that you're sure of, and then going back to the remaining questions. An advantage to this strategy is that often a later question provides the answer, or at least some insight, to a previous question.

You are allowed to write in the exam booklet, so you might try answering 50 questions at a time, writing your answers in the exam booklet, crossing out any obviously wrong answers, then going back to fill in the circles. By using this method, you'll be sure that you don't complete the exam and find that you have only 10 minutes to fill in 250 circles! Answers in your exam booklet aren't scored, so be sure to fill in the answer sheet neatly and completely. Another advantage to this method is that it helps you keep your place on the answer sheet. (Everyone has probably had the same nightmare — not the one about showing up without any clothes — the one about losing your place on the answer sheet and filling in the wrong circles, then having to erase your entire answer sheet and start over.) You might also factor in a short break every 50 questions and then getting a fresh start on the next 50.

Guessing is a desperate but effective method when all else fails. An unanswered question is definitely wrong, so don't leave any questions unanswered. If you can eliminate 2 possible choices, then you have a 50/50 chance of getting the answer right. Another strategy for guessing is to count up the total number of A, B, C, and D answers. You should have a fairly even distribution of answers (although not always). Also, be sure to leave sufficient time for guessing and filling in answer circles. Instead of 5 minutes, consider reserving the final 15 minutes for guessing: It takes a lot longer to fill in answer circles than to point and click.

Practice Drawing Circles!

This might sound silly, but filling in those little answer circles takes some effort. It's probably been a long time since you've taken a paper-based exam with pesky little answer circles (like the SAT in high school). You want to be sure that you can fill in the circles neatly and completely so that they're properly scored. Also, get an idea of how long it takes to fill in the circles so that you can plan your test-taking strategy accordingly. Check out the sample answer sheets that you can print out from the accompanying CD-ROM. Try filling in a page of 50 circles and see how long it takes you (and how badly your hand cramps).

Plan Your Travel

You might have to travel some distance to get to your scheduled exam. If this is the case, make sure that you make all travel arrangements well in advance, including airline, hotel, and rental car reservations. Ensure that you have all the required documents for travel (including your passport and visa if you're traveling to another country for the exam). If you'll be traveling halfway around the world, also be sure to account for jet lag.

If you're driving to your exam, remember that you'll be sitting for a six-hour exam. For example, if you drive from Indianapolis to Chicago (normally a four-hour jaunt), don't plan on leaving at 3 a.m., miraculously finding the test center before 8 a.m. somewhere in downtown Chicago during morning rush hour, and then driving back to Indy at the end of the day. Spend $100 for a hotel room the day before so that you can relax and enjoy the Windy City.

Most exams are scheduled around 8 a.m., so I recommend that you arrive the day before your exam (not just the evening before) so that you can relax and locate the exam center. You sure don't want to be lost at 7:45 a.m. on test day. Also, be sure that you don't schedule a departure flight for 3 p.m. on the day of your exam. You don't want to feel pressured during the exam to rush so that you can make your flight. If possible, stay an extra night, review the material that you were tested on (regardless of whether you believe you passed or failed), and then have some fun!

Chapter 17

Ten Test Day Tips

In This Chapter

▶ Preparing yourself physically and mentally

▶ What to bring to the exam

*W*ell, your big day has finally arrived. After months of study and mind-numbing stress, you cram all night before the exam, skip breakfast because you're running late, argue with the proctor about the way that you're dressed, and then forget everything you know because you've got a splitting headache for the next four hours while sitting for your exam! Not exactly a recipe for success — but the following ten test day tips are.

Get a Good Night's Rest

The night before the exam is not the time to do any last-minute cramming. Studies have proven that a good night's rest is essential to doing well on an exam. Have a nice dinner (I recommend going for some carbohydrates and avoiding anything spicy) and then get to bed early. Save the all-night party for the day after the exam.

Dress Comfortably (And Appropriately)

You should address in attire that's comfortable — remember, this is a six-hour exam. If you're taking your test in a colder climate, dress in layers. Also, be sure to dress appropriately because some test locations may have specific dress requirements, such as business casual.

Eat a Good Breakfast

Breakfast is the most important meal of the day. Even if you're not a breakfast person, try to get something down before sitting for the CISSP exam. No extra time is allotted for lunch breaks, so plan on eating a good, hearty breakfast.

Arrive Early

Absolutely, *under no circumstances*, do you want to arrive late for this exam. Make sure that you know where the exam site is located, what the traffic is like that time of the day, and where you can park. Arrive at the testing site at least a half an hour before the exam time to take care of registration. The exam proctor will provide a brief introduction, discussing rules for breaks and restroom locations. Also before the exam begins, you will receive instructions for filling out the answer sheets. You don't want to miss any of this information. Remember, this is not a Prometric Testing Center: You're not the only person taking the exam, and everybody starts at the same time.

Bring Your Registration Letter and ID

After you register online, International Information Systems Security Certifications Consortium [(ISC)^2] e-mails you a confirmation letter twice. Print out the e-mail and the confirmation letter and bring both with you to the exam. You also need to bring your driver's license, government-issued ID, or passport.

Forward the e-mail to a Hotmail or Yahoo! account. You can download it in your hotel room if you lose your hard copy letter.

Bring Snacks and Drinks

Some test centers provide coffee, sodas, pastries, and light snacks . . . but don't count on it. Bring a small bag with some essentials. A *big* bottle of water is essential. Also, consider bringing a soda and some chips, a sandwich, candy bars, and so on. At most test centers, you're allowed to eat at the back of the room to avoid disturbing others.

Bring Prescription or Over-the-Counter Medications

If you're taking any prescription medication, *bring it with you*. Nothing can ruin your chances (as well as others in the room) of succeeding on the CISSP exam like a medical emergency! Also, consider bringing some basic over-the-counter meds such as acetaminophen or antacids to eliminate any annoying inconveniences such as headaches, heartburn, or a gastrointestinal malady. A box of tissues might also be appropriate — if you have a cold or feel like crying when you see the exam!

Bring Extra Pencils and a BIG Eraser

(ISC)² provides neat little green pre-sharpened No. 2 pencils for the exam. (Grab about $450 worth in case you fail the exam.) But also bring your own pre-sharpened No.2 pencils in case someone else has the same idea and the proctor runs out of pencils. Also, be forewarned — the erasers on these pencils are useless! Do *not* use the erasers on the (ISC)² pencils. You'll smear your pencil marks and risk totally destroying your answer sheet. Instead, invest in one of those click erasers or a good white plastic eraser from Office Depot. And get a *big* one!

Leave Your Cell Phone, Pager, PDA, and Digital Watch at Home

This is the one day that your office is going to have to do without you. Turn off your cell phones, pagers, PDAs, digital watch alarms, or anything else that goes beep. Even better, leave it all in your hotel room or at home. You need to focus on the exam. And (ahem) so does everyone else in the room. In the case of digital watches: Calculators are prohibited during the CISSP exam, and thus some test sites may require you to remove your digital watch. Bring a regular boring watch instead so that you can keep track of the time easily.

Take Frequent Breaks

Finally, six hours is a long time. Be sure to get up and walk around during the exam. I recommend taking a short five-minute break every hour during the exam. Eat a snack, go to the restroom, smoke a cigarette (***Warning:*** The Surgeon General has determined that smoking is hazardous to your health!), walk around, stretch, crack your knuckles, or whatever . . . then get back to the task at hand. You might even incorporate breaks into your test-taking strategy. For example, answer 50 questions and then take a break.

Also, if you find your mind wandering or you have trouble focusing, take a break. Burnout and fatigue can lead to careless mistakes or indifference. If you feel these symptoms coming on, take a break.

But be careful not to overdo your breaks. Most people seem to finish the exam in four to five hours, but it's also fairly common to see several candidates working frantically until the last minute. Stick to frequent but short breaks and you'll be fine.

Chapter 18

Ten Essential Reference Books

In This Chapter
▶ Ten highly recommended information security books
▶ And why!

*I*nformation security is a hot topic, and new books on this important subject are being published every day. Some are better than others. The following list contains ten excellent books on a variety of subjects in information security. Many outstanding information security books have been written and many more are likely to be published. However, the following short list contains ten books that I highly recommend.

Information Security, Protecting the Global Enterprise by Donald L. Pipkin (Prentice Hall PTR). I recommend this book for step-by-step guidance regarding important security management practices.

Computer Security Basics by Deborah Russell and G.T. Gangemi, Sr. (O'Reilly and Associates). Much of the information here is outdated, but this is still an excellent reference for security basics.

Security Engineering: A Guide to Building Dependable Distributed Systems by Ross Anderson (John Wiley & Sons, Inc.). Read this book for excellent, in-depth coverage of some very complex subjects.

Designing Network Security by Merike Kaeo (Cisco Press). Information security Cisco-style! In addition to very technology-specific information, this book also describes basic fundamentals (authentication, authorization, accounting, cryptography, PKI, and security policy) in a very clear and concise manner.

Building Internet Firewalls, 2nd Edition by Elizabeth D. Zwicky, Simon Cooper, D. Brent Chapman, and Deborah Russell (O'Reilly and Associates). This book contains the principles of deploying firewalls to implement an effective security strategy — and how to build one.

RSA Security's Official Guide to Cryptography by Steve Burnett and Stephen Paine (RSA Press). This book contains thorough coverage of a complex subject in an easily understood format.

Fighting Computer Crime: A New Framework for Protecting Information by Donn B. Parker (John Wiley & Sons, Inc.). This book introduces new ways of thinking about information security.

Incident Response: Investigating Computer Crime by Kevin Mandia and Chris Prosise (Osborne/McGraw-Hill). I like this book for its thorough coverage of investigations and evidence gathering.

The CERT Guide to System and Network Security Practices by Julia H. Allen (Addison-Wesley). Read here to discover how to secure your systems and network, step-by-step.

Network Intrusion Detection: An Analyst's Handbook by Stephen Northcutt and Judy Novak (New Riders) and *Intrusion Signatures and Analysis* by Stephen Northcutt, Mark Cooper, Matt Fearnow, and Karen Frederick (New Riders). Okay, that's really two books, but the second one is an excellent (and logical) companion to the first. Both books are from the SANS Institute and provide practical, in-depth information.

Part IV
Appendixes

The 5th Wave   By Rich Tennant

SNOW GLOBE DATA STORAGE

Okay let's shake this thing and see what we come up with.

In this part . . .

Whether you call 'em *appendixes* or *appendices,* they're chock-full of exam-passing goodness. In this book, the appendithingies are a glossary, a practice exam, and the instructions for the CD that is taped inside the back cover.

Appendix A
Practice Exam

Practice Exam Rules

▶ One hour

▶ 50 questions

▶ At least 35 correct answers to pass

▶ Treat this test as closed-book: Don't look ahead (to the answers) or behind (to the chapters)

This 50-question practice exam tests your knowledge on all the CISSP test objectives that I cover in this book. By using this exam, which is similar to the real one, you can identify weak areas that you need to review. At the end of the practice exam, you will find the correct answers, along with explanations and the chapter where the topic is covered.

Questions

1 The individual responsible for protecting information is known as the

 A ○ Owner
 B ○ Custodian
 C ○ Steward
 D ○ Caretaker

2 An example of a protection-based perimeter control is a(n)

 A ○ Firewall
 B ○ IDS
 C ○ TACACS
 D ○ SNMP

3 The process of breaking an encryption is called

 A ○ Decipherment
 B ○ Steganography
 C ○ Cryptanalysis
 D ○ Decryption

4 A system's memory space that is larger than its physical memory is known as

 A ○ Secondary memory
 B ○ Read-only memory
 C ○ Read-ahead cache
 D ○ Virtual memory

5 In the software development lifecycle, Request Control includes which of the following activities?

 A ○ Estimate costs, execute requests
 B ○ Prioritize requests, estimate costs
 C ○ Prioritize requests, estimate costs, execute requests
 D ○ Prioritize requests, execute requests

6 The individual who determines the level of classification for an object is known as the

 A ○ Custodian
 B ○ System Administrator
 C ○ Owner
 D ○ Security Administrator

7 The process of review and approval for modifications to hardware and software is known as

A ○ Change Management
B ○ Configuration Management
C ○ Release Control
D ○ Field Service Control

8 The burden of proof under civil law

A ○ Is greater than under criminal law
B ○ Is less than under criminal law
C ○ Is based solely upon circumstantial evidence
D ○ Is the same as under criminal law

9 CHAP would most likely be used with

A ○ Message digests
B ○ Digital signatures
C ○ Encryption
D ○ Remote access

10 The Software Capability Maturity Model is a measure of

A ○ The security features of software applications
B ○ The performance of modern compilers
C ○ The quality of the software development process
D ○ The longevity of applications

11 A security policy that an organization is required to implement because of legal requirements is known as a

A ○ Regulatory policy
B ○ Legal policy
C ○ Required policy
D ○ Mandated policy

12 A knowledge-based IDS uses

A ○ Learned patterns
B ○ Neural networks
C ○ Heuristics
D ○ Signatures

13 **The effect that a disaster would have on business operations is described in a**

A ○ Business Impact Assessment
B ○ Vulnerability Assessment
C ○ Risk Assessment
D ○ Recovery Plan

14 **Least privilege**

A ○ Is known as Ring 9 in the Ring Protection Model
B ○ Ensures that people have only the privileges they need to do their job
C ○ Is the default permissions for a Guest account
D ○ Is another term for read-only

15 **Civil penalties include**

A ○ Fines and jail time
B ○ Incarceration
C ○ Compensatory damages, punitive damages, and statutory damages
D ○ Financial restitution and incarceration

16 **The primary function of Risk Management is to**

A ○ Identify vulnerabilities
B ○ Identify threats
C ○ Measure risk
D ○ Mitigate risk

17 **An encryption algorithm that uses a key that is the same length as the message is known as a**

A ○ Running Key Cipher
B ○ Stream Cipher
C ○ Block Cipher
D ○ One-Time Pad

18 **A Criticality Survey determines**

A ○ Which functions are the most important in the business
B ○ Which threats are the most important
C ○ Which vulnerabilities are the most important
D ○ Which facilities are the most important

19 **An unintended communications path between two entities is known as a(n)**

A ○ Covert channel
B ○ Overt channel
C ○ Worm hole
D ○ Leak

20 **RAID is typically used for**

A ○ Host-based IDS
B ○ Mission-critical backups
C ○ Mission-critical storage
D ○ Penetration tests

21 **The absence of a safeguard constitutes a**

A ○ Weakness
B ○ Vulnerability
C ○ Threat
D ○ Risk

22 **The types of fire detectors are**

A ○ Heat-actuated, flame-actuated, and smoke-actuated
B ○ Heat-actuated and smoke-actuated
C ○ Carbon monoxide-actuated and smoke-actuated
D ○ Carbon monoxide-actuated, heat-actuated, and smoke-actuated

23 **In OOT, a method is**

A ○ The method used to normalize an object database
B ○ The model used to test an object
C ○ The analysis model used to design the object
D ○ The code associated with an object

24 **An attack based upon the perpetrator's desire for revenge is known as a(n)**

A ○ Material attack
B ○ Business attack
C ○ Grudge attack
D ○ Anger attack

25 **The Rijndael block cipher**

A ○ Was broken in 1993
B ○ Is the algorithm used for the AES
C ○ Was the first public key algorithm
D ○ Is another name for Triple DES

26 **A Single Loss Expectancy is**

A ○ The dollar figure that is assigned to a single event
B ○ The probability of occurrence of a single event
C ○ The probability of occurrence times the dollar figure of a single event
D ○ The threat of the occurrence times the probability

27 **The access control model using the classification of documents and classifica-tion levels of persons is the**

A ○ Discretionary Use Model

B ○ Clark-Wilson Model

C ○ Bell-LaPadula Model

D ○ Biba Model

28 **The goal of Disaster Recovery Planning is to**

A ○ Prevent disasters from occurring

B ○ Determine which disasters are likely to occur

C ○ Restore damaged facilities

D ○ Keep critical business operations running

29 **The process that records and controls the actual changes to hardware and software is known as**

A ○ Change Management

B ○ Configuration Management

C ○ Release Control

D ○ Field Service Control

30 **Which of the following is NOT contained in an SLA?**

A ○ Transaction volume

B ○ System up-time

C ○ Average compile time

D ○ Average response time

31 **The purpose of security awareness is**

A ○ To make workers aware of security risks and proper security procedures

B ○ To make would-be intruders aware of the site's security controls

C ○ To give risk managers as much information as possible

D ○ To understand Risk Management reports

32 **A building entrance that consists of double interlocked doors is known as a(n)**

A ○ Airlock

B ○ Security door

C ○ Mantrap

D ○ Flytrap

33 **The system component through which the CPU, memory, and I/O communicate is called the**

A ○ Bus
B ○ Plane
C ○ Ring
D ○ Train

34 **A backup that copies files that changed since the last full backup is called a(n)**

A ○ Level 2 backup
B ○ Level 3 backup
C ○ Incremental backup
D ○ Differential backup

35 **MD5 is an example of a(n)**

A ○ One-Time Pad
B ○ Message digest
C ○ Moderated digital signature
D ○ Digital Signature Standard

36 **The three types of controls are**

A ○ Proactive, reactive, and responsorial
B ○ Preventive, detective, and corrective
C ○ Direct, indirect, and passive
D ○ Active, passive, and corrective

37 **The traces of data that remain on a media after its erasure is called**

A ○ Remainder
B ○ Echo
C ○ Remanence
D ○ Halo

38 **The goal of Business Continuity Planning is to**

A ○ Prevent disasters from occurring
B ○ Determine which disasters are likely to occur
C ○ Restore damaged facilities
D ○ Keep critical business operations running

39 **An inference engine and a knowledge base make a(n)**

A ○ Expert system

B ○ Neural network

C ○ Fuzzy logic system

D ○ Program

40 **In the US, intellectual property includes**

A ○ Trade secrets

B ○ Patents, trademarks, copyrights, and trade secrets

C ○ Classified documents

D ○ Patents, attestations, and trade secrets

41 **Examples of detective/physical controls are**

A ○ Audit trails and biometrics

B ○ Clipping levels and noise thresholds

C ○ Fences, badges, and card-entry systems

D ○ Motion sensors and cameras

42 **The system component that enforces access control is called the**

A ○ Domain protector

B ○ Ring model

C ○ Reference monitor

D ○ Security kernel

43 **The most thorough DRP test is a(n)**

A ○ Interruption test

B ○ Parallel test

C ○ Simulation test

D ○ Drill

44 **A SYN attack is one form of a**

A ○ Panic attack

B ○ Man in the middle attack

C ○ Password guessing attack

D ○ Denial of Service attack

45 **Which of the following is NOT a function of a digital signature?**

A ○ Detection of unauthorized modifications
B ○ Encryption of a message
C ○ Authenticating the identity of the sender
D ○ Verifying the integrity of a message

46 **Authentication that is based upon *what you are* is known as**

A ○ Biometrics
B ○ Token
C ○ Userid and password
D ○ Smart card

47 **Proximity cards, photo image cards, and biometric devices are known as**

A ○ Personnel controls
B ○ Identity controls
C ○ Facility access controls
D ○ Smart cards

48 **The rule that states that a printout of computer data is considered original evidence is known as the**

A ○ Circumstantial rule
B ○ Hearsay rule
C ○ Best evidence rule
D ○ Conclusive rule

49 **Which of the following is NOT a penetration testing method?**

A ○ War dialing
B ○ Port scanning
C ○ Sniffing
D ○ Violation analysis

50 **Authentication that is based upon *something you have* is known as**

A ○ One-factor authentication
B ○ Token authentication
C ○ Three-factor authentication
D ○ Biometrics

Answers

1 **B.** Custodian. The custodian is the person who is assigned responsibility for protecting information. *(Chapter 5)*

2 **A.** Firewall. A firewall is an example of a protection-based perimeter control. *(Chapter 4)*

3 **C.** Cryptanalysis. Cryptanalysis is the process of breaking an encryption. *(Chapter 7)*

4 **D.** Virtual memory. Virtual memory is the term that describes a system's memory space that exceeds its physical memory space. *(Chapter 8)*

5 **B.** Prioritize requests, estimate costs. Request control includes prioritization and cost estimating. *(Chapter 6)*

6 **C.** Owner. The Owner determines the level of classification for an object. *(Chapter 5)*

7 **A.** Change Management. Change Management is the process of review and approval of changes. *(Chapter 9)*

8 **B.** Is less than under criminal law. The burden of proof under civil law is based upon the preponderance of the evidence, which is a lower standard than for criminal law, which is based upon guilt beyond a reasonable doubt. *(Chapter 11)*

9 **D.** Remote access. CHAP, or Challenge Handshake Authentication Protocol, is used for remote access authentication. *(Chapter 3)*

10 **C.** The quality of the software development process. The Software Capability Maturity Model is a measure of the processes that support software development. *(Chapter 6)*

11 **B.** Legal policy. A regulatory policy is the type that is mandated by legal requirements. *(Chapter 5)*

12 **D.** Signatures. Knowledge-based Intrusion Detection Systems use signatures. *(Chapter 4)*

13 **A.** Business Impact Assessment. The Business Impact Statement describes the impact of a disaster on business operations. *(Chapter 10)*

14 **B.** Ensures that people have only the privileges they need to do their job. Least Privilege means that people have only the privileges they must have to do their job. *(Chapter 9)*

15 **C.** Compensatory damages, punitive damages, and statutory damages. Civil penalties include compensatory damages, punitive damages, and statutory damages but never incarceration. *(Chapter 11)*

16 **D.** Mitigate risk. Although Risk Management does identify threats and vulnerabilities, its primary function is to mitigate risk. *(Chapter 5)*

17 **D.** One-Time Pad. A One-Time Pad uses a key that is the same length as the message. The key is used only once, for that message only. *(Chapter 7)*

18 **A.** Which functions are the most important in the business. The Criticality Survey ranks business functions in order of importance. *(Chapter 10)*

19 **A.** Covert channel. A covert channel is an unintended communications path between two entities. *(Chapter 8)*

20 **C.** Mission-critical storage. RAID (Redundant Array of Inexpensive [or Intelligent, or Independent] Disks, is a disk-storage technology that is used when availability is a big concern. *(Chapter 4)*

21 **B.** Vulnerability. A vulnerability is the result of the absence of a safeguard. *(Chapter 5)*

22 **A.** Heat-actuated, flame-actuated, and smoke-actuated. The types of fire detectors are heat-actuated, flame-actuated, and smoke-actuated. *(Chapter 12)*

23 **D.** The code associated with an object. A method is the code associated with an object. *(Chapter 6)*

24 **C.** Grudge attack. The attack of revenge is known as a grudge attack. *(Chapter 11)*

25 **B.** Is the algorithm used for the AES. Rijndael was chosen as the Advanced Encryption Standard (AES) algorithm in 2001. *(Chapter 7)*

26 **A.** The dollar figure that is assigned to a single event. A Single Loss Expectancy (SLE) is the dollar figure assigned to a single event. *(Chapter 5)*

27 **C.** Bell-LaPadula Model. The Bell-LaPadula model uses the classification of documents and persons. *(Chapter 8)*

28 **D.** Keep critical business operations running. The main goal of Disaster Recovery Planning is to restore damaged facilities. *(Chapter 10)*

29 **B.** Configuration Management. Configuration Management manages the actual changes to hardware and software. *(Chapter 9)*

30 **C.** Average compile time. Compile time has no bearing on Service Level Agreements (SLA). *(Chapter 6)*

31 **A.** To make workers aware of security risks and proper security procedures. Security awareness is used to train workers on security risks and procedures. *(Chapter 5)*

32 **C.** Mantrap. A mantrap is a pair of interlocked doors at a building entrance where only one door can be open at a time. *(Chapter 12)*

33 **A.** Bus. The bus is the component that the CPU, memory, and I/O communicate through. *(Chapter 8)*

34 **D.** Differential backup. A differential backup copies all files that have changed since the last full backup. *(Chapter 4)*

35 **B.** Message digest. MD5 is a message digest algorithm. *(Chapter 7)*

36 **B.** Preventive, detective, and corrective. The three types of controls are preventive, detective, and corrective. *(Chapter 3)*

37 **C.** Remanence. Remanence is the data that remains on a medium after it is supposedly erased. *(Chapter 9)*

38 **D.** Keep critical business operations running. Business Continuity Planning is concerned with keeping critical business functions running during a disaster. *(Chapter 10)*

39 **A.** Expert system. An expert system consists of an inference engine and a knowledge base. *(Chapter 6)*

40 **B.** Patents, trademarks, copyrights, and trade secrets. Patents, trademarks, copyrights, and trade secrets are the four types of intellectual property in the US. *(Chapter 11)*

41 **D.** Motion sensors and cameras. Detective/physical controls are those which reveal violations of physical security, such as motion sensors and cameras. *(Chapter 3)*

42 **C.** Reference monitor. The reference monitor is the system component that enforces access control. *(Chapter 8)*

43 **A.** Interruption test. The interruption test is the most thorough DRP test because in this test, the production systems are actually switched off. *(Chapter 10)*

44 **D.** Denial of Service attack. A SYN attack, sometimes known as a SYN Flood, is a Denial of Service attack. *(Chapter 4)*

45 **B.** Encryption of a message. Digital signatures don't encrypt the original message. *(Chapter 7)*

46 **A.** Biometrics. Biometrics is the authentication that is based upon *what you are*. *(Chapter 3)*

47 **C.** Facility access controls. Proximity cards, photo image cards, and biometric devices are collectively known as facility access controls. *(Chapter 12)*

48 **C.** Best evidence rule. Best evidence rules states that a computer printout of data is considered original evidence, not a copy of it. *(Chapter 11)*

49 **D.** Violation analysis. Violation analysis is a type of monitoring, but it's not a type of penetration testing. *(Chapter 9)*

50 **B.** Token authentication. Token authentication is based on *something you have*. *(Chapter 3)*

Appendix B

Glossary

3DES (Triple DES): An enhancement to the original DES algorithm that uses multiple keys to encrypt plaintext. *See also **DES**.*

Access control: The ability to permit or deny the use of an *object* (a passive entity such as a system or file) by a *subject* (an active entity such as individual or process).

Access matrix model: Provides object access rights (read/write/execute, or R/W/X) to subjects in a discretionary access control (DAC) system. An access matrix consists of access control lists (ACLs) and capability lists. *See also **DAC** and **ACL**.*

Accountability: The ability to associate users and processes with their actions (what you did).

Accreditation: An official, written approval for the operation of a specific system in a specific environment as documented in a certification report.

ACL (Access Control List): Lists the specific rights and permissions assigned to a subject for a given object.

Address space: Specifies where memory is located in a computer system.

Administrative controls: The policies and procedures that an organization implements as part of its overall information security strategy.

Administrative (or regulatory) laws: Define standards of performance and conduct for major industries (such as banking, energy, and health care), organizations, and officials.

AES (Advanced Encryption Standard): A block cipher based on the Rijndael cipher, which is expected to eventually replace DES. *See also **DES**.*

Aggregation: A database security issue that describes the act of obtaining information classified at a higher sensitivity level by combining lower sensitivity information.

AH (Authentication Header): In IPSec, provides integrity, authentication, and non-repudiation. *See also* **IPSec.**

ALE (Annualized Loss Expectancy): Provides a standard, quantifiable measure of the impact that a realized threat will have on an organization's assets. ALE is determined by the formula

SLE x ARO = ALE

SLE (Single Loss Expectancy) is a measure, Asset Value ($) x Exposure Factor (EF), of the loss incurred from a single realized threat or event, expressed in dollars.

EF (Exposure Factor) is a measure, expressed as a percentage, of the negative effect or impact that a realized threat or event would have on a specific asset.

ARO (Annualized Rate of Occurrence) is the estimated annual frequency of occurrence for a specific threat or event.

ANSI: American National Standards Institute.

Application level firewall (or **proxy server):** A type of firewall that transfers a copy of permitted data packets from one network to another.

Archive: In a PKI infrastructure, an archive is responsible for long-term storage of archived information from the CA. *See also* **PKI** and **CA.**

Asset: A resource, process, product, system, and so on that has some value to an organization and must therefore be protected.

Asymmetric key system (or **asymmetric algorithm; public key):** A cryptographic system that uses two separate keys: one key to encrypt and a different key to decrypt information. These keys are known as *public* and *private key pairs.*

Authentication: The process of verifying a user's claimed identity in an access control system (who you are).

Authorization (or **establishment):** Defines the rights and permissions granted to a user account or process (what you can do).

Availability: Ensuring that systems and data are accessible to authorized users when they need it.

Baselines: Identifies a consistent basis for an organization's security architecture, taking into account system-specific parameters, such as different operating systems.

Bell-LaPadula model: A formal confidentiality model that defines two basic properties:

- ✓ **simple security property (ss property):** A subject can't read information from an object with a higher sensitivity label (no read up, or NRU).
- ✓ **star property (* property):** A subject can't write information to an object with a lower sensitivity label (no write down, or NWD).

Best evidence: Original, unaltered evidence, which is preferred by the court over secondary evidence. *See also **Best evidence rule**.*

Best evidence rule: Defined in the Federal Rules of Evidence, states that "to prove the content of a writing, recording, or photograph, the original writing, recording, or photograph is (ordinarily) required."

Biba model: A formal integrity model that defines two basic properties:

- ✓ **simple integrity property:** A subject can't read information from an object with a lower integrity level (no read down, or NRD).
- ✓ **star integrity property (*-integrity property):** A subject can't write information to an object with a higher integrity level (no write up, or NWU).

Birthday attack: A type of attack that attempts to exploit the probability of two messages using the same hash function and producing the same message digest.

Blackout: Total loss of power.

Block cipher: An encryption algorithm that divides plaintext into fixed-size blocks of characters or bits and uses the same key on each fixed-size block to produce corresponding ciphertext.

Brownout: Prolonged drop in voltage.

Brute force attack: A type of attack in which the attacker attempts every possible combination of letters, numbers, and characters to crack a password, passphrase, or PIN.

Buffer (or stack) overflow attack: A type of attack in which the attacker enters an out-of-range parameter or intentionally exceeds the buffer capacity of a system or application to effect a Denial of Service or exploit a vulnerability.

CA (Certification Authority): In a PKI infrastructure, the CA issues certificates, maintains and publishes status information and Certificate Revocation Lists (CRLs), and maintains archives. *See also **PKI**.*

CBC (Cipher Block Chaining): One of four operating modes for DES. *(See also CFB, ECB, DES,* and *OFB).* Operates on 64-bit blocks of plaintext to produce 64-bit blocks of ciphertext. Each block is XORed *(see also XOR)* with the ciphertext of the preceding block creating a dependency or chain, thereby producing a more random ciphertext result. This is the most common mode of DES operation.

CER (Crossover Error Rate): In biometric access control systems, the point at which the FRR equals the FAR, stated as a percentage. *See also FAR* and *FRR.*

Certification: A formal methodology for comprehensive testing and documentation of information system security safeguards, both technical and non-technical, in a given environment using established evaluation criteria.

CFB (Cipher Feedback): One of four operating modes for DES. *(See also CBC, DES, ECB,* and *OFB.)* CFB is a stream cipher most often used to encrypt individual characters. In this mode, previously generated ciphertext is used as feedback for key generation in the next key stream and the resulting ciphertext is chained together.

Chain of Custody (or **Chain of Evidence):** Provides accountability and protection for evidence throughout its entire life cycle.

CHAP (Challenge Handshake Authentication Protocol): A remote access control protocol that uses a three-way handshake to authenticate both a peer and a server.

Cipher: A cryptographic transformation.

Ciphertext: A plaintext message that has been transformed (encrypted) into a scrambled message that is unintelligible.

Circumstantial evidence: Relevant facts that can't be directly or conclusively connected to other events but about which a reasonable inference can be made.

CIRT (Computer Incident Response Team) or **CERT (Computer Emergency Response Team):** A team comprising individuals properly trained in incident response and investigation.

Civil (or **Tort) law:** Addresses wrongful acts committed against an individual or business, either willfully or negligently, resulting in damage, loss, injury, or death.

Clark-Wilson Model: A formal integrity model that addresses all three goals of integrity and identifies special requirements for inputting data.

Closed system: A system that uses proprietary hardware and/or software that may not be compatible with other systems or components.

Clustering (or Key Clustering): Occurs when identical ciphertext messages are generated from a plaintext message by using the same encryption algorithm but different encryption keys.

Cold site: An alternate computer facility with electricity and HVAC but no computer equipment located on site. *See also* ***HVAC.***

Compensating controls: Controls that are implemented as an alternative to other preventive, detective, corrective, deterrent, or recovery controls.

Compensatory damages: Actual damages to the victim including attorney/legal fees, lost profits, investigative costs, and so forth.

Conclusive evidence: Incontrovertible and irrefutable . . . you know, the *smoking gun.*

Confidentiality: Prevents the unauthorized use or disclosure of information, ensuring that information is accessible only to those authorized to have access to the information.

Copyright: A form of protection granted to the author(s) of "original works of authorship," both published and unpublished.

Corrective controls: Controls that remedy violations and incidents or improve existing preventive and detective controls.

Corroborative evidence: Supports or substantiates other evidence presented in a case.

Covert channels: An unintended communications path. May be a covert storage channel or covert timing channel.

Criminal law: Defines those crimes committed against society, even when the actual victim is a business or individual(s). Criminal laws are enacted to protect the general public.

Cryptanalysis: The science of deciphering ciphertext without the cryptographic key.

Cryptography: The science of encrypting and decrypting information, such as a private message, to protect its confidentiality, integrity, and/or authenticity.

Cryptology: The science that encompasses both cryptography and cryptanalysis.

Cryptosystem: The hardware or software implementation that transforms plaintext into ciphertext (encrypts) and back into plaintext (decrypts).

Cryptovariable (or key): A secret value applied to the algorithm. The strength and effectiveness of the cryptosystem is largely dependent upon the secrecy and strength of the cryptovariable.

Culpable negligence: An organization that fails to follow a standard of due care in the protection of its assets may be held culpably negligent. *See also Due care.*

DAC (Discretionary Access Control): An access policy determined by the owner of a file or other resource. *See also MAC.*

DBMS (Database Management System): Restricts access by different subjects to various objects in a database.

Decryption: The process of transforming ciphertext into plaintext.

Demonstrative evidence: Used to aid the court's understanding of a case.

DES (Data Encryption Standard): A commonly used symmetric key algorithm that uses a 56-bit key and operates on 64-bit blocks.

Detective controls: Controls that identify violations and incidents.

Deterrent controls: Controls that discourage violations.

Dictionary attack: A more focused type of brute force attack in which a predefined word list is used. *See also Brute force attack.*

Diffie-Hellman: A key agreement algorithm based on discrete logarithms.

Direct evidence: Oral testimony or a written statement based on information gathered through the witness's five senses that proves or disproves a specific fact or issue.

Disk Mirroring (RAID Level 1): A duplicate copy of all data is written to another disk or set of disks.

Disk Striping (RAID Level 0): Data is written across multiple disks but doesn't provide redundancy or fault tolerance.

Disk Striping with Parity (RAID Level 5): Data is written across multiple disks along with parity data that provides fault tolerance should one disk fail.

DITSCAP (Defense Information Technology Security Certification and Accreditation Process): Formalizes the certification and accreditation process for US Department of Defense information systems.

Documentary evidence: Includes originals and copies of business records, computer-generated and computer-stored records, manuals, policies, standards, procedures, and log files.

Domain: A collection of users, computers, and resources with a common security policy and single administration.

DSS (Digital Signature Standard): Published by NIST *(see also **NIST**)* in Federal Information Processing Standard (FIPS) 186-1, specifies two acceptable algorithms in its standard: The RSA Digital Signature Algorithm and the Digital Signature Algorithm (DSA). *See also **RSA**.*

Due care: The steps that an organization takes to implement security best practices.

Due diligence: The prudent management and execution of due care.

Dynamic password: A password that changes at some regular interval or event.

EAP (Extensible Authentication Protocol): A remote access control protocol that implements various authentication mechanisms including MD5, S/Key, generic token cards, and digital certificates. Often used in wireless networks.

ECB (Electronic Code Book): One of four operating modes for DES *(see also **CBC, CFB, DES,** and **OFB**)*. Operates on 64-bit blocks of plaintext independently and produces 64-bit blocks of ciphertext. The native mode for DES operation.

EES (Escrowed Encryption Standard): Divides a secret key into two parts and places those two parts into escrow with two separate, trusted organizations. Published by NIST in FIPS PUB 185 (1994). *See also **NIST**.*

EMI (Electromagnetic Interference): Electrical noise generated by the different charges between the three electrical wires (hot, neutral, and ground) and can be *common-mode noise* (caused by hot and ground) or *traverse mode noise* (caused by hot and neutral).

Encryption: The process of transforming plaintext into ciphertext.

End-to-end encryption: Packets are encrypted once at the original encryption source and then decrypted only at the final decryption destination.

Enticement: Luring someone toward certain evidence after that individual has already committed a crime.

Entrapment: Encouraging someone to commit a crime that the individual may have had no intention of committing.

ESP (Encapsulating Security Payload): In IPSec, provides confidentiality (encryption) and limited authentication. *See also IPSec.*

Evidence life cycle: Describes the various phases of evidence from its initial discovery to its final disposition. The evidence life cycle has the following five stages: collection and identification; analysis; storage, preservation, and transportation; presentation in court; and return to victim (owner).

Exigent circumstances: If probable cause exists and the destruction of evidence is imminent, property or persons may be searched and/or evidence may be seized without a search warrant.

Expert systems: A type of artificial intelligence system based on an inference engine and knowledge base.

Fail-safe: When a hardware or software failure is detected, program execution is terminated, and the system is protected from compromise.

Fail-soft (or resilient): When a hardware or software failure is detected, certain, non-critical processing is terminated, and the computer or network continues to function in a degraded mode.

Failover: When a hardware or software failure is detected, the system automatically transfers processing to a hot back-up component, such as a clustered server.

FAR (False Accept Rate or Type II Error): In biometric access control systems, the percentage of unauthorized users that are incorrectly granted access. *See also CER and FRR.*

Fault: Momentary loss of power.

Fault-tolerant: A system that continues to operate following failure of a computer or network component.

Felony: More serious crimes that normally result in jail/prison terms of more than one year. *See also Misdemeanor.*

FIPS: Federal Information Processing Standards.

Forensics (or Computer Forensics): The science of conducting a computer crime investigation to determine what has happened and who is responsible, and collecting legally admissible evidence for use in a computer crime case.

FRR (False Reject Rate or Type I Error): In biometric access control systems, the percentage of authorized users who are incorrectly denied access. *See also CER and FAR.*

Fuzzy logic: Used to address uncertain situations to determine whether a given condition is true or false.

Guidelines: Similar to standards but considered recommendations rather than compulsory requirements.

Hearsay evidence: Evidence that isn't based on personal, first-hand knowledge of the witness but was obtained through other sources.

Hearsay rule: Under the Federal Rules of Evidence, hearsay evidence is normally not admissible in court.

HIPAA (Health Insurance Portability and Accountability Act): Federal act that addresses security and privacy requirements for medical systems and information.

Hot site: A fully configured alternate computer facility with electrical power, HVAC, and functioning file/print servers and workstations. *See also HVAC.*

HVAC: Heating, ventilation, and air conditioning.

Identification: The means by which a user claims a specific identity to a system.

Inference: The ability of users to infer or deduce information about data at a higher sensitivity level for which they are not authorized.

Inference channel: A link that allows inference to occur.

Information custodian (or custodian): The individual with day-to-day responsibility for protecting information assets.

Information flow model: A lattice-based model in which objects are assigned a security class and value and their direction of flow is controlled by a security policy.

Information owner (or owner): The individual who decides who is allowed access to a file and what privileges are granted.

Inrush: Initial power rush.

Integrity: Safeguards the accuracy and completeness of information and processing methods and ensures that

- Modifications to data aren't made by unauthorized users or processes.
- Unauthorized modifications to data aren't made by authorized users or processes.
- Data is internally and externally consistent; that is, a given input produces an expected output.

Intellectual property: Includes patents, trademarks, copyrights, and trade secrets.

IPSec (Internet Protocol Security): An IETF open standard for secure communications over public IP-based networks.

ITSEC (European Information Technology Security Evaluation Criteria): Formal evaluation criteria that addresses confidentiality, integrity, and availability, and also evaluates an entire system.

Kerberos: A ticket-based authentication protocol developed at the Massachusetts Institute of Technology (MIT).

KryptoKnight: A ticket-based SSO authentication system developed by IBM.

Lattice-based access controls: A method for implementing mandatory access controls in which a mathematical structure defines greatest lower-bound and least upper-bound values for a pair of elements: for example, subject and object.

Least privilege: A principle requiring that a subject is granted only the minimum privileges necessary to perform an assigned task.

Link encryption: Packet encryption and decryption at every node along the network path. Requires each node to have separate key pairs for its upstream and downstream neighbors.

MAC (Mandatory Access Control system): Access policy is determined by the system rather than the owner. *See also* **DAC**.

Man-in-the-middle attack: A type of attack in which an attacker intercepts messages between two parties and forwards a modified version of the original message.

Mantrap: A physical access control method consisting of a double set of locked doors or turnstiles.

Meet-in-the-middle attack: A type of attack in which an attacker encrypts known plaintext with each possible key on one end, decrypts the corresponding ciphertext with each possible key, and then compares the results *in the middle*.

Memory addressing: Describes the method used by the CPU to access the contents of memory.

Memory space: Describes the amount of memory available in a computer system.

Message digest: A condensed representation of a message producing using a one-way hash function.

Misdemeanor: Less serious crimes, normally resulting in fines or jail/prison terms of less than one year. *See also **Felony.***

Monoalphabetic substitution: A cryptographic system that uses a single alphabet to encrypt and decrypt an entire message.

MOSS (MIME Object Security Services): Provides confidentiality, integrity, identification and authentication, and non-repudiation using MD2 or MD5, RSA asymmetric keys, and DES. *See also **RSA** and **DES.***

MPLS (Multi-Protocol Label Switching): An extremely fast method for forwarding packets through a network using labels inserted between Layer 2 and Layer 3 headers in the packet.

Multi-level system: A single computer system that handles multiple classification levels between subjects and objects.

Multiprocessing: A system that executes multiple programs on multiple processors simultaneously.

Multiprogramming: A system that alternates execution of multiple programs on a single processor.

Multitasking: A system that alternates execution of multiple subprograms or tasks on a single processor.

NCSC: National Computer Security Center.

Need-to-know: A status granted to an individual that define his requirements regarding only the essential information needed to perform his or her assigned job function.

Neural networks: A type of artificial intelligence system that approximates the function of the human nervous system.

NIACAP (National Information Assurance Certification and Accreditation Process): Formalizes the certification and accreditation process for US government national security information systems.

NIST: National Institute of Standards and Technology.

Non-interference model: Ensures that the actions of different objects and subjects aren't seen by, and don't interfere with, other objects and subjects on the same system.

Non-repudiation: A user can't deny an action because his identity is positively associated with his actions.

Object: A passive entity such as a system or file.

OFB (Output Feedback): One of four operating modes for DES *(see also CBC, CFB, DES, and OFB)*. OFB is a stream cipher often used to encrypt satellite communications. In this mode, previous plaintext is used as feedback for key generation in the next key stream; however, the resulting ciphertext isn't chained together (unlike CFB).

One-time Pad: A keystream that can only be used once.

One-time Password: A password that is valid for one logon session only.

One-way Function: A problem that is easy to compute in one direction but not in the reverse direction.

Open message format: A message encrypted in an asymmetric key system by using the sender's private key. The sender's public key, which is available to anyone, is used to decrypt the message. This format guarantees the message's authenticity. *See also Secure message format and Secure and signed message format.*

Open system: A vendor-independent system that complies with an accepted standard. This promotes interoperability between systems and components made by different vendors.

Packet filtering firewall: A type of firewall that examines the source and destination address of an incoming packet and either permits or denies the packet based on an access control list (ACL). *See also ACL.*

Packet (or password) sniffing: A type of attack in which an attacker uses a sniffer to capture network packets and analyze their contents.

PAP (Password Authentication Protocol): A remote access control protocol that uses a two-way handshake to authenticate a peer to a server when a link is initially established.

Patent: As defined by the US Patent and Trademark Office (PTO), a patent is "the grant of a property right to the inventor."

PEM (Privacy Enhanced Mail): Provides confidentiality and authentication using 3DES for encryption, MD2 or MD5 message digests, X.509 digital certificates, and the RSA asymmetric system for digital signatures and secure key distribution. *See also 3DES* and *RSA*.

PGP (Pretty Good Privacy): A freely available, open source e-mail application that provides confidentiality and authentication using the IDEA cipher for encryption and the RSA asymmetric system for digital signatures and secure key distribution. *See also RSA.*

Physical controls: Controls that ensure the safety and security of the physical environment.

PKI (Public Key Infrastructure): Enables secure e-commerce through the integration of digital signatures, digital certificates, and other services necessary to ensure confidentiality, integrity, authentication, non-repudiation, and access control.

Plaintext: A message in its original readable format or a ciphertext message that has been properly decrypted (unscrambled) to produce the original readable plaintext message.

Policies: A formal high-level statement of an organization's objectives, responsibilities, ethics and beliefs, and general requirements and controls.

Polyinstantiation: Allows different versions of the same data to exist at different sensitivity levels.

PPP (Point-to-Point Protocol): Used in remote access service (RAS) servers to encapsulate IP packets and establish dial-in connections over serial and Integrated Services Digital Network (ISDN) links.

Preventive controls: Controls that reduce risk.

Procedures: Provides detailed instructions on how to implement specific policies and meet the criteria defined in standards.

Protection domain: Prevents other programs or processes from accessing and modifying the contents of address space that has already been assigned to an active program or process.

Protection rings: A security architecture concept that implements multiple domains with increasing levels of trust near the center.

Proximate causation: An action taken or not taken as part of a sequence of events that resulted in negative consequences.

Prudent man rule: Under the Federal Sentencing Guidelines, requires senior corporate officers to perform their duties in good faith, in the best interests of the enterprise, and with the care and diligence that ordinary, prudent persons in a like position would exercise under similar circumstances.

Punitive damages: Determined by a jury and intended to punish the offender.

RA (Registration Authority): In a PKI infrastructure, the RA is responsible for verifying certificate contents for the CA. *See also PKI* and *CA.*

RADIUS (Remote Authentication Dial-In User Service): An open-source, User Datagram Protocol (UDP)-based client-server protocol used to authenticate remote users.

RBAC (role-based access control): A method for implementing discretionary access controls in which access decisions are based on group membership according to organizational or functional roles.

Real (or physical) evidence: Tangible objects from the actual crime, such as the tools or weapons used and any stolen or damaged property.

Recovery controls: Controls that restore systems and information.

Reference monitor: An abstract machine that mediates all access to an object by a subject.

Repository: In a PKI infrastructure, a repository is a system that accepts certificates and CRLs from a CA and distributes them to authorized parties. *See also CA* and *PKI.*

RFI (Radio Frequency Interference): Electrical noise caused by electrical components, such as fluorescent lighting and electric cables.

Risk acceptance: Accepting the loss associated with a potential risk.

Risk assignment (or transference): Transferring the potential loss associated with a risk to a third party, such as an insurance company.

Risk mitigation: Reducing risk to a level that is acceptable to an organization.

Risk reduction: Mitigating risk by implementing the necessary security controls, policies, and procedures to protect an asset.

Rotation of duties (or job rotations): Regularly transferring key personnel into different positions or departments within an organization.

RSA (Rivest, Shamir, Adleman): A key transport algorithm based on the difficulty of factoring a number that is the product of two large prime numbers.

Rule-based access control: A method for applying mandatory access control by matching an object's sensitivity label and a subject's sensitivity label to determine whether access should be granted or denied.

Safeguard: A control or countermeasure implemented to reduce the risk or damage associated with a specific threat.

Sag: Short drop in voltage.

SBU (Sensitive but Unclassified): A US government data classification level for information that's not classified but requires protection, such as private or personal information.

Secondary evidence: A duplicate or copy of evidence, such as tape backup, screen capture, or photograph.

Secure and signed message format: A message encrypted in an asymmetric key system using the recipient's public key and the sender's private key. This protects the message's confidentiality and guarantees the message's authenticity. *See also Open message format and Secure message format.*

Secure message format: A message encrypted in an asymmetric key system using the recipient's public key. Only the recipient's private key can decrypt the message. This protects the message's confidentiality. *See also Open message format and Secure and signed message format.*

Security kernel: The combination of hardware, firmware, and software elements in a Trusted Computing Base (TCB) that implements the reference monitor concept. *See also TCB.*

Security perimeter: The boundary that separates the Trusted Computing Base (TCB) from the rest of the system. *See also TCB.*

Sensitivity labels: In a MAC-based system, a subject's sensitivity label specifies its level of trust, whereas an object's sensitivity label specifies the level of trust required for access. *See also MAC.*

Separation (or segregation) of duties and responsibilities: A concept that ensures that no single individual has complete authority and control of a critical system or process.

SESAME (Secure European System and Applications in a Multi-vendor Environment): A ticket-based authentication protocol similar to Kerberos, with additional security enhancements. *See also Kerberos.*

Session hijacking: Similar to a man-in-the-middle attack except that the attacker impersonates the intended recipient rather than modifying messages in transit. *See also Man-in-the-middle attack.*

SET (Secure Electronic Transaction): Developed by MasterCard and Visa to provide secure e-commerce transactions by implementing authentication mechanisms while protecting the confidentiality and integrity of cardholder data.

S-HTTP (Secure HyperText Transfer Protocol): An Internet protocol that provides a method for secure communications with a Web server.

S/MIME (Secure Multipurpose Internet Mail Extensions): Provides confidentiality and authentication for e-mail using the RSA asymmetric key system, digital signatures, and X.509 digital certificates. *See also* **RSA.**

Social engineering: A low-tech attack method employing techniques such as dumpster diving and shoulder-surfing.

Spike: Momentary rush of power.

SSL/TLS (Secure Sockets Layer/Transport Layer Security): A Transport layer protocol that provides session-based encryption and authentication for secure communication between clients and servers on the Internet.

SSO (Single Sign-On): Allows a user to present a single set of logon credentials, typically to an authentication server, which then transparently logs the user on to all other enterprise systems and applications for which that user is authorized.

Standards: Specific, mandatory requirements that further define and support higher-level policies.

State machine model: A secure state is defined and maintained during transitions between secure states.

Stateful inspection firewall: A type of firewall that captures and analyzes data packets at all levels of the OSI model to determine the state and context of the data packet and whether it is to be permitted.

Static password: A password that's the same for each logon.

Statutory damages: Mandatory damages determined by law and assessed for violating the law.

Steganography: The art of hiding the very existence of a message; for example, in a picture.

Stream cipher: An encryption algorithm that operates on a continuous stream of data, typically bit-by-bit.

Subject: An active entity such as an individual or process.

Substitution cipher: Ciphers that replace bits, characters, or character blocks in plaintext with alternate bits, characters, or character blocks to produce ciphertext.

Surge: Prolonged rush of power.

Symmetric key system (or **symmetric algorithm, secret key, single key, private key**)**:** A cryptographic system that uses a single key to both encrypt and decrypt information.

TACACS (Terminal Access Controller Access Control System): A UDP-based access control protocol that provides authentication, authorization, and accounting.

TCB (Trusted Computing Base): The total combination of protection mechanisms within a computer system, including hardware, firmware, and software, which is responsible for enforcing a security policy.

TCSEC (Trusted Computer System Evaluation Criteria): Commonly known as the *Orange Book*. Formal systems evaluation criteria developed for the US Department of Defense by the National Computer Security Center (NCSC) as part of the Rainbow Series.

Teardrop attack: A type of stack overflow attack that exploits vulnerabilities in the IP protocol.

Technical (or logical) controls: Hardware and software technology used to implement access control.

Threat: Any natural or man-made circumstance or event that could have an adverse or undesirable impact, whether minor or major, on an organizational asset.

TNI (Trusted Network Interpretation): Commonly known as the *Red Book* (of the Rainbow Series; *see also **TCSEC**).* Addresses confidentiality and integrity in trusted computer/communications network systems.

Trademark: As defined by the US Patent and Trademark Office (PTO), a trademark is "any word, name, symbol, or device, or any combination, used, or intended to be used, in commerce to identify and distinguish the goods of one manufacturer or seller from goods manufactured or sold by others."

Trade secret: Proprietary or business-related information which a company or individual uses and has exclusive rights to.

Transient: A momentary electrical line noise disturbance.

Transposition cipher: Ciphers that rearrange bits, characters, or character blocks in plaintext to produce ciphertext.

Trusted computer system: A system that employs all necessary hardware and software assurance measures and meets the specified requirements for reliability and security.

View: A logical operation that can be used to restrict access to specific information in a database, hide attributes, and restrict queries available to a user. Views are a type of constrained user interface that restricts access to specific functions by not allowing a user to request it.

Vulnerability: The absence or weakness of a safeguard in an asset, which makes a threat potentially more harmful or costly, more likely to occur, or likely to occur more frequently.

Warm site: An alternate computer facility that is readily available and equipped with electrical power, HVAC, and computers, but not fully configured. *See also **HVAC**.*

Work factor: Describes the difficulty, in terms of time, effort, and resources, required to break a cryptosystem.

WTLS (Wireless Transport Layer Security): A protocol that provides security services for the Wireless Application Protocol (WAP) commonly used for Internet connectivity by mobile devices.

XOR (Exclusive Or): A binary operation applied to two input bits. If the two bits are equal, the result is zero. If the two bits are not equal, the result is one.

Appendix C

About the CD-ROM

*The CD-ROM that comes with this book contains test questions and documents to help you prepare for the exam.

System Requirements

Make sure that your computer meets the minimum system requirements listed here. If your computer doesn't match up to most of these requirements, you may have problems using the contents of the CD:

- ✔ A Pentium class Windows PC with a 200 MHz or faster processor recommended.

- ✔ At least 32MB of total RAM installed on your computer. For the best performance, we recommend at least 64MB and preferably 96MB of main memory.

- ✔ At least 800MB of hard drive space available to install all the software from the CD.

- ✔ A CD-ROM drive.

- ✔ A monitor capable of displaying at least 256 colors.

- ✔ A keyboard and a mouse.

Contents

We've included valuable resources on this CD to help your exam preparation:

- ✔ Dummies Test Engine. This is a tool for you to create custom practice tests with just a few steps. You can concentrate on domains you need to emphasize, or take a full 250-question practice test. The practice test contains questions related to the CISSP certification. The questions are similar in format and content to those you can expect to find on the actual exam. Its purpose is to familiarize you with the test format and help you to get comfortable with the CISSP testing environment.

✔ Boson Test Engine. The folks who make these valuable practice tests have included a sample here for your personal perusal. Of course, they hope you'll be so delighted and impressed that you'll buy more of their products, but the stuff on this CD is completely free and at no extra charge. You can order the complete practice exam from www.boson.com.

✔ RFC 1087, *Ethics and the Internet*. An important series of guidelines from The Internet Society. The complete Request For Comments for your reading pleasure! Familiarize yourself with its contents for the CISSP exam (Law, Investigation, and Ethics domain) and for your professional career!

✔ Adobe Acrobat Reader. The popular reader from Adobe which allows you to view and print documents in portable document format (pdf).

If You Have Problems (Of the CD Kind)

We tried our best to test various computers with the minimum system requirements. Alas, your computer may differ.

The likeliest problem is that you don't have enough RAM for the programs you want to use. If you have trouble with corrupt files on the CDs, please call the Wiley Customer Care phone number: 800-762-2974 (outside the United States: 317-572-3994). You can also contact Customer Service by e-mail at techsupdum@wiley.com. Customer service won't be able to help with complications relating to the program or how it works.

Index

• **F** •

● *P* ●

Wiley Publishing, Inc.
End-User License Agreement

READ THIS. You should carefully read these terms and conditions before opening the software packet(s) included with this book "Book". This is a license agreement "Agreement" between you and Wiley Publishing, Inc."WPI". By opening the accompanying software packet(s), you acknowledge that you have read and accept the following terms and conditions. If you do not agree and do not want to be bound by such terms and conditions, promptly return the Book and the unopened software packet(s) to the place you obtained them for a full refund.

1. **License Grant.** WPI grants to you (either an individual or entity) a nonexclusive license to use one copy of the enclosed software program(s) (collectively, the "Software" solely for your own personal or business purposes on a single computer (whether a standard computer or a workstation component of a multi-user network). The Software is in use on a computer when it is loaded into temporary memory (RAM) or installed into permanent memory (hard disk, CD-ROM, or other storage device). WPI reserves all rights not expressly granted herein.

2. **Ownership.** WPI is the owner of all right, title, and interest, including copyright, in and to the compilation of the Software recorded on the disk(s) or CD-ROM "Software Media". Copyright to the individual programs recorded on the Software Media is owned by the author or other authorized copyright owner of each program. Ownership of the Software and all proprietary rights relating thereto remain with WPI and its licensers.

3. **Restrictions On Use and Transfer.**

   (a) You may only (i) make one copy of the Software for backup or archival purposes, or (ii) transfer the Software to a single hard disk, provided that you keep the original for backup or archival purposes. You may not (i) rent or lease the Software, (ii) copy or reproduce the Software through a LAN or other network system or through any computer subscriber system or bulletin- board system, or (iii) modify, adapt, or create derivative works based on the Software.

   (b) You may not reverse engineer, decompile, or disassemble the Software. You may transfer the Software and user documentation on a permanent basis, provided that the transferee agrees to accept the terms and conditions of this Agreement and you retain no copies. If the Software is an update or has been updated, any transfer must include the most recent update and all prior versions.

4. **Restrictions on Use of Individual Programs.** You must follow the individual requirements and restrictions detailed for each individual program in the "About the CD-ROM" appendix of this Book. These limitations are also contained in the individual license agreements recorded on the Software Media. These limitations may include a requirement that after using the program for a specified period of time, the user must pay a registration fee or discontinue use. By opening the Software packet(s), you will be agreeing to abide by the licenses and restrictions for these individual programs that are detailed in the "About the CD-ROM" appendix and on the Software Media. None of the material on this Software Media or listed in this Book may ever be redistributed, in original or modified form, for commercial purposes.

5. Limited Warranty.

(a) WPI warrants that the Software and Software Media are free from defects in materials and workmanship under normal use for a period of sixty (60) days from the date of purchase of this Book. If WPI receives notification within the warranty period of defects in materials or workmanship, WPI will replace the defective Software Media.

(b) WPI AND THE AUTHOR OF THE BOOK DISCLAIM ALL OTHER WARRANTIES, EXPRESS OR IMPLIED, INCLUDING WITHOUT LIMITATION IMPLIED WARRANTIES OF MERCHANTABIL-ITY AND FITNESS FOR A PARTICULAR PURPOSE, WITH RESPECT TO THE SOFTWARE, THE PROGRAMS, THE SOURCE CODE CONTAINED THEREIN, AND/OR THE TECHNIQUES DESCRIBED IN THIS BOOK. WPI DOES NOT WARRANT THAT THE FUNCTIONS CONTAINED IN THE SOFTWARE WILL MEET YOUR REQUIREMENTS OR THAT THE OPERATION OF THE SOFTWARE WILL BE ERROR FREE.

(c) This limited warranty gives you specific legal rights, and you may have other rights that vary from jurisdiction to jurisdiction.

6. Remedies.

(a) WPI's entire liability and your exclusive remedy for defects in materials and workmanship shall be limited to replacement of the Software Media, which may be returned to WPI with a copy of your receipt at the following address: Software Media Fulfillment Department, Attn.: *CISSP For Dummies,* Wiley Publishing, Inc., 10475 Crosspoint Blvd., Indianapolis, IN 46256, or call 1-800-762-2974. Please allow four to six weeks for delivery. This Limited Warranty is void if failure of the Software Media has resulted from accident, abuse, or mis-application. Any replacement Software Media will be warranted for the remainder of the original warranty period or thirty (30) days, whichever is longer.

(b) In no event shall WPI or the author be liable for any damages whatsoever (including without limitation damages for loss of business profits, business interruption, loss of business information, or any other pecuniary loss) arising from the use of or inability to use the Book or the Software, even if WPI has been advised of the possibility of such damages.

(c) Because some jurisdictions do not allow the exclusion or limitation of liability for consequential or incidental damages, the above limitation or exclusion may not apply to you.

7. U.S. Government Restricted Rights.
Use, duplication, or disclosure of the Software for or on behalf of the United States of America, its agencies and/or instrumentalities "U.S. Government" is subject to restrictions as stated in paragraph (c)(1)(ii) of the Rights in Technical Data and Computer Software clause of DFARS 252.227-7013, or subparagraphs (c) (1) and (2) of the Commercial Computer Software - Restricted Rights clause at FAR 52.227-19, and in similar clauses in the NASA FAR supplement, as applicable.

8. General.
This Agreement constitutes the entire understanding of the parties and revokes and supersedes all prior agreements, oral or written, between them and may not be modified or amended except in a writing signed by both parties hereto that specifically refers to this Agreement. This Agreement shall take precedence over any other documents that may be in conflict herewith. If any one or more provisions contained in this Agreement are held by any court or tribunal to be invalid, illegal, or otherwise unenforceable, each and every other provision shall remain in full force and effect.